Josuah Sylvester--From Drawing by Winifred Winans

THE DIVINE WEEKS

OF

Josuah Sylvester

Mainly translated from the French of William de Saluste,
Lord of the Bartas.

DU BARTAS, Guillaume de Salluste, Seigneur

Edited, with introduction, notes, emendations and excisions,

BY THERON WILBER HAIGHT

Collated with the quarto editions of 1608, 1611 and 1613, and the folios
of 1621, 1633 and 1641

Waukesha, Wis., U. S. A.
H. M. YOUMANS, PUBLISHER
1908

TO THE MEMORY OF
THE BOY MILTON
THIS ABRIDGMENT OF
THE BOOK HE LOVED
BEST IS INSCRIBED

Copy of inscription on a fly leaf following the printed text of "The Divine
Weeks" in a quarto volume belonging
to the edition of 1611. John Hampden
was seventeen years old at the date of
the publication, and the writing may very
possibly be his genuine autograph.

The Divine Weeks of Josuah Sylvester

CONTENTS

THE FOURTH DAY.—

THE FIFTH DAY.—

THE SIXTH DAY.—

A PERSONAL PREFACE

This edition of The Divine Weeks includes five hundred exemplars only, and no copies thereof will be printed hereafter.

As the original work has been ignored by most English writers of dates subsequent to the Stuart restoration, and has not been re-published during all that period, (except in a privately printed edition of one hundred copies by A. B. Grosart, which I have not seen,) it can not be reasonably expected that this abridgment will attract much attention outside of a select circle composed of lovers and admirers of Milton, with whose poetry its lines are most intimately related, and including other readers whose tastes incline them towards explorations of the obscurer vistas of the past.

If another edition shall be called for, however, it will be revised and more or less enlarged from this. And in any case the editor will feel obliged for suggestions from every source in regard to changes that may be thought desirable in text or comment.

That the footnotes now appearing are not so full or so elaborate as could be wished is sufficiently obvious to slight examination. The diligent and industrious research necessary for making them so has not yet been practically attainable, but it is believed that a considerable fund of somewhat valuable and interesting information is contained in them as they now stand. Several of them were suggested by the Rev. Charles Dunster's "Considerations on Milton's Early Reading," published in London in 1800. Mr. Dunster's observations do not cover any part of Paradise Lost, however, and the echoes cited here from the great epic, as well as most of the other comparisons, are such only as have occurred to the recollection of the present editor from his own earlier reading.

Grateful acknowledgment is due to Miss Ina Reid of Waukesha, for her careful and intelligent oversight of the proof sheets of the volume, and for other important assistance in the course of the transition of the manuscript into printed pages.

The pen and ink drawing of Sylvester by Miss Winans is not only a faithful picture, but is also distinguished as the unique example of a portrait of the poet in which an absurd laurel wreath does not figure. The artist has successfully demonstrated the proposition that the Jacobean roundhead had no need of arboreal adornment in order to "make him fit to be seen."   T. W. H.

Waukesha, Wisconsin, September, 1908.

INTRODUCTORY SKETCH

BY THE EDITOR

Josuah Sylvester was born in the county of Kent, in England, in 1563, the year preceding that of the birth of Shakespeare in Warwickshire. The two were contemporaries from 1564 until the death of the dramatist at about the time Sylvester left England for the Low Countries, where he remained the rest of his life in the nominal capacity of secretary of one of the trading companies established on the northwestern coast of the continent by English dissenters and puritans.

These companies were preparing the way and making the paths straight for the New England emigration which began in 1620. Sylvester died September 28, 1618, at Middleburgh in the island of Zealand, being at that time the most famous of English poets after Chaucer. His vogue as a versifier antedated that of Shakespeare by nearly three years, although he himself was not at all well known to the reading public until he was twenty-seven years old, the preceding fifteen years having been spent in coastwise trade along the shores of western Europe.

In his boyhood he had attended school, from the age of nine to that of twelve, and the taste of classical literature which he obtained there seems not to have been forgotten during his marine career, for he was still able to write Latin when he retired from active commercial business in 1590 to adopt literature as a profession. Apparently he had at that time accumulated a moderate competence which seemed sufficient for his maintenance if his literary efforts should prove unremunerative.

A combination of circumstances was responsible for Sylvester's change of vocation, but the weightiest must have been the love of letters which had never been quenched since his school days, and needed only opportunity to blaze forth into living flame. He had become an accomplished French scholar while engaged in trading operations, and in his dealings with the thrifty Huguenots of the northern and western ports of France, had absorbed their religious views and in particular had contracted a fervent admiration for the chief poet of that cult, Guillaume de Saluste, Seigneur du Bartas, a nobleman by birth and training, and a favorite at the court of Navarre from his youth. Queen Jeanne, mother of Henry IV, had commanded him, before he reached the age of twenty-two, to turn the story of Judith at Bethulia into an epic poem, of which he gives the following account in a preface to the edition of 1579:

"M'ayant esté commandé, il y a enuiron quatorze ans, par feu tresillustre et tres vertueuse princesse Ianne reine de Nauarre, de rediger l'histoire de Iudit en forme d'un poème epique, ie n'ay pas tant suyui l'ordre de la frase du texte de la Bible, comme i'ay taché, sans toute fois m'eloigner de la verité de l'histoire, d'imiter Homere" etc.

The following thirteen years were spent by Du Bartas mostly in diplomatic service at the courts of Queen Elizabeth, King James of Scotland and the king of Denmark. James was a great admirer of the "Judith" and in 1584 directed one of his household, Thomas Hudson, to turn that poem into English verse. The task was so well performed that Hudson's version was incorporated with all the editions of the Divine Weeks printed in London after 1605.

Du Bartas was about thirty-four years old when he published, in 1578, his astonishingly successful epic of the creation of the world which he called "La Sepmaine," or The Week. Edition after edition was issued in several French cities besides Paris, and also in Geneva and Brussels. Translations were made into Latin and modern European tongues, King James of Scotland and Sir Philip Sidney being among those who undertook to prepare English versions, without carrying their work to completion.

Undoubtedly the religious conditions of the time had very much to do with the acclamations that were heard in every direction, but there were some praises unmixed with the religious sentiment. For instance Ronsard wrote to his fellow poet that the latter had accomplished more in one "Week" than he himself had been able to do in a lifetime; and the author of the "Faerie Queene" in a sonnet addressed to Du Bellay in the "Ruins of Rome" had the following:

> Needes must to all eternitie survive
> That can to other give eternall dayes;
> Thy days therefore are endles and thy prayse
> Exceeding all that ever went before,
> And after thee gins Bartas hie to rayse
> His heavenly muse th'Almighty to adore.
> Live, happy spirits, th'honour of your name,
> And fill the world with never dying fame.

Such a general chorus of approval had an effect upon Du Bartas something like that produced upon Lord Byron by like applause more than two hundred years afterwards. It caused him to seek for more permanent fame both as a soldier and as a poet. In the intervals of peace in France he applied himself to the extension of his later poem so that it should cover the history of the world (beginning with Adam's installation in Paradise) and be divided for poetical purposes into seven equal parts, each of which should be styled one "Day" and be itself subdivided into four sections for no other perceptible reason than that of convenience of the reader. The first complete "Day" was to cover the narrative of Genesis from the creation of man to the era of the Flood, the second to that of Abraham and so on to the sixth, to be devoted to the story of the divine redemption of man, and the seventh, of a prophetic character, descriptive of the millennial Sabbath.

During the twelve years following the first printing of La Sepmaine, Du Bartas completed four of his proposed "Days," bringing his version of the biblical narrative down to the capture of Jerusalem by Nebuchadnezzar, and thus adding more than twice its bulk to the original poem on the creation of the world.

At the same time the author held a cavalry command under Henry of Navarre in the many civil wars that were intermittently raging over France, and in March, 1590, he was fighting at the decisive battle of Ivry, afterward celebrated in the "Henriade" of Voltaire, and in Macaulay's stirring ballad. Here he was wounded, though not in appearance so seriously as to interfere with his enthusiasm for the cause. He therefore produced a triumphal poem descriptive of the battle, comprising something more than five hundred lines; but he did not long survive the exertion.

Dying thus in the 46th year of his life, the event was saddening to all the protestants of Europe, who had come to look upon the poet as probably inspired by the Almighty to rehearse the language of the Holy Ghost in such wise as should enable it to be easily "understanded of the people." Sylvester immediately proceeded to turn the swan song of Du Bartas into English verse, and before the end of the year his translation was on sale in the bookshops of London.

The English were in a mood to appreciate the publication at its full value, at least. They had not yet entirely recovered from the agitation caused by the supreme effort of the Spanish Armada two years before, to overturn the English government and bring the subjects of Elizabeth under the rule of the Inquisition. To repel that attempt nearly all the merchant shipping attainable in the country was pressed into the naval service of the government, and very likely Sylvester's among the rest. The Spaniards, beaten on the sea, were now helping the League in its endeavor to prevent the accession of Henry IV to the throne that he had inherited, and although driven from the field of Ivry, they had compassed the death of the leading poet of the Huguenot party, and were not yet so overcome as to be no longer a menace to religious liberty, as understood by protestants generally.

Sylvester's first serious attempt at figuring in the field of poetry was therefore very encouraging in the immediate results. The edition was rapidly sold, and in 1592 another was issued in a thicker volume with extracts from the Divine Weeks and the whole of a rather extended poem entitled "The Triumph of Faith." The new publication was also well received and conditions appeared to justify the translator's divinations by anagrams — his favorite superstition. Without greater changes in spelling than were understood to be allowable in the construction of anagrams he had discovered that "Iosua Silvester" by appropriate transposition became "Vere Os Salustii," or "The real Mouth of Saluste." By a second shifting of the name into a French phrase, he was able to read, "Voy, Sire, Saluste," thus giving him ground for thinking that Du Bartas's personality had been in some sense transferred to himself. So he settled down to steady work, and in 1598 was able to produce a 16mo volume containing all of his Du Bartas translations that were ready for publication; but no entire copy of it is known to be now in existence, so that it is impossible to present an authentic table of its contents. In the following year he published a translation from the French of the sonnets on the "Miracle of Peace," a specimen of which is to be found in the notes to "The Handicrafts" in this volume.

It now seems necessary for the purpose of making clear certain literary conditions of the time to return to Shakespeare, although the dramatist was engaged in a business which the puritan poet esteemed a prerogative of the Devil himself, and not to be touched by the fingers of men who were endeavoring to become worthy of eternal salvation.

Up to 1593 the principal occupation of Shakespeare appears to have been that of editor of the plays, old and new, that came into the hands of a certain stage management for production at the theater. Although Shakespeare was also an actor, it is not shown that his services in that capacity were considered indispensable; but in respect to the requirements of the stage for lines to be spoken by the actors his judgment was depended on as that of the managing editor of a great daily newspaper is now depended on in regard to what shall go into its columns, and what shall stay out, when matter is more plentiful than space.

In the performance of these duties he cut out portions and inserted other portions of plays as he pleased, and some writers complained of his methods; as for instance Robert Greene in his "Groatsworth of Wit," (1592,) says that "Shakescene" is "an upstart crow, beautified with our feathers, . . . who supposes he is as well able to bombast our blank verse as the best."

It is difficult to imagine what the theater would be today, if there were no railroads, no telegraphs or telephones, and no newspapers to bring all quarters of the earth within easy reach of one another. Under such circumstances the reading classes would have to be addressed exclusively by means of books, broadsides and pamphlets, and the non-readers by word of mouth. Current local happenings would assume a high degree of prominence above events abroad in the case of every locality, and most emphatically so in the case of any large city.

If the decade next following our civil war had presented such conditions in the American metropolis, and Charles A. Dana, for example, had desired to impress his sentiments upon the citizenship, as the columns of the New York Sun of that period show that he actually did desire, he would have found the theater the most available medium for the accomplishment of his wish, and instead of the polished and incisive sentences that actually came from his pen and from the pens of the "young men" who wrote under his supervision, he might probably have produced dramatic compositions of great excellence, viewed from the standpoint of literature alone, sparkling with allusions to classical and contemporary writings, and also redolent with odors of local and ephemeral significance, the flavor of which could not be restored under other circumstances and in another age.

The situation in which the Elizabethan dramatists found themselves may have been somewhat of this character. Whether their productions were afterwards to become literature or not did not trouble them at all, it may be reasonably supposed, their great object being to get into touch with the generation then engaged in working out the destinies of England. To understand their views in detail would probably be as hopeless an attempt as it would be for them, if they could revisit the terrestrial regions today, to understand why current theatrical announcements are accompanied by pictures of grinning female idiots having eyes rolled upward and heads tipped backward or to one side. In every generation there are developments that become insoluble mysteries to the people of any other period of time.

Much of the meaning of the drama of Elizabeth's age is therefore undoubtedly lost to us forever; but Shakespeare at least has left a monument in which the stuff of immortality is visible in every course of the building. At the same time, if we are able to pick up a fragment now and then of the ephemeral among its massive stones, with strong probability that we are making a correct guess as to how such fragments found places there, we naturally have a feeling of pleasurable gratification at the supposed discovery.

That there are such fragments to be found in the text of the Divine Weeks as set forth in this volume I think will be evident to any fairly attentive reader. If this is the case, it constitutes a valid reason why these and other works of Sylvester should receive more respectful consideration than has been awarded them in public, at any rate, for the two centuries last past.

Hudibras Butler and Turncoat Dryden made it an essential part of their literary business to curry favor with the sons of the first Charles Stuart, and one of their methods was to abuse all the poets of the puritan party as well as Independents and Presbyterians, including some of their predecessors whose verses are just now in the 20th century coming to the front again after a longer sleep that that of the enchanted princess in Tennyson's "Day Dream." As Sylvester was the most conspicuous of them all, the poetical panders discreetly poured upon him the vilest dregs of their contempt while seizing many of his expressions for their own use. Their efforts were in high degree successful, so far as the depreciation of Sylvester and his coadjutors was concerned, and Wycherly and Dryden in drama, and Dryden, Butler and a mob of their followers in didactic, satiric and narrative verse took the places that had been occupied by better men, though for the most part religiously inclined, at the beginning of the century. Milton's poetical efforts preceding the Paradise Lost and including such masterpieces as Comus, Lycidas, L'Allegro, Il Penseroso and the rest were wholly ignored by the Restoration group, who thought such things beneath even unfriendly notice.

Sylvester and his religious friends were narrow minded, without any doubt, but honestly so. They would not deign to read the text of the plays performed in theaters any more than the leaders of "holiness" organizations now would devote their leisure moments to the perusal of the "yellow" newspapers that make daily evening and morning appearances on the streets of all of our large cities, and on those of

most of the smaller towns. Perhaps the insertion here of a
few lines from an original poem of Sylvester's on the subject
of tobacco will indicate clearly enough the strength of detes-
tation with which he regarded attendance at theaters. Of
the weed he says:

> It best becomes a stage or else a stews,
> Or dicing-house where all disorders use.
> It ill becomes a college, church or court,
> Or any place of any civil sort.
> It fits blasphemers, Russians, atheists, etc.

There was one aspect, however, in which Shakespeare had
to be noticed, even by so rigid a puritan as his "silver-
tongued" contemporary. In the year 1593 there was an
epidemic of the plague in London of so severe a character
that the authorities decided to take all available measures
for the prevention of large gatherings of people of any
kind, and among other orders issued one for the closing of
all theaters within their jurisdiction. This deprived Shakespeare of his ordinary employment, and he therefore turned
his attention to composition outside of the drama. His
"Venus and Adonis" was the first fruit of his endeavor in the
new direction and it achieved a prompt and continuous pop-
ularity the same year so that successive editions of the poem
appeared in 1594, 1596, 1599 and 1600. The "Rape of
Lucrece" was published in 1594 and was also received by the
London public with wide approval. It was in this character
of an "heir of Ovid", therefore, that he was entreated in the
English version of the Divine Weeks, along with other poets
of like proclivities, to turn his pen to the service of God,
instead of "charming senses, chaining souls in hell." (Adam,
1st interpolation.)

My object in giving so much space to Shakespearean relations is to make it clearly apparent, if possible, that in any
case where it seems evident that one of the two writers ap-
propriated words, phrases or sentences from the other, it is
in the highest degree improbable that Sylvester was the bor-

rower. A very strong corroboration of this view is to be found in the fact that none of Shakespeare's plays was printed before the year 1597, and only three of them—Romeo and Juliet, Richard II and Richard III—during that year, while the volume which purported to be a complete translation of Du Bartas's biblical poem was given to the public by Sylvester in 1598; and some parts of it had been printed as early as 1592, others in 1596. As a general statement it may be said that in no instance of parallel passages of Shakespeare and Sylvester cited in the notes herein was the drama quoted from printed before the other.

There is, then, occasion for a feeling of interest in the poems now first published for general circulation since Charles I began his war against parliament, because the greatest literary genius of all recorded time did not disdain to read them and to make use of them as he thought proper; but such a feeling should be intensified by the knowledge that to Milton as a child they became what it is hardly an exaggeration to call an integral part of his intellectual and emotional life. Shakespeare used them as the editorial writers of New York dailies now use Tennyson and Longfellow —because of their convenience. Milton exhibited their spirit because his own was pervaded by it.

At fifteen years of age the boy wrote a paraphrase of the 114th Psalm which his most distinguished biographer, Professor Masson, pronounced to be so close an imitation of Sylvester that it might easily have been accepted as the genuine work of that author. At twenty-one he drew a picture in the 15th stanza of the "Hymn" in the "Ode on the Morning of Christ's Nativity" which is an exact description of the most striking features of the full page cut here reproduced in the first "Day" of the Divine Weeks. In all Milton's poems (except, perhaps, the Paradise Regained and Samson Agonistes,) there are so many echoes from Sylvester as to leave no room for doubt that the lines of the elder poet were so woven into the fiber of his own nervous system as to make it impossible for him to tear them out.

The now current calendar year, besides being the tercentenary of Milton's birth, is the three hundredth anniversary of the publication of the second quarto edition of Sylvester's poems, made "more complete," the printer, Humfrey Lownes, said in his address to the reader, by annexing to the text Thomas Hudson's translation of Judith, "perceiving our divine Du Bartas so generally applauded, even of the greatest and gravest of the kingdom, and all his works so welcome to all."

The printing was done in a shop in Bread street, the short thoroughfare where Milton's father had his residence and place of business—and which led from Cheapside, a little east of St. Paul's, southerly to the Thames. If the elder Milton had not been one of those whom Printer Lownes spoke of as applauders of Du Bartas, Sylvester's quarto could not have been made so familiar to the son as the internal evidence of Milton's poetry shows that it was.[1] The volume was probably read aloud over and over in the family before the lad had learned to read for himself, and was dwelt upon by him more than any other book through all the impressible years of his boyhood after he had acquired the art of reading. The "King James" version of the bible was printed when little Milton was two years old, but there is no indication in his published works that he ever absorbed it as thoroughly as he absorbed the matter and spirit of the puritan's translations from the French. Spenser's Faerie Queene was also printed by Lownes, and

---

[1]By way of example of the effect often produced upon Milton's verse by memories of his predecessor's, the following quotation from the beginning of Paradise Lost is presented along with lines from

must have influenced the tastes of Milton, though at a later period of his youth.

Psychologists are all agreed, I believe, on the proposition that impressions received in childhood and apparently

---

various translations of Sylvester's with which comparisons of form or of sentiment may be made:

                    If Sion hill
Delight thee more, and Siloa's brook that flowed
Fast by the oracle of God, I thence
Invoke thy aid to my adventurous song,
That with no middle flight intends to soar
Above th'Aonian mount. . . . .

Instruct me, for Thou know'st. Thou from the first
Wast present, and with mighty wings outspread
Dovelike sat'st brooding o'er the vast abyss
And mad'st it pregnant: What in me is dark
Illumine; what is low raise and support,
That to the height of this great argument
I may assert eternal Providence.—Par. Lost, 1, 10 et seq.

                    The Isaacians still,
As law enjoined, should mount on Sion hill
To sacrifice.—David.—Schism.

He falls asleep fast by a silent river.—Adam,—Eden.

                    Mine adventurous rime
Circling the world may search out every clime.—Noah,—The
                                               [Colonies.

Anon I sacred to the Aonian band
My country's story.—Urania, stanza 5.

                    Grant that soaring near the sky
Among our authors eagle-like I fly.—Adam.—The Imposture.

Eternal issue of eternal sire,
Tell, for I know Thou know'st; for compassed ay
With fire by night, and with a cloud by day,
Thou, my soul's hope, wert their sole guide and guard.—Abra-
                                               [ham,—The Law.

Tell, for thou know'st, what sacred mystery
Under this shadow doth in secret lie.—Abraham,—The Fathers.

Even in such sort seemèd the Spirit eternal
To brood upon this gulf, with care paternal
Quickening the parts, inspiring power in each.—Building the
                                               [World,—Day 1.

Base argument a base style ever yields.—Urania, Stanza 57.

Lest thou be at fault in this vast argument.—Abraham,—The Vocation.

In honor of these gifts, this gift I bring
Small for my pains, great for the argument.—Triumph of Faith,—Dedi-
                                               [cation.

forgotten in middle age are likely to recur to the mind with all their original force in the decline of life, and on the other proposition that images of little vividness in the light of day are often far more apparent to the mental vision in the midst of surrounding physical darkness.

It is claimed that the former of these propositions is so applicable to the case of words memorized in very early life that even the unmeaning formularies used in "counting out" for childish games are to all intents and purposes unforgettable, and many believe that the present insane orthography of our language cannot be cured, because it is learned during the childhood of those who use it, and therefore remains fixed in their minds.

Probably no one who has ever suffered from unwelcome wakefulness at night could fail to remember instances when little noises made by the wind or by the rubbing of branches of trees against the house walls, have not only magnified themselves inordinately, but have sometimes brought to the front visions of burglars or worse.

The relations between Miton and the writings of Sylvester are illustrative of both the tendencies here mentioned. His early poems contain ample demonstrations of the intimate familiarity of the little boy with his predecessor's verses, and also of his boyish habit of amplifying and exalting the mental pictures so obtained. The Paradise Lost was composed in his old age, when his eyes, with "dim suffusion veiled," could "find no dawn;" and under such conditions the earliest recollections of words and phrases would recur to him naturally with the insubstantial pageants long before suggested to his young imagination. All these were of course modified by his maturer judgment, but there is enough of the early thought remaining to afford an interesting subject for contemplation.

The frescoed walls of the Campo Santo at Pisa, says

De Musset, are not very interesting in themselves; but they were the objects of Raphael's early studies, and are therefore regarded with reverence by admirers of the great painter. The autograph signatures of famous men are esteemed more highly than fac similes because of the closer personal association with the writers; and even the Homeric poems, important as they are intrinsically, acquire additional interest from the fact that they were studied by Virgil, Horace, Dante and many other great poets and philosophers. A like association of Sylvester with succeeding English poets is almost as certain as that with Shakespeare and Milton. Gray took the form of his "Elegy" from "Memorials of Mortality" of the old puritan, a quatrain of which is copied below with two additional lines from other poems in the same collection, the whole to be read with reference to the ninth stanza of the "Elegy."

> And that ambition which affords thee wings
>> To seek new seas beyond our ocean's arms
> For mounts of gold and pearls and precious things,
>> Shall not preserve thy carcass from the worms.
>
> The eye of Providence, the hand of power.
>
> Still, still repels the inevitable stour.

The two last quoted lines are from Sylvester's "Elegiac Epistle" and "Job Triumphant" respectively. Other instances are mentioned in the footnotes of this volume; but there is besides an aspect in which the Divine Weeks should be expected to call for attention from Americans at least. The author died two years before the Mayflower sailed for New England, and his poems were probably the only versified productions of considerable magnitude which our ancestors of the seventeenth century brought across the Atlantic. A result of this is that linguistic peculiarities of Sylvester have become imbedded in American colloquial speech to an extent that is very noticeable. Besides the instances cited in the footnotes further on, there appear

among Sylvester's verses such Americanisms as—bear the
brunt, lug, rense, hellhound, peart, afterclaps, upside-down,
wedges and beetles, give the start, grub (for dig out),
kiff nor kin, scarecrows, lets fly, his cake is dough, in at one
ear out at t'other, truck, yerk, and many more.

These and their like are worth looking after; but of yet
greater actual importance to the general reader having
limited leisure is the condensed panoramic view here given
of the theories of natural science prevalent among the
learned circles of Europe at the close of the sixteenth century and later, up to the time when Sir Isaac Newton revealed the innermost secret of the whirling worlds and Sir
Thomas Browne exposed many common errors by bringing cool observation to bear upon the alleged facts. The
credulity of the earlier age was of a character so amazing
that it is now hard to understand without the aid of some
of its clearest headed writers, and there is no other that I
know of who has written about such matters so intelligently,
sympathetically and entertainingly as Du Bartas.

The version of his principal poem here given is pruned
somewhat, (though it cannot be fairly claimed that all worthless lines are cut out,) and it is modernized to the extent
that seemed practicable without destroying the flavor of
Sylvestrian expression. That is to say, the antique spelling has been made to conform to present usage in every
instance where it was thought that the change would not
essentially injure the rhythm or the rhyme. In a few cases
the order of words in a sentence has been rearranged for
the sake of euphony or of easier understanding by twen-
tieth century readers, and in a very few places a modern
word has been substituted for one that is obsolete or has
taken on an offensive meaning; but in no case has a word
so eliminated been replaced by another of unusual occur-
rence. Whatever is uncommon is Sylvester's.

It follows that the text has not been edited especially for the laudable uses of minute scholars who require all that can be found of any subject of investigation; but rather with the object of presenting Sylvester's work as faithfully as appears consistent with the controlling intention of avoiding the serious danger of "that tired feeling" among its intelligent readers; and it is believed that the differences to be found between the portions of the Divine Weeks here produced and the same portions as printed in Lownes's quarto of 1613 are not greater comparatively than the differences between the text of a modern edition of Shakespeare and that of the now familiar folio of 1623.

As regards the discretion used in making such alterations as have been made here in the original text, that is a matter for future judgment, and there should be no great doubt but that credit or discredit will be finally accorded as deserved. There is at any rate no such violent emendation as that of Theobald in substituting in the text of Mrs. Quickly's story of Falstaff's death a sentence that could not possibly have been written by Shakespeare himself.

It is the earnest hope of the editor of the present volume that its perusal will tend to promote the study of Milton's verse—the stateliest that was ever written by man—and that such study will tend to a more thorough examination of the whole of the work of his humbler predecessor, to the benefit of all lovers of English literature.

As a beginning in this direction there is no reason why he should not be permitted to appear in other aspects at this time, if his appearance is to be tolerated at all. Some of his earlier and later poems have therefore been made to follow the abridgment of the Divine Weeks which is the main feature of the present publication. These are gathered in an appendix that will not, it is hoped, be found less interesting than the translation upon which Sylvester based his own claim to public attention.

Of these verses a part have been chosen with the view of showing the origin of sundry expressions employed by later poets; and others, as illustrations of the personal experience of Sylvester himself. His first "Epistle" to his friend, Nicolson, is especially informing as to the individuality of the writer, and when taken in connection with the eulogy by Vicars, throws more light upon this point than is to be obtained elsewhere.

His amatory effusions, (only a few of which are used here,) are apparently productions of an early stage of life, and partake of the general character of such verses in Elizabethan times—not particularly better or worse. He says of one:

> My chief desire
> Was for the dam to damn her to the fire
> Lest, if she should outlive me, she defame
> My lineal heirs, and scandalize my name.

Sylvester's exercises in elegiac poetry abound in the old folios, but they are not given places in this collection, because they do not strike me as worth reprinting. In this opinion I may be as badly deceived as Dr. Samuel Johnson was in respect of Lycidas. If he had a dog that would read Lycidas a second time, he declared, he would have the animal killed. For the present, however, the elegies, touching the deaths of neighbors, of warriors and of royalties, must be permitted to rest in peace.

The "Hebrew Courtship" is a translation from DuBartas, and is reproduced on account of the similarity apparent between some of its lines and some of those of Shelley, "To an Indian Air." "Virtue's her own reward" is a catch-phrase of Sylvester's. Many writers, beginning with Dryden, have since used it or something essentially the same, in their own works and always without credit.

Such treatment is not at all fair, and it is because I think so that this compilation has been made. The translator of the Divine Weeks certainly did a good deal of valuable work for the benefit of English literature, and the notes and comments found here are intended to bring as much of it to the light of day as is practicable within the limits decided on. For the accomplishment of the purpose it has been considered best to make the volume rather readable than profoundly learned. No more original writing of the present appears in its pages than has seemed absolutely necessary for the attainment of the results mentioned above.

But in addition to what I have had to say, it seems proper that readers should know something of the estimation in which these poems have been held by other writers, and a few lines have therefore been taken from each of a large number of laudatory and other pieces by contemporaneous and later authors, and placed before the poet's own text. The first selection is from a dedication to Sylvester of one of Drayton's works. Those following, as far as the last Latin lines inclusive, are excerpts from the commendatory verses in the edition of Sylvester published in 1608, and retained in the succeeding quartos and folios.

COMMENDATIONS AND CONDEMNATIONS

Sallust, to thee and Sylvester, thy friend,
  Comes my high poem, peaceably and chaste,
Your hallowed labors humbly to attend,
  That wreckful Time shall not have power to waste.
                                —Michael Drayton.
I dare confess; of muses more than nine
Nor list nor can I envy none but thine.
                                —Bishop Joseph Hall.
                    We may boast
Much to have won, and others nothing lost
  By taking such a famous prize away,
As thou, industrious Sylvester, hast wrought
  And hast enriched us with th'immortal store
Of others' sacred lines, which from them brought,
  Comes by thy taking, greater than before.
                                —Samuel Daniel.

A true interpreter,

Whom fame nor gain, but love of heaven and us
Moved to un-French his learned labors thus:
Thus loves, thus lives, all-loved Sylvester.

—G. Gay-Wood.

Bartas doth wish thy English now were his;
   So well in that are his inventions wrought,
   As his will now be the translations thought,
Thine the original.

—Ben Johson.

Achilles' fame with him had been interred,
   Had Homer's lines not tied it to the stars;
And of Aeneas had we never heard,
   Had Virgil's strains not been his trumpeters.   .   .
Laura had ne'er so greenly grown above
   Her peers as now she doth to aftertimes,
Had she not had a Petrarch to her love,
   Which made her mount with nectar-dripping rimes...
And Josuah, the sun of thy bright praise
   Shall fixed stand in Art's fair firmament
Till dissolution date Time's nights and days,
   Since right thy lines are made to Bartas' bent.

—John Davies of Hereford.

Let not thy fairest, heaven-aspiring muse
   Disdain these humble notes of my affection;
My faulty lines let faithful love excuse,
   Since my defects shall add to thy perfection.

—E. G. (Guilpin?)

So while Du Bartas and our Sylvester,
   The glorious lights of England and of France,
Had hid their beams, each glow-worm durst prefer
   His feeble glimpse of glimmering radiance;
But now these suns begin to gild the day,
Those twinkling sparks are soon dispersed away.

—R. H. (Robert Hasill?)

My busy fantasy

Bade me awake, open my eyes and see
How Salust's English sun, our Sylvester,
Makes moon and stars to veil.

—R. R. (Richard Rous?)

Shall not Du Bartas, poets' pride and glory,
  In after ages be with wonder heard,
Lively recording th'universal story?
  Undoubtedly he shall, and so shalt thou,
Ear-charming echo of his sacred voice.
            —R. N., Gent. (Robert Nicolson?)

Ut prodesse suis possit, Salustius offert
  Gallis quod nobis Josua noster, opus;
Ille ergo eximiis hoc uno nomine dignus
  Laudibus.
            —Jo. Bo., Miles. (John Bodenham?)

  Non translata mihi, sed genuina canis,
Quin et posteritas, si pagina prima taceret,
  Interpres dubitet tu ne vel ille sit.
         —Car: Fitz-Geofridus Lati-Portensis.

(Fitzgeffrey entered Broadgate Hall at seventeen years old, in 1592. He was later a clergyman and wrote English poetry of good repute. See Collier's Poetical Decameron, Chapter 1.)

Quod Gallus factus modo sit, mirare, Britannus,
  Galle? Novum videas, nec tamen invideas:
Sylvester vester, noster Bartassius, ambo
  Laude quidem gemina digni, ut et ambo pari.
           —E. L., Oxon. (Edw. Lewicke?)

Carmina Bartasi Sylvester carmine vertit,
  Et, si successu non meliore, pari.
            Jo: Mauldeus Germanus.

Coelum percuriat Gallia vertice,
Ipso coelicolas terra Britannica,
  Quae vates tulerint duos
  Claros prae reliquis novos.
            —G. B., Cantabrig.

Musa tua est Bartas dulcissima; Musa videtur
  Ipsa tamen nostri, dulcior esse mihi.
            —Si. Ca., Gent.

Behold the man whose words and works were one,
Whose life and labors have few equals known;
Whose sacred lays his brows with bays have bound,
And him his age's poet-laureate crowned;

Whom envy scarce could hate; whom all admired,
Who lived beloved and a saint expired.

—John Vicars

Thou that with ale or viler liquors
Didst inspire Withers, Pryn and Vicars,
Who, ...
With vanity, opinion, want,
The wonder of the ignorant,
The praises of the author penned
By'mself or wit-insuring friend;
The itch of picture in the front,
With bays and wicked rime upon't—
All that is left o' th' forked hill
To make men scribble without skill—
Canst make a poet spite of fate,
And teach all people to translate,
Though out of languages in which
They understood no part of speech.

—Butler's Hudibras, I, 1, 653.

I remember when I was a boy I thought inimitable Spenser a mean poet in comparison of Sylvester's Du Bartas, and was rapt in ecstasy when I read these lines. . . . . I am much deceived now if this be not abominable fustian. —Dryden, Preface to "Spanish Friar."

But I will sweeten this discourse also out of a contemplation in Divine Du Bartas in the Fifth Day.—Walton's Complete Angler.

To which purpose divine Du Bartas, that noble poet, brings in our father Adam, speaking of those ages thus, as in the sound of Sylvester we have it.—John Swan's Speculum Mundi.

Home and to bed with some pain, having taken cold this morning in sitting too long bare-legged to pare my corns. My wife and I spent a good deal of this evening reading Du Bartas' "Imposture," and other parts, which my wife of late has taken up to read—and is very fine, as anything I meet with.—Pepys' Diary, Nov. 2, 1662.

Ronsard, Du Bellay, Du Bartas, and Des Portes in the last age were the admiration of all the world, and now nobody will read them.—Boileau's Reflections on Longinus.

Sylvester's language is at times admirably condensed, and it abounds in passages which, I conceive, cannot but claim our most unbounded admiration, and which, I firmly believe, made a forcible appeal to the finely tuned ear of Milton.—Charles Dunster.

Such are the occasional strength, energy and harmony of certain portions of this old version that it is probable, had Sylvester been more fortunate in the choice of his original, he had in a great measure been exempt from the numerous faults which now disgrace his composition.—Dr. Drake's "Literary Hours."

The divine Du Bartas as rendered by the not less divine Sylvester.—Southey's "The Doctor, &c."

Of late, partly on Milton's account, the interest in Sylvester has somewhat revived; and such recent English critics as can relish poetry under an uncouth guise find much to like in Sylvester's Du Bartas, just as some recent foreign critics, Goethe among them, have found a good deal to admire, even yet, in the French original.
—Masson's Life of Milton.

The Divine Weeks and Works, whether in Du Bartas's French or Sylvester's English, has now become intolerably tedious and unattractive; but the translator, had he concentrated his powers on a happier object, might have enriched the language.
—Garnet & Gosse, Eng. Lit. (An echo of Drake.)

No publication of the era was more successful than that one, for in a very few years thirty editions were sold, issuing from Rouen, Lyons and Geneva as well as Paris. The illustrious Goethe held La Sepmaine in high esteem, finding it worthy of occupying a place on the same shelf with the most honored productions of the French muse. Unfortunately this favorable judgment does not commend itself to the French critics, who look on Du Bartas as deplorably lacking in taste, although endowed with lofty sentiment along with a certain poetic exaltation of spirit.
—Brunet's Manuel du Libraire.

DU BARTAS

HIS

Diuine Weekes and Workes Translated:

And Dedicated to the Kings most excellent Maiestie by Iosuah Syluester. Now thirdly corrected &c. mcm

Reproduction of Title-Page, (slightly reduced) from the Edition of 1611.

Milton at Ten Years of Age.

THE DIVINE WEEKS

PART I.—BUILDING THE WORLD

THE FIRST DAY

Thou glorious Guide of Heaven's star-glistering motion,
True Neptune thou, the Tamer of the ocean,
The earth's dread Shaker, at whose only word
Th'Æolian scouts are quickly stilled or stirred—
Lift up my soul; my drossy[1] spirits[2] refine;
With learned art enrich this work of mine.
   O, Father, grant I sweetly warble forth[3]
Unto our seed the world's renowned birth.
Grant, gracious God, that I record in verse
The rarest beauties of the universe;
And grant Thy power I may therein discern,

---

[1] This word is printed "drousie" in the folios, but the reading of the quartos as here given is evidently correct.

[2] The word "spirit" is most commonly made a monosyllable by verse makers of three centuries ago, and often by Milton. The first vowel in the word seems to have been suppressed in pronunciation.

[3] This phrase approved itself to Milton in his 16th year so that he wrote in his version of the 136th Psalm, "Let us therefore warble forth," etc. Sylvester pictures King David in a later poem as "shrill-sweetly warbling forth."

That, teaching others, I myself may learn.[4] . .
In sacred sheets of either Testament
'Tis hard to find a higher argument,
More deep to sound, more busy to discuss,
More useful known, unknown more dangerous.
So bright a sun dazzles my tender sight;
So deep discourse my sense confoundeth quite;
My reason's edge is dulled in this dispute,
And in my mouth my fainting words be mute.
This Trinity (which rather I adore
In humbleness than busily explore,)
In th' infinite of nothing builded all
This artificial, great, rich, glorious ball,
Wherein appears, engraven on every part,
The Builder's beauty, greatness, wealth and art,
Art, beauty, wealth and greatness that confounds
The hellish barking of blaspheming hounds.
Climb they that list the battlements of Heaven,
And by the whirlwind of ambition driven,
Beyond the world's walls let those eagles fly,
And gaze upon the Sun of majesty.
Let other some, whose fainting spirits droop,
Down to the ground their meditations stoop,
And so contemplate on these workmanships
That th' Author's praise they in their own eclipse.
My heedful muse, trained in true religion,
Divinely human, keeps the middle region,[5]
Lest, if she should too high a pitch presume,
Heaven's glowing flame should melt her waxen plume,

---

[4]The omission here is of lines relating to possible conditions before the terrestrial creation, a summary of which is condensed into one of the couplets, namely:

> Before all time, all matter, form and place,
> God all in all, and all in God it was.

Which recalls Emily Bronte's stanza:—

> "Though earth and man were gone,
>   And suns and universes ceased to be,
> And Thou wert left alone,
>   Every existence would exist in Thee."

[5]Compare Paradise Lost, I, 14.

Or if too low, near earth or sea she flag,
Laden with mists her moisted wings should lag.
　　It glads me much to view this frame,[6] wherein
As in a glass God's glorious face[7] is seen.
I love to look on God—but in this robe
Of His great works, this universal globe.
For if the sun's bright beams do blear the sight
Of such as fixtly gaze against his light,
Who can behold the empyreal skies,
The lightning splendor of God's glorious eyes?
O, who can ever find the Lord without
His works, which bear His image round about?
God, of Himself incapable to sense,
In works revealed to our intelligence—
Therein our fingers feel, our nostrils smell,
Our palates taste His virtues that excel.
Before our eyes He moves, speaks to our ears,
In th'ordered motions of the spangled spheres.[8]　.　.
　　The world's a stage, where God's omnipotence,
His justice, knowledge, love and providence
Do act their parts, contending in their kinds
Above the heavens to ravish dullest minds.
　　The world's a book in folio, printed all
With God's great works in letters capital.
Each creature is a page, and each effect
A fair character, void of all defect.
But as young truants, toying in a school,
Instead of learning, learn to play the fool,
We gaze but on the babies and the cover,[9]

6"Frame" is often used in the sense of "structure" by Milton
and his predecessors.
7Compare Byron's apostrophe to the ocean in Childe Harold's
Pilgrimage, IV, 183.
8"Leaders are used in this and following instances to indicate
omissions of one or more couplets, believed to be unnecessary for
the general reader, if not entirely superfluous.
9The cherubic images embossed upon elaborate bindings of
ancient books are spoken of in this place as "babies." Du Bartas's
own words, in the original, are:
　　　　—les marges peintures
　　　　Son cuir fleurdelisé, et ses bors surdorés.

The gaudy flowers and edges gilded over;
And never farther for our lesson look
Within the volume of this various book,
Where learned Nature rudest ones instructs
That by His wisdom God the world conducts.   .   .
    Nothing—but nothing—had the Lord almighty
Whereof, wherewith, whereby to build this city;
Yet when He heaven, air, earth and sea did frame,
He sought not far, and sweat not for the same.
As Sol, without descending from the sky
Crowns the fair Spring with painted[10] bravery—
Withouten travail causeth earth to bear,
And, far off, makes the world young every year—
The power and will, th' affection and effect,
The work and project of this Architect
March all at once; all to His pleasure ranges,
Who, always One, His purpose never changes.
    Yet did this nothing not at once receive
Matter and form; for, as we may perceive
That he who means to build a warlike fleet
Makes first provision of all matter meet,
As timber, iron, canvas, cord and pitch,
And when all's ready, then appointeth which
Shall serve for plank, which plank shall line the waist,
The poop, the prow; which fir shall make a mast,
As art and use directeth heedfully
His hand, his tool, his judgment and his eye;
So God, before this frame He fashioned,
I wot not what great word He uttered,
Which summoned all together in a mass
Whats'ever now the heavens' wide arms embrace.
But where the shipwright for his gainful trade
Finds all his stuff to hand already made,
Th' Almighty makes His, all and every part,
Without the help of others' wit or art.

---

[10]Shakespeare uses the verb "paint" in like sense in sc. 1, act
V., of Love's Labor's Lost. The play was of later date than this part
of the poem, but this verbal use may have been of still earlier occur-
rence.

The first world yet was a most formless form,
A confused heap, a chaos most deform,
A gulf of gulfs, a body ill compact,
An ugly medley, where all difference lacked,
Where th' elements lay jumbled all together,
Where hot and cold were jarring with each other—
The blunt with sharp, the base against the high,
Bitter with sweet; and while this brawl[11] did last,
The earth in heaven, the heaven in earth was placed;[12]
Earth, air and fire were with the water mixt;
Water, earth, air within the fire were fixt;
Fire, water, earth did in the air abide;
Air, fire and water in the earth did hide.
For yet the immortal, mighty Thunder Darter,
The Lord High Marshal, unto each his quarter
Had not assigned; the celestial arcs
Were not yet spangled with their fiery sparks.
As yet no flowers with odors earth revived;
No scaly shoals yet in the waters dived,
Nor any birds with warbling harmony
Were borne as yet through the transparent sky.
All was then void of beauty, rule and light,
All without fashion, soul and motion, quite;
Fire was no fire and water was no water,
Air was not air, the earth no earthy matter;
Or, if one could, in such a world spy forth
The fire, the air, the water and the earth,
Th'earth was not firm, the fire was not hot,
Th'air was not light, the water cooled not.
Briefly, suppose an earth poor, naked, vain,

---

[11]"Brawl" is the French "Bransle," a kind of dance in which the figures were especially intricate.

[12]What Du Bartas (and Milton later) called "the world" comprised not the earth with only its immediate surroundings; but outside of the globe, made up of four "elements"—earth, water, air and clear fire—were included the several spheres in which the planets, the sun and the moon, were supposed to be respectively placed, and two spheres still farther away, by which the motions of the planetary spheres were regulated as machinery by the use of balance wheels.

All void of verdure, without hill or plain,
A heaven unhanged, unturning, untransparent,[13]
Ungarnished and ungilt with stars apparent;
So may'st thou guess what heaven and earth was that
Where in confusion reigned such debate;
A heaven and earth for my base style most fit—
Not as they were, but as they were not, yet.   .   .
   The dreadful darkness of the Memphitists,[14]
The sad, black horror of Cimmerian mists,
The sable fumes of hell's infernal vault,
Or if aught darker in the world be thought,
Muffled the face of that profound abyss,
Full of disorders and fell mutinies;
So that, in fine, this furious debate
Even in the birth this ball had ruinate,
Save that the Lord into the pile did pour
Some secret mastic of His sacred power,
To glue together and to govern fair
The heaven and earth, the ocean and the air,
Which, jointly jostling, in their rude disorder,
The new born Nature went about to murder.
   As a good wit[15] that on the immortal shrine
Of memory engraves a work divine,
Abroad, abed, at board, forever uses
To mind his theme, and on his book still muses,
So did God's spirit delight itself a space
To move itself upon the floating mass,
No other care th' Almighty's mind possessed—
If care can enter in His sacred breast—
Or as a hen that fain would hatch a brood,
Some of her own, some of adoptive blood,
Sits close thereon, and with her lively heat,

---

[13]The hanging of the sky and its turning movement were necessary to the scheme of the universe accepted three centuries ago by most reputable scholars and thinkers, including Francis Bacon.
  [14]The Egyptians; so called from Memphis, the former capital of Egypt.
  [15]It is perhaps needless to say that by "a wit" was meant in Sylvester's day a person of unusual mental ability.

Of yellow-white balls doth live birds beget;
Even in such sort seemed the Spirit eternal
To brood upon this gulf;[16] with care paternal
Quick'ning the parts, inspiring power in each,
From so foul lees so fair a world to fetch.   .   .
   Now, though the great duke[17] that in dreadful awe
Upon Mount Horeb learned the eternal law,
Had not assured us that God's sacred power
In six days built this universal bower,
Reason itself doth overthrow the grounds
Of those new worlds that fond Leucippus sounds;
Since, if kind Nature many worlds could clip,[18]
Still th' upper worlds' water and earth would slip
Into the lower, and so, in conclusion,
All would return into the old confusion.
Besides, we must imagine empty distance
Between these worlds, wherein without resistance
Their wheels may whirl, not hindered in their courses
By the inter-jostling of each other's forces.
   But all things are so fast together fixt
With so firm bonds that there's no void betwixt.
Thence comes it that a cask, pierced to be spent,
Though full yet runs not till we give it vent.
Thence is't that bellows, while the snout is stopt,
So hardly heave, and hardly can be op't.
Thence is't that water doth not freeze in winter
Stopt close in vessels where no air may enter.
Thence is't that garden-pots, the mouths kept close,
Let fall no liquor from their sieve-like nose;
And thence it is that the pure, silver source,
In leaden pipes running a captive course

---

16 "Dove-like satst brooding on the vast abyss" is Milton's language at the beginning of Paradise Lost, in speaking of the same matter.
   17 "Duke," that is to say, "Leader." Compare Par. Lost, I, 6-10.
   18 "Clip," meaning "embrace," was a word unfamiliar to Sylvester in that sense, evidently, since he explained it by a marginal interpretation in the old editions. Shakespeare uses it, however, and it is found in much earlier English writing.

Contrary to its nature, spouteth high;
To all so odious is vacuity.
　God, then, not only framed nature one,
But also set it limitation
Of form and time; exempting ever solely
From quantity His own self's essence holy.
How can we call the heavens unmeasured,
Since measured time their course hath measured?
How can we count this universe immortal,
Since many ways the parts prove hourly mortal—
Since its commencement proves its consummation,
And all things ay　decline to alteration?
　Let bold Greek sages feign the firmament
To be composed of a fifth element;
Let them deny, in their profane profoundness,
End and beginning to the heavens' roundness,
And let them argue that death's laws alone
Reach but the bodies under Cynthia's throne;
The sandy grounds of their prophetic brawling
Are all too weak to keep the world from falling.
　One day the rocks from top to toe shall quiver,
The mountains melt, and all in sunder shiver;
The heavens all rent for fear; the lowly fields,
Puffed up, shall swell to huge and mighty hills;
Rivers shall dry, or if, in any flood
Rest any liquor, it shall all be blood.
The seas shall be on fire, and on the shore
The thirsty whales with horrid noise shall roar;
The sun shall seize the black coach of the moon
And make it midnight when it should be noon;
With rusty mask the heavens shall hide their face,
The stars shall fall, and all away shall pass;
Disorder, dread, horror and death shall come,
Noise, storms and darkness shall usurp the room;
And then the chief Chief Justice, venging wrath
Which He already often threatened hath,
Shall make a bonfire of this mighty ball,
As once He made it a vast ocean all.
Alas, how faithless and how modestless

Are you that in your ephemerides
Mark year and month and day which evermore
'Gainst years, months, days, shall dam up Saturn's door!
At thought whereof even now my heart doth ache,
My flesh doth faint, my very soul doth shake.
You have miscast in your arithmetic,
Mislaid your counters;[19] graspingly you seek
In night's black darkness for the secret things
Sealed in the casket of the King of kings.
'Tis He that keeps the eternal clock of time,
And holds the weights of that appointed chime.
He in His hand the sacred book doth bear
Of that close clasped, final calendar,
Where, in red letters,[20] not with us frequented,
The certain date of that great day is printed—
That dreadful day which doth so swiftly post
That 'twill be seen before foreseen, of most.
Then, then, good Lord, shall Thy dear Son descend,
Though He seem yet in feeble flesh ypend,
In complete glory from the glistering sky—
Millions of angels shall about Him fly;
Mercy and Justice, marching cheek by jowl,
Shall His divine, triumphant chariot roll,
Whose wheels shall shine with lightning round about,
And beams of glory each where blazing out.
Those that were laden with proud marble tombs,
Those that were swallowed in wild Monsters' wombs,
Those that the sea hath swilled, those that the flashes
Of ruddy flames have burned all to ashes,
Awakened, all shall rise and all revest
The flesh and bones that they at first possessed.
All shall appear and hear before the throne
Of God the judge without exception,

---

[19] A reminder of a method of reckoning which survived in America well into the 19th century, especially in schools for young children.

[20] As red letters for noting holidays in calendars are coming into vogue again after nearly a century of general disuse, a note on this phrase seems unnecessary.

The final sentence, sounding joy and terror,
Of everlasting happiness or horror.
Some shall His justice, some His mercy taste,
Some called to joy, some into torments cast,
When from the goats He shall His sheep dissever;
These blest in Heaven, those cursed in hell forever. . .
O, Father of the light![21] of wisdom fountain!
Out of the bulk of that confused mountain
What should—what could issue before the light
Without which beauty were no beauty hight? . . .
The Ephesian temple and high Pharian tower
And Carian tomb, trophies of wealth and power,
In vain had they been builded, every one,
By Scopas, Sostrates and Ctesiphon,
Had all been wrapped up from all human sight
In th' obscure mantle of eternal night.
What one thing more doth the good architect
In princely works more specially respect
Than lightsomeness—to th' end the world's bright eye,
Careering daily once about the sky,
May shine therein, and that, in every part
It may seem pompous both for cost and art?
   Whether God's spirit, moving upon the ball
Of bubbling waters which yet covered all,
Thence forced the fire, as when amid the sky,
Auster and Boreas, jousting furiously
Under hot Cancer, make two clouds to clash,
Whence th' air at midnight flames with lightning flash;
Whether, when God the mingled lump dispacked,
From fiery element did light extract;
Whether about the vast, confused crowd
For twice six hours He spread a shining cloud,
Which after He re-darkened, that in time
The night as long might wrap up either clime;[22]
Whether that God made then those goodly beams

---

[21]See Pope's "Universal Prayer."
[22]"Clime" or "climate," meaning territory, is still in good English use, though seldom seen in American writings.

Which gild the world, but not as now it seems;
Or whether else some other lamp He kindled
Upon the heap yet all with waters blindled,[23]
Which, flying roundabout, gave light in order
To th' unplaced climates of that deep disorder;
As now the sun, circling about the ball,
The light's bright chariot, doth enlighten all.
  No sooner said He, "Be there light," but lo!
The formless lump to perfect form 'gan grow,
And all illustred with light's radiant shine,
Doffed mourning weeds and decked it passing fine.
All hail, pure lamp, bright, sacred and excelling;
Sorrow and care, darkness and dread repelling;
The world's great taper, wicked men's just terror,
Mother of truth, true beauty's only mirror—
God's eldest daughter![24] O, how thou art full
Of grace and goodness! O, how beautiful!
Since thy great Parent's all-discerning eye
Doth judge thee so, and since His Majesty—
Thy glorious Maker—in His sacred lays
Can do no less than sing thy modest praise.
  But yet, because all pleasures wax unpleasant
If without pause we still possess them present
And none can right discern the sweets of peace
That have not felt war's irksome bitterness, . . .
Th' all's Architect alternately decreed
That night the day and day should night succeed.
The night, to temper day's exceeding drought,
Moistens our air and makes our earth to sprout.
The night is she that all our travails eases,
Buries our care and all our griefs appeases.
The night is she that, with her sable wing
In gloomy darkness hushing everything,
Through all the world dumb silence doth distil,
And wearied bones with quiet sleep doth fill.

23"Blindled" seems to be a word of Sylvester's manufacture, perhaps from "blindfolded."
24"Offspring of Heaven, first-born." Par. Lost, III, 1.

Sweet night, without thee—without thee, alas,
Our life were loathsome—e'en a hell to pass;
For outward pains and inward passions still
With thousand deaths would soul and body thrill.[25]
Oh night, thou pullest the proud mask away
Wherewith proud actors in this world's great play
By day disguise them; for no difference
Night makes between the peasant and the prince,
The poor and rich, the prisoner and the judge,
The foul and fair, the master and the drudge,
The fool and wise, barbarian and the Greek;
For night's black mantle covers all alike.

He that, condemned for some notorious vice,
Seeks in the mines the baits of avarice,
Or swelt'ring at the furnace, 'fineth bright
Our soul's dire sulphur, resteth yet at night.
He that, still stooping, tugs against the tide
His laden barge along a river's side,
And filling shores with shouts, doth melt him quite,
Upon his pallet resteth yet at night.
He that in summer in extremest heat,
Scorched all day in his own scalding sweat,
Shaves with keen scythe the glory and delight
Of motley meadows,[26] resteth yet at night;
And in the arms of his dear fere[27] foregoes
All former troubles and all former woes.

Only the learned sisters' sacred minions,
While silent night under her sable pinions
Folds all the world, with painless pain they tread
A sacred path that to the heavens doth lead,
And higher than the heavens their readers raise
Upon the wings of their immortal lays.[28]

---

[25]It should be borne in mind that the word "thrill" is generally used by Sylvester as a synonym for "pierce."

[26]"Smooth-shaven green."—Il Penseroso.

[27]The usual meaning of "fere" is "companion."

[28]The poets, servants of the muses, do their writing or composition, at night. Du Bartas's original says nothing of "painless pain,"
and is otherwise somewhat less inflated in this passage.

E'en now I listened for the clock to chime
Day's latest hour, that for a little time
The night might ease my labors; but I see
As yet Aurora scarce hath smiled on me.
My work still grows; for now before mine eyes
Heaven's glorious host in nimble squadrons flies.[29]
Whether this day God made you angels bright
Under the name of heaven or the light,
Or whether after, in the instant born
With those bright spangles which the heavens adorn;
Or whether you derive your high descent
Long time before the world and firmament,
(For I will stiffly argue to and fro
In nice opinions whether so or no,
Especially where curious search, perchance,
Is not so safe as humble ignorance,)
I am resolved that once the Omnipotent
Created you immortal, innocent,
Good, fair and free; in brief, of essence such
As from His own not differed very much.
But even as those whom princes' favors oft
Above the rest have raised and set aloft,
Are oft the first that without right or reason
Attempt rebellion and do practice treason,
And so at length are justly tumbled down
Beneath the foot that raught[30] above the crown.
Even so some legions of those lofty spirits,
Envy'ng the glory of their Master's merits,
Conspired together, strove against the stream
T' usurp His scepter and His diadem.
But He, whose hands do never lightnings lack,
Proud, sacrilegious mutineers to wrack,
Hurled them in air or in some lower cell;
For where God is not, everywhere is hell.[31]

---

[29]Waiting for midnight, he is overtaken by the dawn. Compare, as to the concluding couplet, Milton's "The spangled hosts keep watch in squadrons bright."—Morning of Nativity, III.
[30]Old preteric of reach.
[31]Doubtless the eighteen lines concluding here were the origin-

This cursed crew, with pride and fury fraught,
Of us at least have this advantage got,
That by experience they can truly tell
How far it is from highest heaven to hell;
For by a proud leap they have ta'en the measure,
When headlong thence they tumbled in displeasure.
These fiends are so far off from bettering them
By this hard judgment, that still more extreme,
The more their plague the more their pride increases—
The more their rage; as lizards, cut in pieces,
Threat with more malice, though with lesser might,
And even in dying show their living spite.
For ever since, against the King of Heaven
The apostate Prince of Darkness still hath striven,
Striven to deprave His deeds, t'inter their story,
T' undo His church, to undermine His glory,
To 'reave the world's great body, ship, and state,
Of head, of master and of magistrate.
But finding still the majesty divine
Too strongly fenced for him to undermine—
His ladders, cannons, and his engines all
Forceless to batter the celestial wall,
Too weak to hurt the head, he hacks the members;
The tree too hard, the branches he dismembers.
The fowlers, fishers, and the foresters
Set not so many toils and baits and snares
To take the fowl, the fish, the savage beasts
In woods and floods and fearful wilderness,
As this false spirit sets engines to beguile
The cunningest that practice naught but wile.
With wanton glance of Beauty's beaming eye

---

al inspiration of Paradise Lost, as the picture facing page 11 was the basis of the "Hymn" in the nativity ode of Milton's earlier years. The publication office of The Divine Weeks was very near the dwelling of the Miltons; and from the time that John Milton learned to read until he was past twelve years old Sylvester's quarto was the constant companion of the boy-poet, in whose mind many of the crudities of the older versifier suffered "a sea change into something rich and strange," and were thus transferred to life everlasting.

He snares hot youth in sensuality;
With gold's bright luster doth he age entice
To idolize detested avarice;
With praise of princes, with their pomp and state,
Ambitious spirits he doth intoxicate;
With curious skill, pride and vain dreams he witches
Those that condemn pleasure and state and riches;
Yea, faith itself and zeal he sometimes angles,
Wherewith this juggler heaven-bent[32] souls entangles,
Much like the green worm that in spring devours
The buds and leaves of choicest fruit and flowers,
Turning their sweetest sap and fragrant verdure
To deadly poison and detested ordure.

Alas, who but would have been gulled erewhiles
With night's black monarch's most malicious wiles?
To hear stones speak, see wooden miracles,
And golden gods to utter oracles;
To see him play the prophet and inspire
So many sibyls with a sacred[33] fire;
To raise dead Samuel from his silent tomb,
(To tell his king calamities to come,)
T' inflame the flamen of Jove-Ammon[34] so
With heathen-holy fury fits to know
Future events, and sometimes truly tell

---

[32]In New England, and in those of the United States where the New England element of population predominates, the expression, "Hell-bent," is very familiar; as in the old campaign song, "Maine went, Hell-bent, for Governor Kent," etc. "Bent" appears to have been used, even in England, in a closer relation with the "inclined," of Latin derivation, than has been the case since. Compare Hosea, XI, 7: "My people are bent on backsliding from me."

[33]"Sacred " in this volume is not restricted in meaning as in the present uses of English. It is here as likely to be intended to imply devotion to evil as good. See also Par. Lost, IX, 204, where "sacred" implies taboo.

[34]This line affords a rather more conspicuous example than the others of Sylvester's tendency towards repetitions of similar or identical sounds in single lines. The practice seems to have been a survival of the Old English alliterations which served in preference to rhymes to assist in memorizing verses. The next following line is a somewhat less pronounced example of the same thing. So Milton's "O Eve, in evil hour thou didst give ear," Par. Lost, IX, 1067.

The blinded world what afterwards befell;
To counterfeit the wondrous works of God—
His rod turn serpent and his serpent, rod—
To change the pure streams of the Egyptian flood
From clearest water into crimson blood—
To rain down frogs, and grasshoppers to bring
In the bedchambers of the stubborn king?
   For, as he is a spirit, unseen he sees
The plots of princes and their policies.
Unfelt, he feels the depths of their desires—
Who harbors vengeance, and whose heart aspires; . . .
Besides, to circumvent the quickest sp'rited,
To blind the eyes of even the clearest sighted
And to enwrap the wisest in his snares
He oft foretells what he himself prepares.
For, if a wise man—though man's days be done
As soon, almost, as they be here begun,
And his dull flesh be of too slow a kind
T'ensue the nimble motions of his mind—
By power alone of plants and minerals,
Can work a thousand supernaturals,
Who but will think much more these spirits can
Work strange effects, exceeding sense of man?
Since, being immortal, long experience brings
Them certain knowledge of the effects of things;
And free from body's clog, with less impeach
And lighter speed their bold designs they reach.
   Not that they have the bridle on their neck
To run at random without curb or check,
T'abuse the earth, and all the world to blind,
And tyrannize our body and our mind.
God holds them chained in fetters of His power,
That without leave, one minute of an hour
They cannot range. It was by His permission
The lying spirit trained Ahab to perdition,
Making him march against that foe with force,
That should his body from his soul divorce . . .
For th'only Lord sometimes, to make a trial
Of firmest faith, sometimes with errors vile

To drench the souls that errors, sole, delight,
Lets loose these furies, who with fell despite
Drive still the same nail, and pursue, incensed,
The damned drifts in Adam first commenced.
    But as these rebels, maugre all that will,
T'assist the good be forced t'assault the ill,
Th'unspotted spirits that never did intend
To mount too high, nor yet too low descend,
With willing speed they every moment go
Whither the grace of divine grace doth blow.
Their aims had never other limitation
Than God's own glory and His saints' salvation.
Lawless desire ne'er enters in their breast;
The Almighty's face is their ambrosial feast;
Repentant tears of strayed lambs returning
Their nectar sweet, their music, sinners' mourning.
    Ambitious man's greedy desire doth gape,
Scepter on scepter, crown on crown to clap.
These never thirst for greater dignities;
Travail's their ease; their bliss in service lies:
For God no sooner hath His pleasure spoken,
Or bowed his head, or given some other token,
Or almost thought on an exploit, wherein
The ministry of angels shall be seen,
But these quick posts with ready expedition
Fly, to accomplish their divine commission. . .
    One trusty servant for divine decrees,
The Jews' apostle from close prison frees;
One in few hours a fearful slaughter made
Of all the first-born that the Memphians had,
Exempting those upon whose door-posts stood
A sacred token of lambs' tender blood;
Another mows down in a moment's space
Before Jerusalem, God's chosen place,
Sennacherib's proud, over-daring host
That threatened Heaven, and 'gainst the earth did
    boast,
In his blasphemous brains, comparing even
His idol gods unto the God of Heaven.

His troops, victorious in the East before,
Besieged the city which did sole adore
The only God; so that, without their leave,
A sparrow scarce the sacred walls could leave.
   Then Hezekiah, as a prudent prince,
Poising the danger of these sad events, . . .
The massacre of infants and of eld,
His royal self with thousand weapons quelled,
The temple razed, th'altar and censer void
Of sacred use, God's servants all destroyed—
Humbled in sackcloth and in ashes, cries
For aid to God, the God of victories,
Who hears his suit and thunders down His fury
On those proud, pagan enemies of Jewry.
   For, while they watch, within their corps de garde,
About the fire securely snorted hard,
From Heaven th'Almighty, looking sternly down,
Casting His friends a smile, His foes a frown,
A sacred fencer 'gainst the Assyrians sent,
Whose two-hand sword, at every veney, slent[35]
Not through a single soldier's feeble bones,
But keenly slices through whole troops at once,
And hews broad lanes before it and behind,
As swiftly whirling as the whirling wind.
Now 'gan they fly, but all too slow to shun
A flying sword that followed every one.
A sword they saw, but could not see the arm
That in one night had done so dismal harm;
As we perceive a windmill's sails to go,
But not the wind that doth transport them so.
   Blushing Aurora had yet scarce dismissed
Mount Libanus from the night's gloomy mist,
When th'Hebrew sentinels, discovering plain
An hundred four score and five thousand slain,
Exceeding joyful, 'gan to ponder stricter
To see such conquest and not know the victor.

---

[35] Fell slantwise at every stroke. The "two-hand sword" is suggestive of the "two-handed engine at the door" in Lycidas.

O, sacred tutors of the saints! You guard
Of God's elect, you pursuivants, prepared
To execute the counsels of the Highest!
You heavenly courtiers, to your King the nighest,
God's glorious heralds, Heaven's swift harbingers,
'Twixt Heaven and Earth you true interpreters! .
I could be well content and take delight
To follow farther your celestial flight,
But that I fear, here having ta'en in hand
So long a journey both by sea and land—
I fear to faint if at the first too fast
I cut away and make too hasty haste;
For travelers that burn in brave desire
To see strange countries, manners and attire,
Make haste enough if only the first day
From their own sill they set but on their way.

THE SECOND DAY

Clear source of learning! Soul of th'universe!
Since thou art pleased to choose my humble verse
To sing Thy praises, make my pen distil
Celestial nectar, and this volume fill
With th'Amalthean horn; that it may have
Some correspondence to a theme so grave.
Rid Thou my passage and make clear the way
From all incumbers. Shine upon this Day,
That, guided safely by Thy sacred light,
My rendezvous I may attain ere night.
   That huge broad-length, that long-broad height pro-
      found,
Th'infinite finite, that great moundless mound,—
I mean that chaos, that self-jarring mass
Which in a moment made of nothing was,
Was the rich matter and the matrix, whence
The heavens should issue, and the elements. . .
   Since[1] then the knot of sacred marriage
Which joins the elements from age to age,
Brings forth the world's babes,—since their enmities
With full divorce kill whatsoever dies,
And since, but changing their degree and place

---

[1] Sylvester uses two contractions of the word, "Sithence." In the sense in which it appears in this line, "Sith" is always employed by him. Meaning "Subsequently," he writes "Since." The former contraction having been dropped from later English use, the latter is substituted for it in all instances occurring in this volume except where its retention seems necessary on account of the exigencies of the verse.

They frame the various forms wherewith the face
Of this fair world is so embellished,
As six sweet notes, curiously varied
In skillful music, make a hundred kinds
Of heavenly sounds, that ravish hardest minds,
And with division of a choice device,
The hearers' souls out at their ears entice;
Or as of twice twelve letters, thus transposed,
This world of words is variously composed,
And of these words, in diverse order sown,
This sacred volume that you read is grown—
Through gracious succor of th'eternal Deity—
Rich in discourse, with infinite variety;[2]
It was not causeless that so carefully
God did divide their common seignory,
Assigning each a fit, confined sitting,
Their quantity and quality befitting.

Whoso sometime hath seen rich ingots tried,
When, forced by fire, their treasures they divide;
How fair and softly[3] gold to gold doth pass,
Silver seeks silver, brass consorts with brass,
And the whole lump, of parts unequal, severs
Itself apart in white, red, yellow rivers,
May understand how, when the mouth divine
Opened, (to each its proper place t'assign,)
Fire flew to fire, water to water slid,
Air clung to air, and earth with earth abid.

Earth, as the lees and heavy dross of all,
After its kind did to the bottom fall.
Contrariwise, the light and nimble fire
Did through the crannies of th'old heap aspire
Unto the top, and by its nature light

---

[2]Shakespeare's Antony and Cleopatra, in which this phrase is used, was not published until five years after Sylvester's death, and there is no evidence of the representation of the play on any stage before its publication.

[3]Cowper's adoption of the expression, "Fair and softly," in the "History of John Gilpin" has made it familiar to the general reader. Sylvester uses it frequently, and a second time in this Day.

No less than hot, mounted in sparks upright;
As, when we see Aurora, passing gay,
With opals paint the ceiling of Cathay,
Sad floods do fume, and the celestial tapers,
Through earth's thin pores, in air exhale their vapors
　　But lest the fire, (which all the rest embraces)
Being too near, should burn the earth to ashes,
As chosen umpires the great All-Creator
Betweeen these foes placed the air and water;[4]
For one sufficed not their stern strife to end.
Water, as cousin, did the earth befriend;
Air for its kinsman fire as firmly deals,
But both, uniting their divided zeals,
Took up the matter and appeased the brawl
Which doubtless else had discreated all.
Air lodged aloft and water under it—
Not casually, but so disposed fit
By Him who, nature in her kind to keep,
Kept due proportion in His workmanship,
And in this store-house of His wondrous treasure
Observed in all things number, weight and measure.
　　For, had the water next the fire been placed,
Fire, seeming then more wronged and more disgraced,
Would suddenly have left its adversary
And set upon the umpire, more contrary.
But all the links of th'holy chains that tether
The many members of the world together
Are such as none but only He can break them
Who at the first did of mere nothing make them.
Water, as armed with moisture and with cold,
The cold, dry earth with its one hand doth hold,
With th'other, th'air; the air, as moist and warm,
Holds fire with one, water with th'other arm;
As country maidens, in the month of May,
Merrily sporting on a holiday,

---

[4]The ancient cosmography as commonly accepted in the era of
Du Bartas and long afterwards, is as clearly elucidated here, perhaps,
as in any other brief description.

And lusty, dancing of a lively round
About the maypole, by the bagpipe's sound,
Hold hand in hand, so that the first is fast,
By means of those between, unto the last.
  For since 'tis so that the dry element
Not only yields her own babes nourishment,
But with the milk of her abundant breasts
Doth also feed air's nimble-winged guests,
And also all th'innumerable legions
Of greedy mouths that haunt the briny regions, . .
'Twas meet, her slow, sad body to digest
Farther from heaven than any of the rest;
Lest, of heaven's course th'eternal, swift careers,
Rushing against her with their whirling spheres
Should her transport as swift and violent
As ay they do their neighbor element.
  And since, on th'other side, th'harmonious course
Of heaven's bright torches is th'immortal source
Of earthly life, and since all alterations
Almost are caused by their quick agitations,
In all the world God could not place so fit
Our mother earth as in the midst of it.
For all the stars reflect their lively rays
On fire and air and water various ways,
Dispersing so their powerful influence _
On, in and through these various elements;
But on the earth they all in one concur,
And all unite their severed force in her;
As in a wheel, which with a long deep rut
Its turning passage in the dirt doth cut,
The distant spokes nearer and nearer gather
And in the nave unite their points together. . .
Air, host of mists, the bounding tennis ball
That stormy tempests toss and play withal,
Of winged clouds the wide, inconstant house,
Th'unsettled kingdom of swift Æolus,
Great warehouse of the winds, whose traffic gives
Motion of life to everything that lives,
Is not throughout all one. Our elder sages

Have fitly parted it into three stages;
Whereof because the highest still is driven
With violence of the first-moving heaven
From east to west, and from the west returning
To the honored cradle of the rosy morning,
And also seated next the fiery vault,
It, by the learned, very hot is thought.
That which we touch, with times doth variate;
Now hot, now cold, and sometimes temperate.
Warm tempered showers it sendeth in the spring;
In autumn likewise, but more varying;
In winter time, continual cold and chill,—
In summer season hot and sultry still;
For then the fields, scorched with flames, reflect
The sparkling rays of thousand stars' aspect,
And chiefly Phoebus, to whose arrows bright
Our globy grandam serves for butt and white.[5]

But now, because the middle region's set
Far from the fiery ceiling's flagrant heat,
And also from the warm reverberation
Which ay the earth reflects in diverse fashion,
That circle shivers with eternal cold,
For into hail how should the water mould
Even when the summer hath gilt Ceres' gown,
Except those climes with icicles were sown?

So soon as Sol, leaving the gentle Twins,
With Cancer or thirst-panting Leo, inns,
The midmost air redoubleth all his frosts,
Being besieged by two mighty hosts
Of heat, more fierce 'gainst his cold force than ever,
Calls from all quarters his chill troops together,
T'encounter them with his united power,
Which than dispersed, hath far greater power.
As Christian armies from the frontiers far,
And out of fear of Turks' outrageous war,
March in disorder and become dispersed,
As many squadrons as were soldiers erst;

---

[5]Referring to targets in the practice of archery.

So that sometimes the untrained multitude
With bats and bows hath beat them and subdued.
But if they once perceive, or understand
The moony standards of proud Ottoman
To be approaching, and the sulph'ry thunder
Wherewith he brought both Rhodes and Belgrade
          under,
They soon unite, and in a narrow place
Entrench themselves; their courage grows apace
Their heart's on fire; and circumcised powers
By their approach double the strength of ours.
    'Tis doubtless this antiperistasis—
Bear with the word; I hold it not amiss
T'adopt sometimes such strangers for our use
When reason and necessity induce,
As, namely, when our native phrase doth want
A word so forceful and significant—
Which makes a fire seem to our sense and reason
Hotter in winter than in summer season.
'Tis it which causeth the cold, frozen Scythia,
(Too often kissed by th'husband of Orithyia,[6])
To bring forth people whose still hungry breast,
Winter or summer, can more food digest
Than those lean starvelings which the sun doth broil
Upon the hot lands of the Libyan soil;
And that ourselves, happily seated fair,
Whose spongy lungs draw sweet and wholesome air,
Hide in our stomachs a more lively heat,
While bifront Janus' frosty frowns do threat;
Than when bright Phoebus, leaving swarthy Chus,[7]
Mounts to our zenith to reflect on us. . .
    For, as a little end of burning wax
By th'emptiness, or of itself, attacks
In cupping glasses, through the scotched skin
Behind the poll, superfluous humors thin,
Which, fuming from the brain, did thence descend

---

[6]Boreas (the North Wind,) was the husband of Orithyia.
[7]Ethiopia.

Upon the sight, and much the same offend,
So the swift coachman, whose bright, flaming hair
Doth every day gild either hemisphere,
Two sorts of vapors by his heat exhales
From floating deeps and from the flowery dales;
One somewhat hot, but heavy, moist and thick,
The other light, dry, burning, pure and quick,
Which, through the welkin roaming all the year,
Make the world diverse to itself appear.
Now, if a vapor be so thin that it
Cannot to water be transformed fit,
And that, with cold-limed wings, it hover near
The flowery mantle of our mother dear,
Our air grows dusky, and moist, drowsy mist
Upon the fields doth for a time persist;
And if this vapor fair and softly fly,
Not to the cold stage of the middle sky,
But 'bove the clouds, it turneth in a trice
To dew in April, in December, ice.
But if the vapor bravely can adventur'
Up to th'eternal seat of shivering winter,
The small, thin humor by the cold is pressed
Into a cloud which wanders east and west
Upon the wind's wings, till in drops of rain
It fall into its grandam's lap again.
Whether from boisterous wind, with stormy puff
Jostling the clouds with mutual counter-buff,
Do break their brittle sides and make them shatter
In drizzling showers their swift distilling water,—
As when a wanton, heedless page, perhaps,
Rashly together two full glasses claps,[8]
Both being broken, suddenly they pour
Both their brewed liquors on the dusty floor,—
Or whether th'upper clouds' moist heaviness
Doth with its weight the under cloud oppress,
And so one humor doth another crush

---

[8] The illustration here given has the air of having been a personal experience of the poet.

Till to the ground their liquid pearls do gush,—
As the more clusters of ripe grapes we pack
In vintage time upon the hurdle's back,
At its pierced bottom the more fuming liquor
Runs in the scummy vat, and falls the thicker.
  Then many heaven-floods in our floods do lose-am[9]
Nought's seen but showers; th'heaven's sad, sable
    bosom
Seems all in tears to melt, and earth's green bed
With odious frogs sometimes is covered;
Either because the floating cloud doth fold
Within itself both moist, dry, hot and cold,
Whence all things here are made, or else for that
The active winds, sweeping this dusty flat,
Sometimes in air some fruitful dust do heap
Whence these new-formed ugly creatures leap.
As on the edges of some standing lake
Which neighbor mountains with their gutters make,
The foamy slime itself transformeth oft
To green half-tadpoles, playing there aloft,
Half made, half unmade, round about the flood
Half dead, half living, half a frog, half mud.
  Sometimes it happens that the force of cold
Freezes the whole cloud. Then we may behold
In silver flakes a heavenly wool to fall.
Then fields seem grassless, forests leafless all,
The world's all white; and through the heaps of snow
The tallest stag can scarce his armor show.
  Sometimes befalls that when by secret power
The clouds new changed to a dripping shower,
Th'excessive cold of the mid air anon
Candies it all in balls of icy stone,
Whose violent storms sometimes, alas, do proin[10]

---

[9]The spelling here is not changed from that of the original and may
have been intended as a writing of "loose 'em" or "lose 'em." The
ensuing description of meteorological phenomena ought to be of interest as an example of scientific investigation in the sixteenth century.
  [10]This form of "prune" can not be modernized here, on account of
its frequent use in making rhymes. It is the invariable orthography
of the word in The Divine Weeks.

Without a knife our orchard and our vine,—
Reap without sickle, beat down birds and cattle,
Degrade our woods, and make our roofs to rattle. . .
   If th'exhalation hot and oily prove
And yet as feeble giveth place above,
To th'airy regions' everlasting frost
Incessantly th'apt-tending fume is tossed
Till it inflame; then like a squib it falls,—
Or fire-wing'd shaft or sulph'ry powder-balls.
   But if this kind of exhalation tower
Above the walls of winter's icy bower
'T inflameth also, and anon becomes
A new, strange star, presaging awful dooms.
And, for this fire hath more fuel in't
Than had the first, 'tis not so quickly spent;
Whether the heaven's incessant agitation
Into a star transforming th'exhalation,
Kindle the same, like as a coal, that winked
On a stick's end and seemed almost extinct,
Tossed in the dark with an industrious hand
To light the night, becomes a fire-brand;
Or whether th'upper fire do fire the same
As lighted candles do th'unlight aflame.
   According as the vapor's thick or rare,
Even or uneven, long, large, round or square,
Such are the forms it in the air resembles;
At sight whereof th'amazed vulgar trembles.
Here in the night appears a flaming spire,
There a fierce dragon folded all in fire,
Here a bright comet, there a burning beam,
Here flying lances, there a fiery stream;
Here seems a horned goat, environed round
With fiery flakes about the air to bound,
There, with long, bloody hair, a blazing star
Threatens the world with famine, plague and war;
To princes, death, to kingdoms, many crosses;
To all estates inevitable losses;
To herdmen, rot; to plowmen, hapless seasons;
To sailors, storms; to cities, civil treasons.

But hark! What hear I in the heavens? methinks
The world's wall shakes, and its foundation shrinks.
It seems even now that horrible Persephone
Loosing Megar', Alecto and Tysiphone,
Weary of reigning in black Erebus
Transports her hell between the heavens and us.
  'Tis held, I know, that when a vapor moist,
As well from fresh as from salt waters hoist
In the same instant with hot exhalations
In the airy region's secondary stations,
The fiery fume, besieged with the crowd
And keen, cold thickness of that dampish cloud,
Strengthens its strength, and with redoubled volleys
Of joined heat, on the cold leaguer sallies.
  Like as a lion, only late exiled
From's native forests; spit at and reviled,
Mocked, moved and troubled with a thousand toys
By wanton children,—idle girls and boys,—
With hideous warring doth his prison fill,
In's narrow cloister ramping wildly, still
Runs to and fro, and, furious, less doth long
For liberty, than to revenge his wrong;
This fire, desirous to break forth again
From's cloudy ward, cannot itself restrain,
But without resting, loud it groans and grumbles,
And rolls and roars, and round, round, round it
    rumbles,
Till, having rent the lower side in sunder,
With sulphury flash it have shot down its thunder.
  Though willing to unite, in these alarms,
To's brother's forces its own fainting arms,
And th'hottest circle of the world to gain,
To issue upward oft it strives in vain.
For 'tis then fronted with a trench so large,
And such an host, that though it often charge
On this and that side, the cold camp about,
With its hot skirmish, yet still, still, the stout
Victorious foe repelleth every push,
So that, despairing, with a furious rush,

Forgetting honor, it is fain to fly
By the back door, with blushing infamy.
  Then th'ocean boils for fear; the fish do deem
The sea too shallow to safe-shelter them;
The earth doth shake; the shepherd in the field
In hollow rocks himself can hardly shield;
Th'affrighted heavens open, and in the vale
Of Acheron, grim Pluto's self looks pale.
Th'air flames with fire; for the loud roaring thunder,
Rending the cloud that it includes, asunder,
Sends forth those flashes which so blear our sight;
As wakeful students in a winter's night
Against the steel glancing with stony knocks
Strike sudden sparks into their tinder-box.
  Moreover, lightning of a fume is framed,
Through 'tself's hot dryness evermore inflamed,
Whose power, past credit, without razing skin,
Can bruise to powder all our bones within;
Can melt the gold that greedy misers hoard
In barred coffers, and not burn the board;
Consume the shoes and never hurt the feet;
Empty a cask, yet not demolish it. . .
  Shall I omit a hundred prodigies
Oft seen in forehead of the frowning skies?
Sometimes a fiery circle doth appear,
Proceeding from the beauteous beams and clear
Of sun and moon, and other stars' aspect,
Down looking on a thick, round cloud direct;
When not of force to thrust their rays throughout it,
In a round crown they cast them round about it;
Like as, almost, a burning candle, put
Into a closet with the door close shut,
Not able through the boards to send its light,
Out at the edges round about, shines bright.
  But, in's declining, when Sol's countenance
Direct upon a waterish cloud doth glance,—
A waterish cloud, which cannot easily
Hold any longer her moist tympany,—
On the moist cloud he limns his lightsome front,

And with a gaudy pencil paints upon't
A blue-green-gilt bow, bended over us;
For th'adverse cloud which first receiveth thus
Apollo's rays, the same direct repels
On the next cloud, and with his gold it mells
Her various colors; like as when the sun
At a bay window peepeth in upon
A bowl of water, his bright beams' aspect
With trembling luster it doth far reflect
Against th'high ceiling of the lightsome hall,
With stately fretwork overcrusted all.
  On th'other side, if the cloud sidelong sit,
And not beneath—or justly opposite—
To sun or moon; then either of them forms
With strong aspect, double or triple forms
Upon the same. The vulgar's then in fright
To see at once three chariots of the light,
And in the welkin, on night's gloomy throne,
To see at once more shining moons than one.   .   .
  Methinks I hear, when I do hear it thunder,
The voice that brings swains up and Cæsars under.
By that tower-tearing stroke I understand
Th'undaunted strength of the divine right hand.
When I behold the lightning in the skies
Methinks I see th'Almighty's glorious eyes.
When I perceive it rain down timely showers,
Methinks the Lord His horn of plenty pours.
When from the clouds excessive water spins,
Methinks God weeps for our unwept-for sins;
And when in heaven I see the rainbow bent,
I hold it for a pledge and argument
That nevermore shall universal floods
Presume to mount over the tops of woods
Which hoary Atlas in the clouds doth hide,
Or on the crowns of Caucasus do ride.
But, above all, my pierced soul inclines,
When th'angry heavens threat with prodigious signs,
When nature's order doth reverse and change
Preposterously into disorder strange. . . .

God, the great God of heaven, sometimes delights
From top to toe to alter nature's rites,
That His strange works, to nature contrary
May be forerunners of some misery.
The drops of fire which weeping heaven did shower
Upon Lucania, when Rome sent the flower
Of Italy into the wealthy clime
Which Euphrates fats with his fruitful slime,
Presaged that Parthians should, the next year, tame
The proud Lucanians, and nigh quench their name. . .
    Jews,—no more Jews; no more of Abram's sons;
But Turks, Tartareans, Scythians, Lestrigons,—
Say what you thought:—What thought you when so·
        long
A flaming sword over your temple hung,
But that the Lord would, with a mighty arm,
The righteous vengeance of his wrath perform
On you and yours? That what the plague did leave
Th'insatiate gorge of famine should bereave?
That sucking infants, crying for the teat
Self-cruel mothers should unkindly eat;
And that, ere long, the share and coulter should
Rub off their rust upon their roofs of gold?
And all because you, cursed, crucified
The Lord of Life who for our ransom died.
    The ruddy fountain that with blood did flow,—
The fiery rock the thundering heavens did throw
Into Liguria,—and the bloody crosses
Seen on men's garments,—seemed with open voices
To cry aloud that the Turks' swarming host
Should pitch his proud moons on the Genoan coast.
O frantic France! why dost not thou make use
Of strangeful signs whereby the heavens induce
Thee to repentance? Canst thou tearless gaze
Night after night on that prodigious blaze,—
That hairy comet,—that long streaming star
Which threatens earth with famine, plague and war?
Th'Almighty's trident and three-forked fire
Wherewith He strikes us in His greatest ire.

But what, alas, can heaven's bare threatenings urge,
Since all the sharp rods which so hourly scourge
Thy senseless back cannot so much as wrest
One single sigh from thy obdurate breast?
Thou drinkest thine own blood; thine own flesh thou
    eatest;
In what most harms thee, thy delight is greatest.
O senseless folk, sick of a lethargy,
Who to the death despise your remedy!
Like froward jades that for no striking stir,
But wax more restive still, the more we spur,
The more your wounds, the more secureness[11] grows,
Fat with afflictions, as an ass with blows,
And as the sledge hardens with strokes the steel,
So the more beaten, still the less ye feel.[12] . .

  Yet once again, dear country, must I call:[13]
England, repent! fall, to prevent thy fall!
Though thou be blind, thy wakeful watchmen see
Heaven's ireful vengeance hanging over thee
In fearful signs, threatening a thousand woes
To thy sin's deluge, which all overflows.

  Thine uncontrolled, bold, open atheism;
Close idol service; cloaked hypocrism;
Common blaspheming of God's name in oaths;
Usual profaning of His Sabaoths;
Thy blind, dumb, idle shepherds, choked with steeples,
That fleece thy flocks, and do not feed thy peoples;
Strifeful ambition; Florentizing states;
Bribes and affection swaying magistrates;
Wealth's merciless wrong, usury, extortion;
Poor's idleness, repining at their portion;
Thy drunken surfeits, and excess in diet,

11Carelessness.
12Du Bartas wrote during the civil wars of the reign of Henri III
of France.
13The thirty lines beginning here are part of a still longer interpolation of Sylvester's own. Compare with it that portion of Milton's Lycidas beginning, "How well could I have spared," and ending
with the couplet referring to the "two-handed engine at the door."

Thy sensual wallowing in lascivious riot;
Thy huffed, puffed, painted, curled, pearled, wanton
    pride,
(The bawd to lust and to all sins beside);
These are thy sins. These are the signs of ruin
To every state that doth the same pursue in.
Such cost the Jews and Asians desolation,
Now turned Turks, that were the holy nation.
Happy who take, by others' dangers, warning
"All that is writ is written for our learning;"
So preach thy prophets, but who heeds their cry,
Or who believes? Then much less hope have I.
Wherefore, dear Bartas, having warned them,
From this digression turn we to our theme. . .
   So, next the heavens, God marshaled th'element
Which seconds them in swift, bright ornament,
And then the rest, according as of kin
To th'azure spheres or th'erring fires they bin.
Yet some, more crediting their eyes than reason,
From's proper place this essence do disseisin,
And vainly strive, after their fancy's sway,
To cut the world's best element away,—
The nimble, light, bright flaming, heatful fire,
Fountain of life, smith, founder, purifier,
Cook, surgeon, soldier, gunner, alchymist,
The source of motion;—briefly what not is't?
Apt for all, acting, all, whose arms embrace
Under heaven's arms this universal mass.
"For if," they say, "the fire were lodged between
The heavens and us, it would by night be seen,
Since then, so far off, as in meads we pass,
We see least glow-worms glister in the grass;
Besides, how should we through the fiery tent
Perceive the bright eyes of the firmament,
Since here the soundest and the sharpest eye
Can nothing through a candle-flame descry?"
   O, hard believing wits, if Zephyrus'
And Auster's sighs were never felt of us
You would suppose the space between earth's ball

And heaven's bright arches void and empty all;
And then you would no more the air allow
For element than th'hot, bright flamer now.
Now, even as far as Phoebus' light excels
The light of lamps and every taper else
Wherewith we use to lengthen th' afternoon
Which Capricorn ducks in the sea too soon;
So far in pureness th'elemental flame
Excels the fire that for our use we frame.
For ours is nothing but a dusky light,
Gross, thick and smoky, enemy to sight;
But that above, for being neither blent
With fumy mixture of gross nourishment,
Nor tossed with winds, but far from us, comes near
Its neighbor, heaven, in nature pure and clear.

   But of what substance shall I after Thee,
O matchless Master, make heaven's canopy?
Uncertain here, my resolutions rock
And waver, like th'inconstant weathercock,
Which, on a tower turning with every blast,
Changeth its master and its place as fast.
Learned Lyceum now awhile I walk in,
Then th'academian shades I stalk in.

   Treading the way that Aristotle went
I do deprive the heavens of element
And mixture too, and think th'omnipotence
Of God did make them of a quintessence;
Since of the elements two still erect
Their motion upward, and two down direct;
But th'heaven's course, not wandering up or down,
Continually turns only roundly round.
The elements have no eternal race,
But settle ay in their assigned place;
But th' azure circle, without taking breath,
Its certain course forever gallopeth.
It keeps our pace, and moved with weightless weights,
It never takes fresh horse, nor never baits.

   Things that consist of th'elements' uniting
Are ever tossed with an intestine fighting;

Whence springs, in time, their life and their deceasing,
Their diverse change, their waxing and decreasing;
So that, of all that is or may be seen
With mortal eyes under night's horned queen,[14]
Nothing retaineth the same form and face
Hardly the half of half an hour's space.
But the heavens feel not fate's impartial rigor;
Years add not to their stature or their vigor;
Use wears them not, but their green-ever age
Is all in all still like their pupilage.[15]
    Then suddenly, turned studious Platonist,
I hold the heavens of elements consist.
'Tis earth whose firm parts make their lamps apparent,
Their bodies fast. Air makes them all transparent.
Fire makes their restless circles pure and clear,
Hot, lightsome, light and quick in their career;
And water, 'nointing with cold moist the beams
Of th'interkissing, turning globe's extremes,
Tempers the heat caused by their rapid turning,
Which else would set all th'elements a burning. . .
    See, see the rag of human arrogance!
See how far dares man's erring ignorance,
That with unbridled tongue, as if it oft
Had tried the mettle of that upper loft,
Dares, without proof or without reason yielded,
Tell of what timber God His palace builded.
But in these doubts much rather rest had I
Than with my error draw my reader 'wry,
Till a Saint Paul do re-descend from heaven,
Or till myself—of sinful robe bereaven,
This rebel flesh, whose counterpoise oppresses
My pilgrim soul, and ever it depresses,—
Shall see the beauties of that blessed place,
If then I aught shall see, save God's bright face.
    But even as many or more quarrels cumber
Th'old heathen schools about the heavens' number.

14"The horned moon"—Milton in his translation of Psalm 136.
15See Shakespeare's Antony and Cleopatra, II, 2, 241.

One holds but one, making the world's eyes shine
Through the thin thickness of that crystalline,[16]
As through the ocean's clear and liquid flood
The slippery fishes up and down do scud.
Another, judging certain by his eye,
And seeing seven bright lamps, moved diversely,
Turn this and that way; and on th'other side
That all the rest of th'heaven's twinkling pride
Keep all one course; ingeniously he varies
The heaven's rich building into eight round stories.
    Others, amid the starriest orb perceiving
A triple cadence, and withal conceiving
That but one natural course one body goes,
Count nine; some, ten; not numbering yet with those
Th'empyreal palace, where th'eternal treasures
Of nectar flow,—where everlasting pleasures
Are heaped up,—where an immortal May
In blissful beauties flourisheth for ay,—
Where life still lives,—where God His 'sizes holds,
Environed round with seraphim and souls
Bought with His precious blood, whose glorious flight
Erst soared from earth above the heavens bright.
Nor shall my faint and humble muse presume
So high a song and subject to assume.
    O fair, five-double round, sloth's foe apparent,
Life of the world, days', months' and years' own parent!
Thine own self's model, never shifting place,
And yet thy pure wings with so swift a pace
Fly over us that but our thoughts alone
Can, as thy babe, pursue thy motion.
Infinite finite! free from growth and grief,
Discord and death! dance-lover,—to be brief
Still like thyself, all thine own in thee all,
Transparent, clear, light,—law of this low ball;
Which in thy wide bout, boundless, all dost bound
And claspest all under or in thy round!

---

[16]See Par. Lost, III, 479.

Throne of th'Almighty, I would fain rehearse
Thy various dances in this very verse,
If it were time; and but my bounded song
Doubteth to make this second day too long.
For notwithstanding yet another day
I fear some critic will not stick to say
My babbling muse did sail with every gale
And mingled yarn to length her web withal.   .   .
   Yet have I not so little seen and sought
The volumes which our age hath chiefest thought,
But that I know how subtly greatest clerks
Presume to argue in their learned works
T'o'erwhelm these floods, this crystal to deface
And dry this ocean which doth all embrace.
But as the beauty of a modest dame
Who, well content with nature's comely frame
And native fairness, as 'tis freely given
In fit proportion by the hand of Heaven,
Doth not with painting prank,[17] nor set it out
With helps of art, sufficient fair without,
Is more praiseworthy than the wanton glance,
Th'affected gait, th'alluring countenance,
The mart of pride, the periwigs and painting,
Whence courtesans refresh their beauty's fainting;
So do I more the sacred tongue esteem,
Though plain and rural it do rather seem
Than schooled Athenian, and divinity,
For only varnish, have but verity—
Than all the golden wit-pride of humanity
Wherewith men burnish their erroneous vanity.
   I'd rather give a thousand times the lie
To mine own reason than but once defy
The sacred voice of th'everlasting Spirit
That doth so often and so loud aver it,
That God, above the shining firmament,
(I wot not, I, what kind) of waters pent,
Whether that pure, super-celestial water

---

[17]"Prank" so used by Milton, Comus, Verse 759.

With our inferior have no likely nature;
Whether, turned vapor, it have round embowed
Heaven's highest stage in a transparent cloud;
Or whether, as they say, a crystal case
Do, round about, the heavenly orb embrace.
But with conjectures wherefore strive I thus?
Can doubtful proofs the certainty discuss?
I see not why man's reason should withstand,
Or not believe, that He whose powerful hand
Bayed up the Red Sea with a double wall
That Israel's host might 'scape Egyptian thrall,
Could prop, as sure, as many waves on high
Above the heavens' star-spangled[18] canopy.   .   .
Let us observe, and boldly weigh it well,
That this proud palace where we rule and dwell,
Though built with matchless art, had fallen long since,
Had 't not been ceiled round with moist elements.
For like as in man's litttle world, the brain
Doth highest place of all our frame retain,
And tempers with its moistful coldness so
Th'excessive heat of other parts below;
Th'eternal Builder of this beauteous frame
To intermingle meetly frost with flame
And cool the great heat of the great world's torches
This day spread water over heaven's bright arches.

---

[18]Apparently the origin of a common appellation for the American flag.

THE THIRD DAY

All those steep mountains, whose high, horned tops
The misty cloak of wandering clouds enwraps,
Under first waters their crump shoulders hid,
And all the earth as a dull pond abid,
Until th'All-Monarch's bounteous majesty,
Willing t'enfeoff man this world's empery,
Commanded Neptune straight to marshal forth
His floods apart, and to unfold the earth;
And in his waters now contented rest
To 've all the world for one whole day possessed.
    As when the muffled heavens have wept amain
And foaming streams, assembling on the plain,
Turned fields to floods,—soon as the showers do cease
With unseen speed the deluge doth decrease,
Sups up itself, in hollow sponges sinks,
And 's ample arms in straiter channel shrinks;
Even so the sea to 'tself itself betook,
Mount after mount, field after field forsook,
And suddenly in smaller casks did tun
Her waters, that from every side did run.
Whether th'imperfect light did first exhale
Much of that primer humor, wherewithal
God, on the second day, might frame and found
The crystal spheres that he hath spread so round;—
Whether th'Almighty did new place provide
To lodge the waters;—whether opening wide
Th'earth's hollow pores, it pleased Him to convey
Deep underground some arms of such a sea;
Or whether, pressing water's gloomy globe

That covered all, as with a cloudy robe,
He them imprisoned, in those bounds of brass,
Which to this day the ocean dare not pass,
Without His license; for th'Eternal, knowing
The sea's commotive and inconstant flowing,
Thus curbed her, and 'gainst her envious rage
Forever fenced our flowery mantled stage;
So that we often see those rolling hills
With roaring noise threatening the neighbor fields,
Through their own spite to split upon the shore
Foaming with fury that they dare no more.

For what could not that great High Admiral
Work in the waves, since at His servants' call
His dreadful voice,[1] to save His ancient sheep,
Did cleave the bottom of th'Erythrean deep,[2]
And toward the crystal of his double source
Compelled Jordan to retreat his course,
Drowned with the deluge the rebellious world,
And from dry rocks abundant rivers purled?

Lo, thus the weighty waters did erewhile
With winding turns make all this world an isle;
For, like as molten lead, being poured forth
Upon a level plat of sand or earth,
In many fashions mazeth to and fro,—
Runs here direct,—there crookedly doth go,—
Here doth divide itself, there meets again;
And the hot riv'let of the liquid rain
On the smooth table crawling like a worm,
In th'instant almost every form doth form;
God poured the waters on the fruitful ground
In sundry figures; some in fashion round,
Some square, some crossed, some long, some lozenge-
 wise,

1Compare with this account Par. Lost, VII, 276 et seq.
2"The ruddy waves He cleft in twain
 Of the Erythrean main."—Milton's Psalm 136. In Sylvester's translation of Du Bartas's "Judith" he speaks of "the Erythrean ruddy
billows." Du Bartas, in the original work, does not speak of cleaving.
"En l'aer l' onde pendit," are his words, supposed to be translated
here.

Some triangles, some large, some lesser-size;
Amid the floods by this fair difference
To give the world more wealth and excellence.
Such is the German sea, such Persian sine,
Such th'Indian gulf and such th'Arabian brine,
And such our sea, whose diverse-branched retorsions
Divide the world in three unequal portions.
And though each of these arms, how large soever,
To the great ocean seems a little river,
Each makes a hundred sundry seas besides,
(Not sundry in waters, but in names and tides),
To moisten kindly, by their secret veins,
The thirsty thickness of the neighbor plains;
To bulwark nations, and to serve for fences
Against th'invasion of ambitious princes;:
To bound large kingdoms with eternal limits;
To further traffic through all earthly climates;
T'abridge long journeys, and with aid of wind
Within a month to visit either Ind. . . .
    And all the highest, heaven-approaching rocks
Contribute hither with their snowy locks;
For soon as Titan, having run his ring,
To th'icy climates bringeth back the spring,
On their rough backs he melts the hoary heaps;
Their tops grow green, and down the water leaps.
On every side it foams, it roars, it rushes,
And through the steep and stony hills it gushes,
Making a thousand brooks; whereof, when one
Perceives his fellow striving to be gone,
Hasting his course, he him accompanies.
After, another and another hies
All in one race; joint-losing, all of them,
Their names and waters in a greater stream;
And he that robs them shortly doth deliver
Himself and his into a larger river;
And that at length, however great and large,
Lord of the plain, doth in some gulf discharge
His parent tribute to Oceanus
According to th'eternal rendezvous.

Yet, notwithstanding, all these streams that enter
In the main sea do not at all augment her;
For that, besides that all these floods in one
Matched with great Neptune, seem as much as none,
The sun, as erst I said, and winds withal,
Sweeping the surface of the briny ball,
Extract as much still of her humors thin
As weeping air and willing earth pour in.
But as the sweltering heat and shivering cold,
Gnashing and sweat, that th'ague-sick do hold,
Come not at hazard, but in time and order
Afflict the body with their fell disorder,
The sea hath fits; alternate course she keeps
From deep to shore, and from the shore to deeps.
 Whether it were that at the first, the ocean
From God's own hand received this double motion
By means whereof it never resteth stound,
But as a turning whirligig goes round,
Whirls of itself, and good while after, takes
Strength of the strength which the first motion makes;
Whether the sea which we Atlantic call
Be but a piece of the Grand Sea of all,
And that his floods, entering the ample bed
Of the deep main, with fury hurried
Against the rocks, repulsed with disdain
Be thence compelled to turn back again;
Or whether Cynthia, that with changeful laws
Commands moist bodies, doth this motion cause;
As on our shore we see the sea to rise
Soon as the moon begins to mount our skies,
And when, through heaven's vault vailing toward
  Spain,
The moon descendeth, then it ebbs again.
Again, so soon as her inconstant crown
Begins to shine on th'other horizon,
It flows again; and then again it falls
When she doth light th'other meridionals.
 We see, moreover, that th'Atlantic seas
Do flow much farther than the Genoese

Or both the Bosphors; and that lakes which grow
Out of the sea do neither ebb nor flow,
Because, they say, the silver-fronted star
That swells and shrinks³ the seas, as pleaseth her,
Pour with less power her plenteous influence
Upon these strait and narrow-streamed fens,
And inland seas which many a mount immounds,
Than on an ocean vast and void of bounds.
Even as in summer, her great brother's eye
When winds be silent, doth more easily dry
Wide-spreading plains, open and spacious fields,
Than narrow vales vaulted about with hills. . . .
  In fear to've drowned myself and readers too,
(The floods so made my words to overflow,)
Therefore, ashore! and on the tender lee
Of lakes and pools, rivers and springs, let's see
The sovereign virtues of their several waters,
Their strange effects and admirable natures
That with incredible rare force of theirs
Confound our wits, ravish our eyes and ears.
  Th'Ammonian fount, while Phoebus' torch is 'light,
Is cold as ice; and opposite, all night,
Though the cold crescent shine thereon, is hot,
And boils and bubbles like a seething pot.
  They say, forsooth, the river Silarus
And yet another, called Eurimanus,
Convert the boughs, the bark, the leaves and all
To very stone, that in their waters fall.
Nor should I blench the Jews' religious river,
Which every Sabbath dries his channel over,
Keeping his waves from working on that day
Which God ordained a sacred rest for ay.
If near unto the Eleusinian spring
A sportful jig some wanton shepherd sing
The ravished fountain falls to dance and bound,

---

³"Shrink" is never used transitively by Shakespeare, unless we accept as genuine the line in 3 Hen. VI, 3, 2, 156. Milton has, in the ode on the Nativity, "The Lybic Hammon shrinks his horn," and in other places in the same sense.

Keeping true cadence to the rustic sound.
Cerona, Xanth, and Cephisus do make
The thirsty flocks that of their waters take
Black, red and white; and near the crimson deep
Th'Arabian fountain maketh crimson sheep.

Salonian fountain, and thou, Andrian spring,—
Out of what cellars do you daily bring
The oil and wine that you abound with so?
O earth, do these within thy entrails grow?
What, be there vines and orchards underground?
Is Bacchus' trade and Pallas' art there found?

What should I of the Illyrian fountain tell;
What shall I say of the Dodonean well,
Whereof the first sets any clothes on fire;
Th'other doth quench—Who but will this admire?—
A burning torch, and when the same is quenched,
Lights it again, if it again be drenched?
Sure, in the legends of absurdest fables
I should enroll most of these admirables,
Save for the reverence of the unstained credit
Of many a witness where I erst have read it;
And saving that our gain-spurred pilots find
In our days waters of more wondrous kind.

Of all the sources infinite to count,
Which to an ample volume would amount,
Far hence, on foreign unfrequented coast,
I'll only choose some five or six at most,
Strange to report, perhaps believed of few,
And yet no more incredible than true.[4]

In th'isle of iron,—one of those same seven
Whereto our elders "Happy" name had given,
The savage people never drink the streams
Of wells and rivers, as in other realms.
Their drink is in the air; their gushing spring
A weeping tree out of itself doth wring;
A tree whose tender-bearded root, being spread

---

[4]These and other "travelers' tales" cited by Du Bartas are worth attention as indications of how far credulity used to go.

In driest land, its sweating leaf doth shed
A most sweet liquor, and, like as the vine
Untimely cut, weeps at her wound, her wine
In pearled tears incessantly distils
A crystal stream which all their cisterns fills,
Through all the island; for all hither hie,
And all their vessels cannot draw it dry.
   In frosty Iceland are two fountains strange,
One flows with wax; the other stream doth change
All into iron; yet with scalding steam
In thousand bubbles belcheth up its stream.
In golden Peru, near Saint Helen's mount,
A stream of pitch comes from a springing fount.
   What more remains? The new-found world, besides,
Toward the west many a fair river guides,
Whose floating waters, knowing the use aright
Of work-fit day and rest-ordained night
Better than men, run swiftly all the day,
But rest all night and stir not any way. . . .
Now as my happy Gascony excels
In corn, wine, warriors, every country else,
So doth she also in free baths abound,
Where strangers flock from every part around
The barren wife, the palsy-shaken wight,
The ulcerous, gouty, deaf and decrepit,
From east and west arriving, fetch from hence
Their ready help with small or no expense. . . .
   On one side hills hoared with eternal snows
And craggy rocks Baigneres do inclose.
The other side is sweetly compassed in
With fragrant skirts of an immortal green,
Whose smiling beauties far excel in all
The famous praise of the Peneian vale.
There's not a house but seemeth to be new;
Th'even-slated roofs reflect with glistering blue;
To keep the pavement ever clean and sweet
A crystal river runs through every street,
Whose silver stream, as cold as ice, doth slide
But little off the physic water's side,

Yet keeps its nature, and disdains a jot
To intermix its cold with th'other's hot.
　　But all these wonders that adorn my verse
Yet come not near unto the wondrous Lers;
If it be true that the Stagyrian sage,
With shame confused, and driven by desperate rage
Because his reason could not reach the knowing
Of Euripus's seven-fold ebb and flowing,
Leapt in the same, and there his life did end,
Comprised in what he could not comprehend.
　　What had he done, had he beheld the fountain
Which springs at Belstat near the famous mountain
Of Foix, whose flood, bathing Maserian plains,
Furnish with wood the wealthy Toulousans?
As oft as Phoebus, in a complete race,
On both horizons shows his radiant face,
This wondrous brook for four whole months doth flow
Four times six times, and ebbs as oft, as low.
For half an hour may dry-shod pass that list;
The next half hour may none its course resist;
Whose foaming stream strives proudly to compare
Even in the birth with fameful'st floods that are.
O learned (nature taught) Arithmetician,
Clockless, so just to measure time's partition![5]　.　.　.
　　This also serveth for probation sound
That th'earth and water's mingled mass is round,—
Round as a ball; seeing on every side
The day and night successively to slide.
Yea, though Vespucio, famous Florentine,
Mark Pole and Columb, brave Italian trine
And thousand gallant modern Typheis[6] else
Had never brought the north pole parallels
Under the south, and sailing still about

---

[5]The twenty-four lines omitted here are interpolated by Sylvester. It should be understood that in all cases where interpolations are noted, they are by Sylvester and not by any other hand.

[6]Du Bartas has "Typhis." The reference seems to be to Tiphys, pilot of the ship, Argo, in the quest of the Golden Fleece. That ancient navigator is said to have died before reaching Colchis.

So many new worlds under us found out,—
Nay, never could they the arctic pole have lost
And found th'antarctic, if in every coast,
Seas, liquid glass, round bowed not everywhere
With sister earth, to make a perfect sphere.

But, perfect artist, with what arches strong,
Props, stays and pillars, hast thou stayed so long
This hanging; thin, sad, slippery water ball
From falling out and overwhelming all?
May it not be, good Lord, because the water
To the world's center tendeth still by nature,[7]
And toward the bottom of this bottom bound,
Willing to fall doth yet remain still round?
Or may 't not be because the surly banks
Keep waters captive in their hollow flanks,
Or that our seas be buttressed, as it were,
With thousand rocks dispersed here and there?
Or rather, Lord, is't not thine only power
That bows it round about earth's branchy bower?

Doubtless, great God, 'tis doubtless thine own hand
Whereon this mansion of mankind doth stand.
For though it hang in air, swim in the water,
Though every way it be a round theater,
Though all turn round about it, though for ay
Itself's foundations with swift motions play,
It rests immovable; that the chosen race
Of Adam there may find fit dwelling-place. . . .

Let any judge whether this lower ball
Whose endless greatness we admire[8] so, all,
Seem not a point, compared with th'upper sphere
Whose turning turns the rest in their career.[9]
Since the least star that we perceive to shine
Above, dispersed in th'arches crystalline,—
If, at the least, star-clerks be credit worth—

---

[7]"Tend de son naturel vers le centre du monde."—Du Bartas.
[8]It is probably superfluous in the case of almost every reader to call attention to the fact that the uniform meaning of "admire" three hundred years ago was—"wonder at."
[9]See Par. Lost, III, 482.

Is eighteen times bigger than all the earth;
Whence, if we but subtract what is possessed
From north to south, and also east to west,
Under the empire of the ocean
Atlantic, Indian and American,
And thousand huge arms issuing out of these,
With infinites of other lakes and seas,
And also what the two intemperate zones
Do make unfit for habitations,—
What will remain? Ah, nothing, in respect.
Lo here, O men! Lo, wherefore you neglect
Heaven's glorious kingdom! Lo, the largest scope
Glory can give to your ambitious hope.
   O princes, subjects unto pride and pleasure,
Who to enlarge but a hair's breadth the measure
Of your dominions, breaking oaths of peace,
Cover the fields with bloody carcasses;
O magistrates, who to content the great,
Make sale of justice on your sacred seat,
And breaking laws for bribes, profane your place,
To leave a leek to your unthankful race;
You strict extorters that the poor oppress,
And wrong the widow and the fatherless,
To leave your offspring rich, of others' good,
In houses built of rapine and of blood;
You city vipers, that, incestuous, join
Use upon use, begetting coin of coin;
You merchant mercers and monopolites,
Gain-greedy chapmen, perjured hypocrites,
Dissembling brokers, made of all deceits,
Who falsify your measures and your weights
T'enrich yourselves, and your unthrifty sons
To gentilize with proud possessions;
You that for gain betray your gracious prince,
Your native country, or your dearest friends;
You that to get you but an inch of ground,
With cursed hands remove your neighbor's bound,
(The ancient bounds your ancestors have set,)
What gain you all? Alas, what do you get?

Yea, though a king by wile or war had won
All the round earth to his subjection,
Lo, here the guerdon of his glorious pains;
A needle's point, a mote, a mite, he gains,
A nit, a nothing, did he all possess,—
Or if than nothing anything be less.
When God, whose words more in a moment can
Than in an age the proudest strength of man,
Had severed the floods, leveled the fields,
Embased the valleys and embossed the hills,—
"Change, change," quoth He, "O fair and firmest globe,
Thy mourning weed to a green, gallant robe.
Cheer thy sad brows and stately garnish them
With a rich, fragrant, flowery diadem." . . .
No sooner spoken but the lofty pine
Distilling pitch, the larch with turpentine,
Th'evergreen box and gummy cedar sprout,
And th'airy mountains mantle round about;
The mastful oak, the useful ash, the holm,
Coat-changing cork, white maple, shady elm,
Through hill and plain ranged their plumed ranks.
The winding rivers bordered all their banks
With slice-sea alders,[10] and green osiers small
With trembling poplars, and with willows pale,
And many trees beside, fit to be made
Fuel or timber, or to serve for shade.
The dainty apricock, of plums the prince,
The velvet peach, gilt orange, downy quince,
Already bear, graven in their tender barks,
God's powerful providence in open marks.
The scent-sweet apple and astringent pear,
The cherry, filbert, walnut, meddelar,
The milky fig, the damson black and white,
The date and olive, aiding appetite,
Spread everywhere a most delightful spring,
And everywhere a very Eden bring.

---

[10]Because alders have the property of remaining under water in-
definitely without decay, they have been much used for sluices.

Here the fine pepper in close clusters hung,
There cinnamon and other spices sprung;
Here dangled nutmegs, that for thrifty pains
Yearly repay the Bandans wondrous gains;
There grows—th'Hesperian plant,—the precious reed
Whence sugary syrups in abundance bleed.
There weeps the balm, and famous trees from whence
Th'Arabians fetch perfuming frankincense.
There th'amorous vine coils, in a thousand sorts
With winding arms her spouse that her supports,—
The vine, as far inferior to the rest
In beauty, as in bounty past the best.   .   .   .

And though through sin, whereby from heavenly state
Our parents barred us, th'earth, degenerate
From her first beauty, bearing still upon her
Eternal scars of her first lord's dishonor;
Though with the world's age her weak age decay,
Though she becomes less fruitful every day,   .   .   .
Yet doth she yield matter enough to sing
And praise the Maker of so rich a thing.

Never mine eyes in pleasant spring behold
The azure flax, the golden marigold,
The violet's purple, the sweet rose's stammel,
The lily's snow, and pansy's various ammel,
But that in them the Painter I admire,
Who in more colors doth the fields attire,
Than fresh Aurora's rosy cheeks display
When in the east she ushers in fair day,
Or Iris' bow, which, bended in the sky,
Bodes fruitful dews whereas the fields be dry,

Here, dear Lord Bartas, give thy servant leave[11]
In thy rich garland one rare flower to weave
Whose wondrous nature had more worthy been
Of thy divine, immortalizing pen,
But from thy sight, when Seine did swell with blood,
It sunk, perhaps, under the crimson flood,
When beldam Medicis, Valois, and Guise,

---

[11]Eighteen lines are interpolated here.

Stained Hymen's robe with heathen cruelties,
Because the sun, to shun so vile a view,
His chamber kept, and wept Bartholomew.
For so, so soon as in the western seas
Apollo sinks in silver Euphrates,
The lotos dives deeper and deeper ay
Till midnight, then remounteth toward day,
But not above the water till the sun
Do re-ascend above the horizon;
So ever true to Titan's radiant flame
That, rise he, fall he, it doth still the same. . . .

God, not content to've given these plants of ours
Precious perfumes, fruits, plenty, pleasant flowers,
Infused physic in their leaves and mores
To cure our sickness and to salve our sores;
Else, doubtless, death assaults so many ways,
Scarce could we live a quarter of our days;
But like the flax, which flowers at once and falls,
One feast would serve our births and burials;
Our birth our death, our cradle then our tomb,
Our tender spring our winter would become.

Good Lord! how many gasping souls have 'scaped
By th'aid of herbs, for whom the grave hath gaped,
Who, even about to touch the Stygian strand,
Have yet beguiled grim Pluto's greedy hand!
Beardless Apollo's bearded son[12] did once
With juice of herbs rejoin the scattered bones
Of the chaste prince that, in th'Athenian court,
Preferred death before incestuous sport.
So did Medea, for her Jason's sake,
The frozen limbs of [13]Aeson youthful make.

O sacred simples that our life sustain
And when it flies us, call it back again;
'Tis not alone your liquor, inly ta'en,
That oft defends us from so many a bane,

---

[12]Æsculapius.
[13]Aeson was the father of Jason, said by Ovid to have experienced a renewal of his youth by the magical practices of Medea.

But even your savor, yea, your neighborhood,
For some diseases is exceeding good,
Working so rare effects that only such
As feel or see them can believe so much.
  Blue succory, hanged on the naked neck,
Dispels the dimness that our sight doth check, .   .   .
The burning sun, the baneful aconite,
The poisonous serpents that unpeople quite
Cyrenean deserts, never endanger them
That wear about them th'Artemisian stem.
About an infant's neck hang peony,—
It cures Alcides' cruel malady.[14]
If fuming bowls of Bacchus in excess
Trouble thy brains with storms[15] of giddiness,
Put but a garland of green saffron on
And that mad humor will be quickly gone.
Th'enchanting charms of Siren's blandishments,
Contagious air, engendering pestilence,
Infect not those that in their mouths have ta'en
Angelica, that happy counter-bane
Sent down from heaven by some celestial scout,
As well the name and nature both avow't. .   .
  Nor, powerful herbs, do we alonely find
Your virtues working in frail human-kind;
But you can force the fiercest animals,
The fellest fiends, the firmest minerals,—
Yea, fairest planets, if antiquity
Have not belied the hags of Thessaly.
The touch alone of choke-pard aconite[16]
Bereaves the scorpion both of sense and might;
As, opposite, helleborus doth make
His vital powers from deadly slumber wake.
With betony fell serpents round beset,
Lift up their heads and fall to hiss and spet,

---

[14]Eczema.
[15]This may be the first record of "brain-storm" which alienists have lately reckoned upon as a foundation for a defense of murderers.
[16]Apparently a plant having a tendency to choke animals of the tiger family, according to popular reports.

With spiteful fury in their sparkling eyes
Breaking all truce with infinite defies.
Puffed up with rage, to't by the ears they go,
Bane against bane, plague against plague they throw,
Charging each other with so fierce a force,
(For friends turned foes have lightly least remorse,)
That, wounded all, or rather all awound,
With poisoned gore they cover all the ground,
And naught can stint their strange, intestine strife,
But only th'end of their detested life.
   As betony breaks friendship's ancient bands,
So willow-wort makes wonted hate shake hands;
For being fastened to proud coursers' collars
That fight and fling, it will abate their cholers,   . . .
And horse that, feeding on the grassy hills
Tread upon moon-wort with their hollow heels,
Though lately shod, at night go barefoot home,
Their master musing where their shoes be come.
O moonwort, tell us where thou hid'st the smith,
Hammer and pincers thou unshoest them with.
Alas, what lock or iron engine is't
That can thy subtile, secret strength resist,
Since the best farrier cannot set a shoe
So sure but thou so shortly canst undo?
   But I suppose not that the earth doth yield
In hill or dale, in forest or in field,
A rarer plant than Candian dittany,
Which, wounded deer eating, immediately
Not only cures their wounds exceeding well,
But 'gainst the shooter doth the shaft repel.
Moreover, Lord, is't not a work of Thine
That everywhere, in every turf, we find
Such multitude of other plants to spring
In form, effect and color, differing?
And each of them, in their due seasons ta'en
To one is physic, to another bane;
Now gentle; sharp anon; now good, then ill;
What cureth now, the same anon doth kill.
Th'herb, sagapen, serves the slow ass for meat,

But kills the ox if of the same he eat.
So branched hemlock for the stares[17] is fit,
But death to man if he but taste of it;
And oleander unto beasts is poison
But unto man a special counter-poison.

What ranker poison, what more deadly bane
Than aconite can there be touched, or ta'en?
And yet his juice but cures the burning bite
Of stinging serpents, if applied to it.
O valiant venom! O courageous plant!
Disdainful poison, noble combatant,
That scorneth aid, and loves alone to fight,
That none partake the glory of his might.
For if he find our bodies prepossessed
With other poison, then he leaves the rest,
And with his rival enters secret duel,
One to one, strong to strong, cruel to cruel,
Still fighting fierce, and never overgive
Till they, both dying, give man leave to live.

And to conclude, whether I walk the fields,
Rush through the woods, or clamber up the hills,
I find God everywhere. Thence all depend.
He giveth frankly what we thankf'ly spend.
Here for our food millions of flowery grains
With long mustachios wave upon the plains;
Here thousand fleeces, fit for princes' robes,
In Serean forests hang in silken globes;
Here shrubs of Malta, for my meaner use,
The fine white balls of bombace[18] do produce;
Here th'azure flowered flax is finely spun
For finest linen by the Belgian nun;
Here fatal hemp, which Denmark doth afford,
Doth furnish us with canvas and with cord,
Cables and sails, that, winds assisting either,
We may acquaint the east and west together,
And dryfoot dance on Neptune's watery front,

17Starlings.
18Cotton.

And in adventure lead whole towns upon't.
Here, of one grain of maize, a reed doth spring
That, thrice a year, five hundred grains doth bring,
Which, after, th'Indians parch and pound and knead,
And thereof make them a most wholesome bread.
  Th'almighty Voice which built this mighty ball
Still, still resounds and echoes over all,
And that alone yearly the world revives;
Through that alone all springs, all lives, all thrives;
And that alone makes that our mealy grain
Our skillful seedman scatters not in vain,
But being covered by the toothful harrow,
Or hid awhile under the folded furrow,
Rots to revive; and warmly wet, puts forth[19]
Its root beneath, its bud above the earth;
Enriching shortly with its springing crop
The ground with green, the husbandman with hope.
The bud becomes a blade, the blade a reed,
The reed an ear, the ear another seed;
The seed, to shut the wasteful sparrows out,
In harvest hath a stand of pikes about,
And chaffy husks in hollow cods enclose it,
Lest heat, wet, wind should roast or rot or lose it,
And lest the straw should not sustain the ear,
With knotty joints 'tis sheathed here and there.
  Pardon me, reader, if thy ravished eyes
Have seen today too great varieties
Of trees, of flowers, of fruit, of herbs, of grains
In these, my groves, meads, orchards, gardens, plains,
Since th'isle of Cebu's admirable tree
Beareth a fruit, called cocos commonly,
The which alone far richer wonders yields
Than all our groves, meads, orchards, gardens, fields.
What, wouldst thou drink? The wounded leaves drop
    wine.
Lack'st thou fine linen? Dress the tender rind,—
Dress it like flax; spin it and weave it well;

---

[19]See Par. Lost, VII, 280.

It shall thy cambric and thy lawn excel.
Long'st thou for butter?   Bite the pulpy part,
And never better came to any mart.
Needest thou oil?   Then bolt it to and fro,
And passing oil it soon becometh so.
Or vinegar, to whet thine appetite?
Then sun it well and it will sharply bite.
Or want'st thou sugar?   Steep the same a stound,
And sweeter sugar is not to be found.
'Tis what you will, or will be what you would.
Should Midas touch it 'twould, I think, be gold;
And God, I think, to crown our life with joys,
The earth with plenty and His name with praise,
Had done enough if He had made no more
Than this one plant, so full of wondrous store;
Save that the world, when one thing breeds satiety,
Could not be fair without so great variety.

But earth not only on her back doth bear
Abundant treasures, glistering everywhere,
But inwardly she's no less fraught with riches,
Nay, rather more, which more our souls bewitches.
Within the deep folds of her fruitful lap
Such boundless mines of treasure doth she wrap
That the hungry hands of human avarice
Cannot exhaust with labor or device.
For they be more than there be stars in heaven,
Or stormy billows on the ocean driven,
Or ears of corn in autumn on the fields,
Or savage beasts upon a thousand hills,
Or fishes diving in the silver floods,
Or scattered leaves in winter in the woods.[20]

Slate, jet and marble shall escape my pen;
I overpass the salt mount Orimene;
I blench the brine-quar hill in Arragon,
Whence there they powder their provision.
I'll only now emboss my book with brass,

---

[20]"Thick as leaves in Vallombrosa," according to the popular perversion of lines 302 and 303, Book I of Paradise Lost.

Dye't with vermilion, deck't with copperas,
With gold and silver, lead and mercury,
Tin, iron, orpine, stigium, lethargy;
And on my gold-work I will only place
The crystal pure which doth reflect each face,
The precious ruby of a sanguine hue,
The seal-fit onyx and the sapphire blue,
The chalcedony, full of circles round,
The tender topaz and rich diamond,
The various opal and green emerald,
The agate by a thousand titles called,
The sky-like turquoise, purple amethysts,
And fiery carbuncle, which flame resists.
  I know to man the earth seems altogether
No more a mother, but a step-dame, rather,
Because, alas, unto our loss she bears
Bloodshedding steel and gold, the ground of cares,
As if these metals, and not man amiss,
Had made sin mount unto the height it is;
But as the sweet bait of abundant riches
Bodies and souls of greedy men bewitches,
Gold gilds the virtuous, and it lends them wings
To raise their thoughts unto the rarest things.
The wise not only iron will apply
For household turns, and tools of husbandry,
But to defend their country when it calls,
From foreign dangers and intestine brawls.
But with the same the wicked never mell
But to do service to the hags of hell;
To pick a lock, to take a neighbor's purse,
To break a house or to do something worse,—
To cut a parent's throat, to kill his prince,
To spoil his country, murdering innocents.
Even so, profaning of a gift divine,
The drunkard drowns his reason in the wine.
So sale-tongued lawyers, wresting eloquence,
Excuse rich wrong, and cast poor innocence;
So antichrists, their poison to infuse

Miscite the scriptures and God's name abuse.[21] . . . .
So God's best gifts, usurped by wicked ones,
To poison turn, through their contagions.
    But shall I balk th'admired adamant
Whose dead-live power my reason's power doth daunt?
Renowned loadstone which on iron acts,
And by a touch the same aloof attracts,—
Attracts it strangely with unclasping crooks,
With unknown cords, with unconceived hooks,
With unseen hands, with undiscerned arms,
With hidden force, with sacred, secret charms,
Wherewith he woos his iron mistress
And never leaves her till he gets a kiss; .
Nay, till he folds her in his faithful bosom,
Never to part, except we, loveless, loose 'em,
With so firm zeal and fast affection
The stone doth love the steel, the steel the stone.
And though some time some make-bate come betwixt,
Still burns their first flame, 'tis so surely fixed;
And while they cannot meet to break their minds,
With mutual skips they show their love by signs,
As bashful suitors, seeing strangers by,[22]
Parley in silence with the hand or eye.
    Who can conceive or censure in what sort
One loadstone-touched amulet doth transport
Another iron ring, and that another
Till four or five hang dangling one from other?
Great as Apollo might he be, methinks,
Could tell the reason of those hanging links;
Since reason-scanners have resolved, all,
That heavy things, hanged in the air, must fall.
    I am not ignorant that he who seeks
In Roman robes to suit the sagest Greeks,—
Whose jealous wife, weening to home revoke him
With a love potion, did with poison choke him,—

---

[21]"The devil can cite scripture for his purpose."—Merch. of Venice, 1, 2.
[22]An interpolated couplet.

Hath sought to show, with arguing subtility,
The secret cause of this rare sympathy.
But say, Lucretius, what's the hidden cause
That toward the north star the needle draws
Whose point is touched with loadstone? Loose this
    knot,
And still green laurel shall be still thy lot;
Yea, thee more learned will I then confess
Than Epicurus or Empedocles.

    We're not to Ceres so much bound for bread,
Neither to Bacchus for his clusters red,
As, Signor Flavio, to thy witty trial,
For first inventing of the seaman's dial, . . .
Whereby, through th'ocean, in the darkest night,
Our hugest carracks are conducted right, ...
Whereby a ship that stormy heavens have whirled
Near in one night into another world,
Knows where she is, and in the card descries
What degrees thence the equinoctial lies.

    Clear-sighted spirits that cheer with sweet aspect[23]
My other rhymes, though subject to defect,—
If in this volume, as you over-read it,
You meet some things that seem to pass all credit,
Because, perhaps, here proved yet by no man,
Their strange effects be not in knowledge common;
Think that to some the loadstone's use is new,
And seems as strange as we have tried it true.
Let, therefore, that which iron draws, draw such
To credit more than what they see and touch.

    Nor is th'earth only worthy praise eternal,
For the rare riches on her back external,
Or in her bosom; but her own self's worth
Solicits me to sound her glory forth.
I call to witness all those weak diseased
Whose bodies oft have by th'effect been eased
Of Lemnos' sealed earth, or Eretrian soil,
Or that of Chios, or of Melos' isle.

---

[23]Ten lines interpolated.

All hail, fair earth, bearer of towns and towers,
Of men, gold, grain, physic and fruits and flowers!
Fair, firm and fruitful, various, patient, sweet,
Sumptuously clothed in a mantle meet
Of mingled color; laced about with floods,
And all embroidered with fresh-blooming buds,
With rarest gems richly about embossed,
Excelling cunning and exceeding cost.
   All hail, great heart, round base and steadfast root
Of all the world![24] The world's strong, fixed foot!
Heaven's chastest spouse! Supporter of this all!
This glorious building's goodly pedestal!
All hail, dear mother, sister, hostess, nurse,
Sovereign of all worlds! Of thy liberal purse
We're all maintained. Matchless emperess,
To do thee service with all readiness,
The spheres before thee bear ten thousand torches;
The fire to warm thee folds his heatful arches
In purest flames about the floating cloud.
Th'air, to refresh thee, willingly is bowed
About the waves, and well content to suffer
Mild Zephyr's blasts, and Boreas' billowing rougher.
Water, to quench thy thirst, about thy mountains
Wraps her moist arms,—seas, rivers, lakes and foun-
    tains. . . .
   O thrice, thrice happy he who shuns the cares[25]
Of city troubles and of state affairs,
And, serving Ceres, tills with his own team
His own free land, left by his friends to him!
   Never pale envy's poisonous heads do hiss
To gnaw his heart, nor vulture avarice.
His field's bounds bound his thoughts. He never sups
For nectar, poison mixed in silver cups;
Neither in golden platters doth he lick,
For sweet ambrosia, deadly arsenic.
His hand's his bowl,—better than plate or glass,—

24Meaning the visible universe.
25Compare Pope's "Ode on Solitude."

The silver brook his sweetest hippocras.
Milk, cheese and fruits, fruits of his own endeavor,
Dressed without dressing, hath he ready ever.
　　False counselors—concealers—of the law,
Turn-coat attorneys that with both hands draw,
Sly pettifoggers, wranglers at the bar,
Proud purse-leeches, harpies of Westminster,
With feigned chiding and foul jarring noise
Rack not his brain nor interrupt his joys;
But cheerful birds, chirping him sweet good morrows[26]
With nature's music do beguile his sorrows,
Teaching the fragrant forests, day by day,
The diapason of their heavenly lay.
　　His wandering vessel, reeling to and fro
On th'ireful ocean, as the winds do blow,
With sudden tempest is not overwhirled
To seek his sad death in another world;
But leading all his life at home in peace,
Always in sight of his own smoke; no seas,—
No other seas he knows, nor other torrent
Than that which waters with its silver current
His native meadows; and that very earth
Shall give him burial which first gave him birth.
　　To summon timely sleep he doth not need
Ethiop's cold rush, nor drowsy poppy seed, . . .
But on green carpets, thrummed with mossy beaver,
Fringing the round skirts of his winding river,
The stream's mild murmur, as it gently gushes,[27]
His healthy limbs in quiet slumber hushes.
　　Drum, fife and trumpet, with their loud alarms,
Make him not start out of his sleep to arms;
Nor dear respect of some great general
Him from his bed unto the block doth call.
The crested cock sings "Hunt is up!" to him,
Limits his rest, and makes him stir betime,

---

[26]"The lark . . . to come in spite of sorrow
　And at my window bid Good morrow."—L'Allegro.
[27]"And gushing brooks."—Lycidas.

To walk the mountains or the flowery meads,
Impearled with tears that sweet Aurora sheds.   .   .   .
 His wretched years in princes' courts he spends not,
His thralled will on great men's wills depends not;
He, changing master, doth not change at once
His faith,—religion and his God renounce;—
With mercenary lies he doth not chant,
Praising an emmet for an elephant,—
Sardanapalus, drowned in soft excess,
For a triumphant, virtuous Hercules;
Thersites foul for Venus' lovely Love,
And every changeling for a turtle dove;
Nor lavishes in his lascivious lays
On wanton Flora chaste Alcestis' praise;
But all self-private, serving God, he writes
Fearless, and sings but what his heart indites.
 No sallow fear doth day and night afflict him;
Unto no fraud doth day or night addict him;
Or if he muse on guile, 'tis but to get
Beast, bird or fish, in toil or snare or net.
 What though his wardrobe be not stately stuffed
With sumptuous silks, pinked and pounced and puffed,
With gold ground velvets and with silver tissue
And all the glory of old Eve's proud issue?
What though his feeble coffers be not crammed
With misers' idols, golden ingots, rammed?
He is warm wrapped in his own grown wool;
Of unbought wines his cellar's ever full;
His garner's stored with grain, his ground with flocks,
His barns with fodder, with sweet streams his rocks. . .
Let me, good Lord, among the great unkenned,
My rest of days in the calm country end. .   .   .
Be Hadley pond my sea, Lambsbourn my Thames,[28]
Lambourn my London, Kennet's silver streams
My fruitful Nile; my singers and musicians

---

[28]These concluding lines are substituted by the translator for similar ones in the original, in which the reference is to the estates of
the author. The half dozen closing lines of the French make a pretty

The pleasant birds, with warbling repetitions;
My company pure thoughts to work Thy will,
My court a cottage on a lowly hill,
Where without let I may so sing Thy name
That times to come may wonder at the same.
Or if the new North Star, my sovereign James,
The secret virtue of whose sacred beams
Attracts th'attentive service of all such
Whose minds did ever virtue's loadstone touch,
Shall ever deign t'invite mine humble fate
T'approach the presence of his royal state;
Or if my duty or the grace of nobles
Shall drive or draw me near their pleasing troubles,
Let not their favors make me drunk with folly;
In their commands still keep my conscience holy;
Let me true honor, not the false, delight,
And play the preacher, not the parasite.

---

rural picture, as follows:—
　　　"Mon etang soit ma mer, mon bosquet mon Ardène,
　　La Gimone mon Nil, le Sarrampin ma Seine:
　　Mes chantres et mes Lucs les mignards oiselés:
　　Mon cher Bartas mon Louvre: et ma cour mes valés:
　　Ou sans nul détourbier si bien ton los l'entone,
　　Que la race future a bon droit s'en étone."

THE FOURTH DAY

Pure Spirit that rapt'st above the firmest sphere
In fiery coach thy faithful messenger,
Who, smiting Jordan with his plaited[1] cloak,
Did erst divide the waters with the stroke,
O, take me up; that far from earth I may
From sphere to sphere see th'azure heavens to-day.
Be Thou my coachman, and now, cheek by jowl,[2]
With Phœbus' chariot let my chariot roll.
Drive on my coach by Mars's flaming coach;
Saturn and Luna let my wheels approach;
That, having learned of their fire-breathing horses,
Their course, their light, their labor and their forces,
My muse may sing in sacred eloquence
To virtue's friends their virtuous eloquence.
And with the loadstone of my conquering verse
About the poles attract the most perverse. . . .
   God's none of these faint, idle artisans
Who, at the best, abandon their designs,
Working by halves; as rather, a great deal,
To do much quickly than to do it well;
But rather as a workman never weary,

---

[1]In the quartos the spelling is "pleighted," and the pronunciation probably made the vowel sound in the first syllable identical with that of our long i. The word may have been related to "ply" and have had the meaning of "folded." Compare Milton's "plighted clouds" in Comus, line 301.

[2]This phrase apparently conveyed no ludicrous meaning in its customary use in the 16th and early 17th centuries. It is employed in the description of the Resurrection, in the first of these "Days."

And all-sufficient, He His works doth carry
To happy end, and to perfection
With sober speed brings what He hath begun.
　　Having therefore the world's wide curtain spread
About the circuit of the fruitful bed
Where, to fill all with her unnumbered kin,
Kind Nature's self each moment lieth in,—
To make the same forever admirable,
More stately-pleasant and more profitable,
He th'azure tester[3] trimmed with golden marks
And richly spangled with bright, glistering sparks.
　　I know those tapers, twinkling in the sky,
Do turn too swiftly from our hand and eye;
That men can never rightly reach to seeing
Their course and force, and much, much less their being,
But if conjecture may extend above
To that great orb whose moving all doth move,
Th'imperfect light of the first day was it
Which for Heaven's eyes did shining matter fit.
For God, selecting lightest of that light,
Garnished heaven's ceiling with those torches bright,
Or else divided it, and pressing close
The parts, did make the sun and stars of those.
　　But if thy wit's thirst rather seek these things
In Grecian cisterns than in Hebrew springs,
I then conclude that, as of moistful matter
God made the people that frequent the water,
And of an earthly stuff the stubborn droves
That haunt the hills and dales and downs and groves,
So did He make of His almighty might
Th'heavens and stars of one same substance bright,
To th'end these lamps, dispersed in these skies,
Might with their orb, it with them, sympathize.
And as with us, under the oaken bark
The knurly knot with branching veins we mark
To be of substance all one with the tree,

---

[3] A tester is such a canopy as was formerly placed above a pulpit, etc., and is now often placed above beds in sleeping apartments.

Although far thicker and more rough it be,
So those gilt studs in th'upper story driven,
Are nothing but the thickest parts of heaven.
　　When I observe their light and heat yblent,
Mere accidents of th'upper element,
I think them fire, but not such fire as lasts
No longer than the fuel that it wastes;
For then I think all th'elements too little
To furnish them with only one day's victual.
And therefore smile I at those fable forges
Whose busy, idle style so stiffly urges
The heaven's bright cressets to be living creatures
Ranging for food, and hungry fodder eaters,
Still sucking up in their eternal motion
The earth for meat, and for their drink, the ocean.
　　Sure I perceive no motion in a star
But certain, natural and regular;
Whereas beasts' motions infinitely vary,
Confused, uncertain, diverse, voluntary.
I see not how so many golden posts
Should scud so swift about heaven's azure coasts,
But that the heavens must ope and shut sometimes,
Subject to passions which our earthly climes
Alter, and toss the sea, and th'air estrange,
From itself's temper with exceeding change.
　　I see not how, in those sound, blazing beams,
One should imagine any food-fit limbs,
Nor can I see how th'earth and sea should feed
So many stars, whose greatness doth exceed
So many times, if star-divines say troth,
The greatness of the earth and ocean both;
Since here our cattle in a month will eat
Seven times the bulk of their own bulk in meat.
　　These torches range not then at random o'er
The lightsome thickness of an unfirm floor,
As here below diversely moving them
The painted birds between two airs do swim;
But rather fixed unto turning spheres
Ay, will they nill they, follow their careers,

As cart nails fastened in a wheel without
Self motion, turn with others' turns about.
   As th'ague-sick, upon his shivering pallet
Delays his health oft to delight his palate,
When willfully his tasteless taste delights
In things unsavory to sound appetites,
Even so some brain-sicks live there now-a-days
That lose themselves still in contrary ways,—
Preposterous wits that cannot row at ease
On the smooth channel of our common seas.
And such are those, in my conceit at least,
Those clerks that think—think how absurd a jest!—
That neither heavens nor stars do turn at all,
Nor dance[4] about this great, round earthly ball,
But th'earth itself, this massy globe of ours,
Turns round about once every twice twelve hours,
And we resemble land-bred novices
New brought aboard to venture on the seas;
Who at first launching from the shore suppose
The ship stands still and that the firm earth goes.
   So twinkling tapers that heaven's arches fill,
Equally distant should continue still.
So never should an arrow shot upright
In the same place upon the shooter light;
But would do rather as at sea a stone
Aboard a ship upward uprightly thrown,
Which not within-board falls, but in the flood
Astern the ship if so the wind be good.[5]
So should the fowls that take their nimble flight
From western marshes towards heaven's light,
And Zephyrus, that in the summer time
Delights to visit Eurus in his clime,
And bullets thundered from the cannon's throat,

---

[4]"Dance" implied orderly movement, and is repeatedly used by Milton in that sense, especially as relating to the heavens. See Par. Lost, VII, 374; VIII, 125.

[5]It is curious that what is here assumed to be a fact could have been proved error by a perfectly easy experiment, within the scope of the daily life of every sailor, especially. And Sylvester had been a sailor all his days up to the time that he turned writer.

Whose roaring drowns the heavenly thunder's note,
Should back recoil; sithence the quick career
That our round earth should daily gallop here
Must needs exceed a hundred fold for swift
Birds, bullets, winds; their wings, their force, their drift.
  Armed with these reasons, 'twere superfluous
T'assail the reasons of Copernicus,
Who, to solve better of the stars' appearance
Unto the earth a three-fold motion warrants,
Making the sun the center of this all,
Moon, earth and water in one only ball.
But sithence here nor time nor place doth suit
His paradox at length to prosecute,
I will proceed, grounding my next discourse
On th'heaven's motions, and their constant course.
  Greatness I oft admire of mighty hills,
And pleasant beauty of the flowery fields,
And countless number of the ocean's sand,
And secret force of sacred adamant;
But much, much more, the more I mark their course,
Stars' glistering greatness, beauty, number, force.
  Even as a peacock, pricked with love's desire,
To woo his mistress, strutting stately[6] by her,
Spreads round the rich pride of his pompous veil,
His azure wings and golden starry tail,
With rattling pinions wheeling still about,
The more to let his beauteous beauty out,—
The firmament, as feeling like above,
Displays its pomp; pranceth about its love,
Spreads its blue curtain mixed with golden marks,
Set with gilt spangles, sown with glittering sparks,
Sprinkled with eyes, specked with tapers bright,
Powdered with stars, streaming with glorious light,
T'inflame the earth the more, with lover's grace,
To take the sweet fruit of his kind embrace.
  He that to number all the stars would seek,
Had need invent some new arithmetic;

---

[6]See L'Allegro, line 52.

And who to count that reckoning takes in hand
Had need for counters take the ocean's sand;
Yet have our wise and learned elders found
Four dozen figures in the heavenly round
For aid of memory; and to our eyes
In certain houses to divide the skies.
Of those are twelve in that rich girdle greft[7]
Which God gave Nature for a New Year's gift,—
When, making all, His voice almighty most
Gave so fair laws unto heaven's shining host—
To wear it bias, buckled overthwart her
Not round about her swelling waist to gird her.

   This glorious baldric,[8] of a golden tinge,
Embossed with rubies, edged with silver fringe,
Buckled with gold, with a bend glistering bright,
Heaven bias-wise environs day and night.
For, from the period when the Ram[9] doth bring
The day and night to equal balancing,
Ninety degrees towards the north it winds,
Thence just as much toward mid-heaven it bends,
As many thence toward the south, and thence
To'ards the year's portal[10] the like difference.

   Nephelean crook-horn, with brass comets crowned,
Thou buttest bravely 'gainst the New Year's bound,
And richly clad in thy fair golden fleece,
Dost hold the first house in heaven's spacious mese.
Thou spiest anon the Bull behind thy back,
Who, lest that fodder by the way he lack,
Seeing the world so naked, to renew't
Coats th'infant earth in a green, gallant suit,
And without plow or yoke doth freely fling
Through fragrant pastures of the flowery spring.
The Twins, whose heads, arms, shoulders, knees and feet
God filled with stars to shine in season sweet,

7Engraved.
8In Drake's "American Flag" the "Baldric of the Skies" is mentioned
as a source of the national colors.
9Of course the reference is to the constellation, "Aries."
10The English calendar year at that time began late in March.

Contend in course who first the Bull shall catch,
That neither will nor may attend their match.
Then summer's guide, the Crab comes rowing soft
With his eight oars through th'heaven's azure loft,
To bring us yearly, in his starry shell,
Many long days the shaggy earth to swell.
  Almost with like pace leaps the Lion out
All clad with flames, bristled with beams about,
Who, with contagion of his burning breath,
Both grass and grain to cinders withereth.
The Virgin next, sweeping heaven's azure globe
With stately train of her bright, golden robe,
Mild, proudly marching, in her left hand brings
A sheaf of corn, and in her right hand, wings.
After the Maiden shines the Balance bright,
Equal divider of the day and night,[11]
In whose gold beam with three gold rings there fastens
With six gold strings a pair of golden basins.
  The spiteful Scorpion, next the Scale addressed,
With two bright lamps covers his loathsome breast,
And fain from both ends with his double sting
Would spet his venom over everything.
But that the brave half-horse Phylirian Scout,[12]
Galloping swift the heavenly belt about,
Ay fiercely threats with his flame-feathered arrow
To shoot the sparkling, starry viper thorow.
And th'hoary Centaur, during all his race,
Is so attentive to this only chase,
That, dreadless of his dart, heaven's shining Kid
Comes jumping light, just at his heels unsped.
  Meanwhile the Skinker[13] from his starry spout
After the Goat a silvery stream pours out,
Distilling still out of his radiant fire
Rivers of water—who but will admire?—
In whose clear channel might at pleasure swim

---

[11]That is to say, the autumnal equinox occurs when the sun has
entered the constellation, "Libra."
[12]Sagittarius.
[13]Aquarius.

Those two bright Fishes that do follow him,
But that the torrent slides so swift away
That it outruns them ever, even as they
Outrun the Ram, who ever them pursues,
And by renewing yearly, all renews.
   Besides these twelve, toward the arctic side
A flaming Dragon doth two Bears divide;
After, the Wainman comes, the Crown, the Spear,
The Kneeling Youth, the Harp, the Hamperer
Of th'hateful Snake,—whether we call the same
By Esculapius' or Alcides' name,—
Swift Pegasus, the Dolphin, (loving man,[14])
Jove's stately Eagle, and the silver Swan,
Andromeda, with Cassiopeia near her,
Her father Cepheus and her Perseus dearer,
The shining Triangle, Medusa's Tress,
And the bright Coachman of Tyndarides.
   Toward th'other pole Orion, Eridanus
The Whale, the Whelp, and hot-breathed Sirius,
The Hare, the Hulk, the Hydra and the Bowl,
The Centaur, Wolf, the Censer and the Fowl,
The twice foul Raven, the Southern Fish, and Crown
Through heaven's bright arches brandish up and down.
   Thus on this day working, th'eighth azure tent[15]
With artless art, divinely excellent,
Th'Almighty's finger fixed many a million
Of golden 'scutcheons in that rich pavilion,
But in the rest, under that glorious heaven,
But one apiece unto the several seven;[16]
Lest of those lamps the number-passing number
Should mortal eyes with such confusion cumber
That we should never, in the clearest night,
Stars' divers courses see or discern aright.
   And therefore also all the fixed tapers
He made to twinkle with such trembling capers;

---

[14]Referring to Arion's adventure.
[15]Again alluding to the supposed structure of spheres in the visible universe.
[16]One sphere for each of the "seven planets."

But the seven lights that wander under them
Through various passage never shake a beam;
Or He perhaps made them not different,
But th'host of sparks spread through the firmament
Far from our sense, through distance infinite,
Seems but to twinkle to our twinkling sight;
Whereas the rest, nearer a thousand-fold
To th'earth and sea, we do more brim[17] behold.
For th'heavens are not mixedly interlaced,
But th'undermost by th'upper be embraced,
And more or less their roundels wider are,
As from the center they be near or far;
As in an egg the shell includes the skin,
The skin the white, the white the yolk within.
 Now, as the wind, buffing upon a hill
With roaring breath against a ready mill,
Whirls with a whiff the sails of swelling clout,
The sails do swing the winged shaft about,
The shaft the wheel, the wheel the trendle turns,
And that the stone which grinds the floury corns;
Or like as also in a clock well tended,
Just counterpoise justly thereon suspended,
Makes the great wheel go round, and that anon[18]
Turns with its turning many a meaner one,
The trembling watch and th'iron maul that chimes
The entire day in twice twelve equal times,
So the grand heaven in four and twenty hours,
Surveying all this various house of ours,
With his quick motion all the spheres doth move
Whose radiant glances gild the world above,
And drives them every day, which swiftness strange is,
From Gange to Tagus and from Tay to Ganges.
 But th' under-orbs, as grudging to be still
So straitly subject to another's will,
Still without change, still at another's pleasure,

---

[17]Middle English "breme" is defined as "sharp, cruel, severe." It
would seem to have had also the meaning, "conspicuous," and was
occasionally written as above, and sometimes "brimme."
[18]"Then to the well-trod stage anon."—L'Allegro.

After one pipe to dance one only measure,
They from-ward turn, and traversing aside,
Each by himself an oblique course doth slide;[19]
So that they all, although it seem not so,
Forward and backward at an instant go,
Both up and down and with contrary paces,
At once they post to two contrary places.
(Like as myself, in my lost merchant years,[20]—
A loss, alas, that in these lines appears,—
Wafting to Brabant England's golden fleece,
A richer prize than Jason brought to Greece,
While toward the sea our then swan-poorer Thames
Bore down my bark upon her ebbing streams,
Upon the hatches, from the prow to poop
Walking, in compass of that narrow coop,
Maugre the most that wind and tide could do,
Have gone at once towards Lee and London too.)
   But now the nearer any of these eight
Approach th' empyreal palace walls in height,
The more their circuit, and more days they spend
Ere they return unto their journey's end.
It's therefore thought that sumptuous canopy
The which th'unniggard hand of Majesty
Powdered so thick with shields so shining clear
Spends in its voyage nigh seven thousand year.
   Ingenious Saturn, spouse of memory,
Father of th'age of gold, though coldly dry,
Silent and sad, bald, hoary, wrinkled-faced,
Yet art thou first among the planets placed,
And thirty years thy leaden coach doth run
Ere it arrive where thy career begun.[21]
Thou, rich, benign, ill-chasing Jupiter
Art rightly next thy father,—sickle bearer,—

---

[19]Sylvester's marginal note says:—"Each of the eight heavens so transported by the primum mobile hath also his proper oblique and distinct course.
[20]This parenthesis is an interpolation.
[21]"Thy (the moon's) pale career."—Il Penseroso.

And while thou dost with thy more mild aspect
His froward beams' disastrous frowns correct,
Thy tinnen chariot, shod with burning bosses,
Through twice six signs in twice six twelve-months
    crosses.
    Brave minded Mars, (yet master of disorder,
Delighting naught but battles, blood and murder),
His furious coursers lasheth night and day,
That he may swiftly pass his course away;
But in the road of his eternal race
So many rubs hinder his hasty pace
That thrice, the while the lively liquor-god
With dabbled heels hath swelling clusters trod,
And thrice hath Ceres shaven her amber tress
Ere his steel wheels have done their business.
    Pure goldy-locks Sol, state's friend, honor giver,
Light bringer, laureate, leech man, all-reviver,
Thou in three hundred three score days and five
Dost to the period of thy race arrive.
For with thy proper course thou measur'st th' year
And measur'st days with thy constrained career.
    Fair, dainty Venus . . . .
Whom wanton dalliance, dancing and delight,
Smiles, witty wiles, youth, love, and beauty bright,
With soft, blind Cupids evermore consort,—
Of lightsome day opens and shuts the port;
For hardly dare her silver doors go far
From bright Apollo's glory-beaming car.
    Not much unlike moves Mercury the witty;
For ship, for shop, book, bar or court, or city;
Smooth orator, swift penman, sweet musician,
Rare artisan, deep reaching politician,
Fortunate merchant, fine prince' humor pleaser,
To end his course takes near a twelve-months' leisure,
For all the while his nimble, winged heels
Dare little budge from Phoebus' golden wheels.
    And lastly Luna, thou cold Queen of Night,[23]

---

[23]See "Two Gentlemen of Verona," IV, 2, 100; "As You Like It,"

Regent of humors, parting months aright,
Chaste emperess, to one Endymion constant,—
Constant in love though in thy mien inconstant,
(Unlike our loves, whose hearts dissemble soonest,)
Twelve times a year through all the zodiac runnest.
   Now if these lamps, so infinite in number,
Should still stand still as in a slothful slumber,
Then should some places, always in one plight,
Have always day and some have always night.
Then should the summer's fire and winter's frost
Rest opposite still on the selfsame coast.
Then naught could spring and nothing prosper would
In all the world for want of heat and cold. . . .
   I'll ne'er believe that the Arch-Architect
With all these fires the heavenly arches decked
Only for show, and with these glistering shields,
T' amaze poor shepherds watching in the fields.
I'll ne'er believe that the least flower that pranks[24]
Our garden borders or the common banks,
And the least stone that in her warming lap
Our kind nurse, Earth, doth covetously wrap,
Hath some peculiar virtue of its own
And that the glorious stars of heaven have none,
But shine in vain, and have no charge precise
But to be walking in heaven's galleries,
And through that palace up and down to clamber,
As golden gulls about a prince's chamber.
   Senseless is he who without blush denies
What to sound senses most apparent lies;
And 'gainst experience he that spets fallacions
Is to be hissed from learned disputations.
And such is he that doth affirm the stars
To have no force on these inferiors,
Though heaven's effects we most apparent see
In number more than heavenly torches be.

III. 2, 2. Sylvester mentions "the pale Queen of Night" towards the
end of the 7th Day.
  [24]"Pranked in Reason's garb."—Comus.

I will allege the seasons' alteration
Caused by the sun in shifting habitation;
I will not urge that never at noondays
His envious sister intercepts his rays
But some great state eclipseth, and from hell
Alecto looses all these furies fell;—
Grim, lean-faced Famine, foul, infectious Plague,
Bloodthirsty War and Treason—hateful hag!
Here pouring down Woe's universal flood
To drown the world in seas of tears and blood.
    I'll overpass how sea doth ebb and flow
As th'horned queen doth either shrink or grow;
And that the more she fills her forked round
The more the marrow doth in bones abound,
The blood in veins, the sap in plants, the moisture
And luscious meat in crayfish, crab and oyster;
That oak and elm and fir and alder, cut
Before the crescent have her cornets shut,
Are never lasting for the builder's turn
In ship or house, but rather fit to burn;
And also that the sick, while she is filling,
Feel sharper fits through all their members thrilling
So that this lamp alone approves what powers
Heaven's tapers have, even on these souls of ours,
Tempering or troubling, as they be inclined,
Our mind and humors, humors and our mind,
Through sympathy, which, while this flesh we carry,
Our souls and bodies doth together marry.
    I'll only say that since the hot aspect
Of th'heavenly Dog-Star kindles with effect
A thousand unseen fires, and dries the fields,
Scorches the valleys, parches up the hills,
And oftentimes unto our panting hearts
The bitter fits of burning fevers darts;
And opposite, the Cup, the dropping Pleiades,
Bright glistering Orion and the weeping Hyades
Never almost look down on our abode
But that they stretch the waters' bounds abroad;
With cloudy horror of their wrathful frown

Threatening again the guilty world to drown;
And to be brief, since the gilt azure front
Of firmest sphere hath scarce a spark upon't
But poureth downward from apparent change
Toward the storing of the world's great grange,
We may conjecture what hid power is given
T'infuse among us from the other seven,—
From each of these which for their virtue rare
Th' Almighty placed in a proper sphere.
  Not that as Stoic I intend to tie
With iron chains of strong necessity
Th' Eternal's hands, and his free feet enstock
In destiny's hard, adamantine rock.
I hold that God, as the first cause, hath given
Light, course and force to all the lamps of heaven;
That still He guides them, and His providence
Disposeth free their fatal influence;
And that therefore the rather we below
Should study all their course and force to know,
To th'end that, seeing through our parents' fall,
T'how many tyrants we are waxen thrall,
Ever since first fond woman's blind ambition
Breaking, made Adam break heaven's high commission,
We might unpuff our heart and bend our knee
T'appease with sighs God's wrathful majesty;
Beseeching Him to turn away the storms
Of hail and heat, plague, death and dreadful arms,
Which oft the angry stars, with bad aspects,
Threat to be falling on our stubborn necks;
To give us curbs to bridle th' ill proclivity
We are inclined to by a hard nativity;
To pour some water, of His grace, to quench
Our boiling flesh's fell concupiscence;
To calm our many passions, spiritual tremors,
Sprung from corruption of our vicious humors.
  Latonian twins,[25] parent of years and months,
Alas, why hide you so your shining fronts?

---

[25]The sun and moon.

What, will you show the splendor of your ray
But through a veil of mourning clouds, I pray?
I pray, pull off your mufflers and your mourning,
And let me see you in your native burning;
And my dear muse by her eternal flight
Shall spread as far the glory of your light
As you yourselves run in alternate ring
Day after night, night after day to bring.
  Thou radiant coachman, running endless course,
Fountain of heat, of light the lively source,
Life of the world, Lamp of this universe,
Heaven's richest gem! O teach me where my verse
May but begin thy praise. Alas, I fare
Much like the one that in the clouds doth stare
To count the quails that with their shadow cover
Th' Italian sea when soaring hither over,
Fain of a milder and more fruitful clime,
They come, with us to pass the summer time.
No sooner he begins one shoal to sum,
But more and more still greater shoals do come,
Swarm upon swarm, that with their countless number
Break off his purpose and his sense encumber.
  Day's glorious eye! Even as a mighty king
About his country, stately, progressing
Is compassed round with dukes, earls, lords and knights,
Orderly marshaled in their noble rights,
Esquires and gentlemen in courtly kind,
And then his guard before him and behind;
And there is naught in all this royal muster
But to his greatness addeth grace and luster,
So, while about the world thou ridest ay,—
Which only lives by virtue of thy ray,—
Six heavenly princes, mounted evermore,
Wait on the coach, three behind, three before,
Besides the hosts of th'upper twinkling bright,
To whom, for pay, thou givest only light.
  And even as man—the little world of cares—
Within the middle of his body bears
His heart, the spring of life, which with proportion

Supplieth spirits to all and every portion;
Even so, O sun, thy golden chariot marches
Amid the six lamps of the six low arches
Which seal the world, that equally it might
Richly impart them beauty, force and light.
   Praising thy heat, which subtilely doth pierce
The solid thickness of our universe,
Which in th'earth's kidneys mercury doth burn,
And pallid sulphur to bright metal turn,
I do digress to praise that light of thine,
Which, if it should but one day cease to shine,
The unpurged air to water would resolve,
And water would the mountain tops involve.
  . . . .Rising from the Indian wave,
Thou seem'st, O Titan, like a bridegroom brave,
Who from his chamber early issuing out
In rich array, with rarest gems about,
With pleasant countenance and lovely face,
With golden tresses and attractive grace,
Cheers at his coming all the youthful throng
That for his presence earnestly did long,
Blessing the day, and with delightful glee
Singing aloud his epithalamy. . . .
   When I record how fitly thou dost guide
Through the fourth heaven thy flaming coursers' pride,
That as they pass their fiery breaths may temper
Saturn's and Cynthia's cold and moist distemper,
(For, if thou galloped'st in the nether room
Like Phaeton, thou wouldst the world consume,
Or, if thy throne were set in Saturn's sky,
For want of heat then everything would die,)
In the same instant I am pressed to sing
How thy return reviveth everything;
How in thy presence fear, sloth, sleep and night,
Snows, fogs and fancies take their sudden flight.
Thou'rt, to be brief, an ocean wanting bound,
Where (as full vessels have the lesser sound,)
Plenty of matter makes the speaker mute,
As wanting words thy worth to prosecute.

Yet glorious monarch, 'mong so many rare
And matchless flowers as in thy garland are,
Some one or two shall my chaste, sober muse
For thine immortal sacred sisters choose.
I'll boldly sing, bright sovereign, thou art none
Of those weak princes flattery works upon;—
No second Edward, nor no Richard Second,
Un-kinged both, as rule-unworthy reckoned,[26]—
Who, to enrich their minions past proportion,
Pill all their subjects with extreme extortion;
And charmed with pleasures,—O exceeding pity!—
Lie always wallowing in one wanton city;
And, loving only that, to mean lieutenants
Farm out their kingdom's care, as unto tenants.
For, once a day, each country under heav'n
Thou bidst good-morrow, and thou bidst good-even.
And thy far-seeing eye, as censor, views
The rites and fashions fish and fowl do use,
And our behaviors, worthy, every one,
Th'Abderian laughter and Ephesian moan.
But true it is, to th'end a fruitful lew
May every climate in its time renew,
And that all men may nearer, in all realms,
Feel the alternate virtue of thy beams;
Thy sumptuous chariot with the light returning
From the same portal mounts not every morning;
But to make known eachwhere thy daily drift,
Dost every day thy coursers' daily shift;
That while the spring, pranked in her greenest pride,
Reigns here, elsewhere autumn as long may bide,
And while fair summer's heat our fruits doth ripe,
Cold winter's ice may other countries gripe.
No sooner doth thy shining chariot roll
From highest zenith toward northern pole
To sport thee for three months in pleasant inns

---

[26]This interpolated couplet may have been destructive of the prospects of the English poet at the court of King James, who had different views in relation to the sacredness of kings.

Of Aries, Taurus, and the gentle Twins,
But that the mealy mountains, late unseen,
Change their white garments into lusty green,
The gardens prank them with their flowery buds,
The meads with grass, with leaves the naked woods,
Sweet Zephyrus begins to buss his Flora,
Swift winged singers to salute Aurora,
And wanton Cupid through this universe
With pleasing wounds all creatures' hearts to pierce.
   When, backward bent, Phlegon, the fiery steed,
With Cancer, Leo and the Maid doth feed,
Earth cracks with heat and summer crowns its Ceres
With gilded ears as yellow as her hair is;
The reaper, panting both for heat and pain,
With crooked razor shaves the tufted plain;[27]
And the good husband that due season takes
Within a month his year's provision makes.
   When from mid-heaven thy bright flame doth fly
Toward the cross stars in th'antarctic sky,
To be three months uprising and down lying
With Scorpio, Libra and the Archer flying,
Earth by degrees her lovely beauty 'bates,
Pomona loads her lap with delicates,
Her apron and her osier basket both
With dainty fruits for her dear Autumn's tooth,—
Her healthless spouse, who barefoot hops about
To tread the juice of Bacchus' clusters out.
   And last of all, when thy proud trampling team
For three months more to sojourn still doth seem
With Capricorn, Aquarius and the Fishes,
While we in vain revoke thee with our wishes,
Instead of flowers, chill, shivering Winter dresses
With icicles her (self bald) borrowed tresses,
About her brows a periwig of snow,
Her white frieze mantle fringed with ice below,
A pair of lamb-lined buskins on her feet;—
So doth she march, Orithyia's love to meet,

---

[27]"On the dry, smooth-shaven green."—Il Penseroso.

Who, with his bristled, hoary, bugle beard,
Coming to kiss her, makes her lips afeard;
Whereat he sighs, a breath so cold and keen
That all the waters crystallized been,
While in a fury with his boisterous wings
Against the Scythian, snowy rocks he flings;
All lusks in sloth, and till three months do end,
Bacchus and Vulcan must us both befriend.[28]

O second honor of the lamps supernal,
Sure calendar of festivals, eternal,
Sea's sovereign, sleep-bringer, pilgrims' guide,
Peaceloving queen; What shall I say beside?
What shall I say of thine inconstant brow
Which makes my brain waver, I wot not how?
But if by th'eye a man's intelligence
May guess of distant things so far from hence,
I think thy body round as any ball,
Whose superfice, nigh equal over all,
As a pure glass, now up, and down anon,
Reflects the bright beams of thy spouse, the sun,
For as a husband's noblesse doth illuster
A mean-born wife, so doth the glorious luster
Of radiant Titan with his beams embright
Thy gloomy front that selfly hath no light.

Yet 'tis not always after one self sort,
For, for thy car doth swifter thee transport
Than doth thy brother's, diversely thou shin'st
As more or less thou from his sight declin'st.
Therefore each month, when Hymen blest, above,
In both your bodies kindles ardent love,
And that the stars' king, all enamored on thee,

---

[28]In justice to Du Bartas it should be stated that the original of all this paragraph may be literally translated as follows:—"Then loitering in the houses of Capricorn, Aquarius and Pisces, Winter clothes himself with ice instead of flowers. Water is suspended in the air from house-tops; and the spouse of Orithyia with a rock-breaking breath blows over Scythia. All lusks in sloth; and Bacchus and Vulcan moderate the cold of the late months of the year." "Lusks," meaning "idles," seems not to be obsolete in England now; but the word is seldom, if ever, heard on this side of the Atlantic.

Full of desire, shines down direct upon thee,
Thy nether half globe toward th' earthly ball,
After its nature, is observed by all.
But him aside thou hast no sooner got
But on thy side a silver file we note,—
A half-bent bow which swells the less thy coach
Doth the bright chariot of thy spouse approach,
And fills his circle.   When the imperial star
Beholds thee just in one diameter,
Then by degrees thy full face falls away
And by degrees westward thy horns display,
Till, fall'n again betwixt the lover's arms,
Thou wink'st[29] again, vanquished with pleasure's charms.
    Thus dost thou wax and wane, thee oft renewing,
Delighting change, and mortal things, ensuing
As subject to thee thyself's transmutation,
Feel th'unseen force of secret alteration.
. Not but that Phoebus always with his shine
Clears half at least of thine aspect divine;
But 't seems not so; because we see but here
Of thy round globe the lower hemisphere.
. Though waxing, usward, heavenward thou dost wane,
And waning usward, heavenward grow'st again.
    Yet it befalls, even when thy face is full,
When at the highest thy pale coursers pull,
When no thick mask of clouds can hide away
From living eyes thy broad, round, glistering ray,
Thy light is darkened and thine eyes are sealed,
Covered with shadow of a rusty shield.
For thy full face, in its oblique design
Confronting Phoebus in th'ecliptic line,
And th'earth between, thou losest for a space
Thy splendor, borrowed of thy brother's grace.
    But to revenge thee on the earth for this
Forestalling thee of thy kind lover's kiss,
Sometimes thy thick orb thou dost interblend

29Does it need be said that winking, with Sylvester, meant merely
a closing of the eyes?

'Twixt Sol and us, toward the latter end
And then, because his splendor cannot pass
Or pierce the thickness of thy gloomy mass,
The sun, as subject to death's pangs, us sees not,
But seems all lightless, though indeed he is not.   . . .
    So from the south to north to make apparent
That God revoked his sergeant Death's sad warrant
'Gainst Hezekiah, and that he would give
The godly king fifteen years more to live;
Transgressing heaven's eternal ordinance,
Thrice in one day thou through the path didst prance,
And, as desirous of another nap,
In thy vermilion, sweet Aurora's lap,
Thy coach turned back, and thy swift, sweating horse,
Full ten degrees lengthened their wonted course.
Dials went false, the forests, gloomy black,
Wondered to see their mighty shades go back.
    So when the incensed heaven did fight so fell
Under the standard of dear Israel
Against the host of odious Amorites,
Among a million of swift flashing lights
Raining down bullets from a stormy cloud
As thick as hail, upon their armies proud;
That such as 'scaped from Heaven's wrathful thunder
Victorious swords might, after, hew in sunder;
Conjured by Joshua, the brave steeds stood still,
In full career stopping thy whirling wheel;
And one whole day in one degree they staid
In midst of heaven for sacred army's aid,
Lest th'infidels, in their disordered flight,
Should save themselves under the wings of night.
    Those that then lived under the other pole,
Seeing the lamp which doth enlight the whole
To hide so long his lovely face away,
Thought never more to have re-seen the day,—
The wealthy Indians and the men of Spain
Never to see sun rise or set again.
In the same place shadows stood, still as stone,
And in twelve hours the dials showed but one.

THE FIFTH DAY

    .   .   .   .   .   .[1] He began
This day to quicken in the ocean.
In standing pools and in the straggling rivers
Whose folding channel fertile champaigns severs,
So many fishes of so many features
That in the waters one may see all creatures;
And all that in this All is to be found,
As if the world within the deeps were drowned.
   Seas have, as well as skies, sun, moon and stars,
As well as air, swallows and rooks and stares,
As well as earth, vines, roses, nettles, melons,
Pinks, gilliflowers, mushrooms and many millions
Of other plants more rare and strange than these,
As very fishes living in the seas;
And also rams, calves, horses, hares and hogs,
Wolves, lions, urchins, elephants and dogs,—
Yea, men and maids; and, which I more admire,
The mitered bishop and the cowled friar,
Whereof examples but a few years since
Were shown the Norway's and Polonian prince.
   You divine wits of elder days, from whom
The deep invention of rare works hath come,—
Took you not pattern of your chiefest tools
Out of the lap of Thetis,—lakes and pools

---

[1] About thirty lines of prefatory matter are omitted, for the reason
that they take too many words to demonstrate what needs no proof—
namely, that the earth without animal life upon it would have been
a flat failure.

Which partly in the waves, part on the edges
Of craggy rocks, among the ragged sedges,
Bring forth abundance of pins, pincers, spokes,
Pikes, piercers, needles, mallets, pipes and yokes,
Oars, sails and swords, saws, wedges, razors, rammers,
Plumbs, cornets, knives, wheels, vises, horns and
    hammers?
And, as if Neptune and fair Panope,
Palaemon, Triton and Leucothoe
Kept public rolls, there is the Calamary,
Who ready pen-knife, pen and ink doth carry. . . .
   Some have their heads groveling betwixt their feet,
As th'inky cuttles and the many-feet;
Some in their breast, as crabs; some headless are,
Footless and finless, as the baneful hare
And heatful oyster, in a heap confused
Their parts unparted, in themselves diffused.
   The Tyrian merchant, or the Portuguese
Can hardly build one ship of many trees;
But of one tortoise, when he list to float
Th'Arabian fisherman can make a boat,
And one such shell him in the stead doth stand
Of hulk at sea, and of a house on land.
   Shall I omit the monstrous whirlabout
Which in the sea another sea doth spout,[2]
Wherewith huge vessels, if they happen nigh,
Are overwhelmed and sunken suddenly?
   Shall I omit the tunnies that durst meet
Th'Eoan monarch's[3] never daunted fleet,
And beard more bravely his victorious powers
Than the defenders of the Tyrian towers,
Or Porus, conquered on the Indian coast,
Or great Darius that three battles lost?

---

  [2]Schiller improved on this figure in his "Diver." Du Bartas's original language is still less forcible than Sylvester's:—"L'enorme Senedete, Qui, crachant dans Tethis, une autre Tethis jette."
  [3]Alexander the Great, who turned the Orient (monde Eoe, morning land,) into a single province of his empire, according to the original lines of the French poet.

When on the surges I perceive from far
Th'ork, whirlpool whale, or huffing physeter,[4]
Methinks I see the wandering isle again,
Ortygian Delos, floating on the main,
And when in combat these fell monsters cross,
Meseems some tempest all the sea doth toss.
   Our fearless sailors in far voyages,[5]
More led by gain's hope than their compasses,
On th'Indian shore have sometimes noted some
Whose bodies covered two broad acres room;
And in the South Seas they have also seen
Some like high-topped and huge-armed treen,
And other some whose monstrous backs did bear
Two mighty wheels with whirling spokes, that were
Much like the winged and wide-spreading sails
Of any windmill turned with merry gales. . . .
As citizens in some intestine brawl
Long cooped up within their castle wall,
So soon as peace is made and siege removed,
Forsake awhile their town so strong approved,
And tired with toil, by leashes and by pairs,
Crowned with garlands, go to take the airs;
So dainty salmon, chevins thunder-scarred,
Feast-famous sturgeon, lampreys speckle-starred,
In the spring season the rough seas forsake
And in the rivers thousand pleasures take;
And yet the plenty of delicious foods,
Their pleasant lodging in the crystal floods,[6]
The fragrant scent of flowery banks about,
Cannot their country's tender love wipe out
Of their remembrance, but they needs will home
In th'ireful ocean to go seek their tomb.
Like English gallants that in youth do go

4A great whale that was said to have the habit of swelling itself
up to much huger dimensions, like the frog in the fable.
5Eight lines interpolated.
6The phrases, "Crystal fountains," and "Glassy floods," both occur
in Milton's paraphrase of Psalm 114, which is only four lines longer
than an orthodox sonnet.

To visit Rhine, Sein, Ister, Arne and Po,
Where, though their sense be dandled days and nights
In sweetest choice of changeable delights,
They never can forget their mother soil,
But hourly home their hearts and eyes recoil,
Long languishing with an extreme desire
To see the smoke of their dear native fire.   .   .
    The subtle smell-strong many-foot that fain
A dainty feast of oyster flesh would gain,
Swims softly down, and to him slily slips,
Wedging with stones his yet wide yawning lips,
Lest else, before that he hath had his prey,
The oyster, closing, clip his limbs away;
And when he thought t'have 'joyed his victories,
Himself become unto his prize a prize.
The cramp-fish, knowing that she harboreth
A plagueful humor, a fell, baneful breath,
A secret poppy and a senseless winter,
Benumbing all that dare too near her venture,
Pours forth her poison and her chilling ice
On the next fishes,—charmed so in a trice
That she not only stays them in the deep
But stuns their sense and lulls them fast asleep;
And then at will she with their flesh is fed,
Whose frozen limbs still living seem but dead.
'Tis this torpedo that when she hath took
Into her throat the sharp, deceitful hook,
Doth not as other fish that wrench and wriggle
When they be pricked, and plunge and strive and
        struggle,
And by their stir thinking to 'scape the angle,
Faster and faster on the hook do tangle;
But, wily, clasping close the fishing line,
Suddenly spews into the silver brine
Her secret-spreading, sudden-speeding bane,
Which up the line and all along the cane
Creeps to the hand of th'angler, who withal
Benumbed and senseless, suddenly lets fall
His hurtful pole and his more hateful prize;

Become like one that as in bed he lies
Seems in his sleep to see some ghastly ghost;
In a cold sweat, shaking and swelt almost,
He calls his wife for aid, his friends, his folks,[7]
But his stuffed stomach his weak clamor chokes.
Then would he strike at that he doth behold,
But sleep and fear his feeble hands do hold.
Then would he run away, but as he strives,
He feels his foot fettered with heavy gyves. . . .
    The thriving Amia, near Abydos breeding,
And subtle sea-fox, in steeds' love exceeding,
Without much risk to their dear life and lining,
Can from the worm-clasp compass their untwining.
For, sucking in more of the twisted hair,
Above the hook they it in sunder shear
So that their foe who for a fish did look
Lifts up a bare line, robbed of bait and hook.
But timorous berbel will not taste a bit
Till with their tails they have unhooked it
And all the baits the fisher can devise
Cannot beguile their wary jealousies.
    Even so almost the many-spotted cuttle
Well near ensnared yet escapeth subtle;
For when she sees herself within the net,
And no way left but one from thence to get,
She suddenly a certain ink doth spew
Which dyes the waters of a sable hue,
That, dazzling so the fisher's greedy light,
She through the clouds of the black water's night
Might 'scape with honor the black streams of Styx,
Whereof already, almost lost, she licks.
    And as a prisoner, of some great transgression
Convict by witness and his own confession,
Kept in dark durance full of noisome breath,
Expecting nothing but the day of death,

---

7 "His folks," meaning the people of his household related to him
by consanguinity and marriage, is a common expression in the inland
counties of New England and New York.

Spies every corner and pries round about
To find some weak place where he may get out,
The delicate, cud-chewing, golden-eye,
Kept in a weir, the widest place doth spy,
And thrusting in his tail, makes th'osiers gape
With his oft flapping, and doth so escape.
But if his fellow find him thus bested,
He lends his tail to the imprisoned,
That thereby holding fast with gentle jaw,
Him from his durance he may friendly draw.
Or if before that he were captivate
He see him hooked on the biting bait,
Hasting to help, he leapeth at the line,
And with his teeth snaps off the hairy twine. . .

  As a great carrack, cumbered and oppressed
With her own burden, wends not east or west,
Starboard or larboard with so quick careers
As a small frigate or swift pinnace steers;
And as a large and mighty limbed steed,
Either of Friesland or the German breed,
Can never manage half so readily
As Spanish jennet or light Barbary;
So the huge whale hath not so nimble motion
As smaller fishes that frequent the ocean;
But sometimes rudely 'gainst a rock he brushes,
Or in some roaring strait he blindly rushes,
And scarce could live a twelvemonth to the end
But for the little musculus, his friend,
A little fish, that, swimming still before,
Directs him safe from rock, from shelf, and shore;
Much like a child that, loving, leads about
His aged father, when his eyes be out;
Still wafting him through every way so right
That, reft of eyes, he seems not reft of sight. . .

  But, Clio, wherefore art thou tedious
In numbering Neptune's busy burghers thus?
If in His works thou wilt admire the worth
Of the seas' Sovereign, bring but only forth
One little fish, whose admirable story

Sufficeth sole to show His might and glory.
Let all the winds in one wind gather them,
And, seconded with Neptune's strongest stream,
Let all at once blow all their stiffest gales
Astern a galley under all her sails,
Let her be holpen with a hundred oars,
Each lively handled by five lusty rowers;
The remora, fixing her feeble horn
Into the tempest-beaten vessel's stern,
Stays her stone still, while all her stout consorts
Sail thence at pleasure to their wished ports.
They loose them all their sheets, but to no boot;
For the charmed vessel budgeth not a foot,
No more than if three fathom under ground
A score of anchors held her fastly bound;
No more than doth an oak that in a wood
Hath thousand tempests thousand times withstood,
Spreading as many massive roots below
As mighty arms above the ground do grow.
    O Stop-Ship, say, say how thou canst oppose
Thyself alone against so many foes?
O tell us where thou dost thine anchors hide,
Whence thou resistest sails, oars, wind and tide!
How, on the sudden, canst thou curb so short
A ship whom all the elements transport?
Whence is thine engine, and thy secret force
That frustrates engines and all force doth force?
    I had in harbor heaved mine anchor o'er,
And even already set one foot ashore,
When lo, the dolphin, beating 'gainst the bank,
'Gan my oblivion moodily misthank.
Peace, princely swimmer, sacred fish, content thee;
For, for thy praise, th'end of this song I meant thee.
Brave admiral of the broad, briny regions,
Triumphant tamer of the scaly legions,
Who, living, ever liv'st,—for never sleep,
Death's lively image, in thine eyes doth creep,—
Lover of ships, of men, of melody,
Thou up and down through the moist world dost ply,

Swift as a shaft.   Whose salt thou lovest so
That, lacking that, thy life thou dost forego.
Thou, gentle fish, wert th'happy boat of yore
Which safely brought th'Amiclean harp ashore.
   Arion, matchless for his music's skill,
Among the Latins having gained his fill
Of gold and glory, and exceeding fain
To re-salute his learned Greece again,
Unwares embarks him in a pirate's ship,
Who, loth to let so good a bounty slip,
Soon weighs his anchors, packs on all his sail,
And winds conspiring with a prosperous gale,
His winged frigate made so speedy flight
Tarentum towers were quickly out of sight,
And all—save skies and seas—on every side,
Where the compass only is the pilot's guide.
   The sailors then, whom many times we find
Falser than seas and fiercer than the wind,
Fall straight to strip him, rifling at their pleasure
In every corner to find out his treasure
And having found it, all with one accord
Hoist th'owner up to heave him overboard ;
Who, weeping, said, "O Nereus' noble issue,
Not to restore my little gold I wish you,
For my chief treasure in my music lies,
And all Apollo's sacred pupils prize
The holy virgins of Parnassus so
That underfoot all worldly wealth they throw.
No, brave triumphers over wind and wave,
Who in both worlds your habitation have,
Who both heaven's hooks in your adventures view,
'Tis not for that with broken sighs I sue.
I but beseech you, offer no impieties
Unto a person dear unto the deities.
So may Messinian sirens for your sake
Be ever mute when you your voyage make,
And Triton's trumpet th'angry surges 'suage
When justly Neptune shall against you rage.
But if, alas, I cannot this obtain,

As my faint eyes read in your frowns too plain,
Suffer at least to my sad dying voice
My doleful fingers to consort their noise,
That so the sea-nymphs, rapt in admiration
Of my divine, sweet, sacred lamentation,
Dragging my corpse to shore, with weeping showers
May dew the same, and it entomb with flowers."
    "Then play," said they, "and give us both together,
Treasure and pleasure, by thy coming hither."
    His sweetest strokes then sad Arion lent
Th'enchanting sinews of his instrument,
Wherewith he charmed the raging ocean so
That crook-toothed lampreys and the congers row
Friendly together, and their native hate
The pike and mullet for the time forgat,
And lobsters floated fearless all the while
Among the polyps, prone to theft and guile.
    But among all the fishes that did throng
To dance the measure of his mournful song,
There was a dolphin did the best accord
His nimble motions to the trembling chord,
Who, gently sliding near the pinnace' side,
Seemed to invite him on his back to ride.
By this time twice the sailors had essayed
To heave him o'er; yet twice himself he stayed,
And now the third time strove they him to cast;
Yet by the shrouds the third time held he fast;
But lastly, seeing they were past remorse
And he too feeble to withstand their force,
The trembling dolphin's shoulders he bestrid,
Who on the ocean's azure surges slid,
So that far off, his charge so cheered him,
One would have thought him rather fly than swim,
Yet fears he every shelf and every surge,—
Not for himself, but for his tender charge,—
And sloping swiftly overthwart the seas,
Not for his own, but for his rider's ease,
Makes double haste to find some happy strand
Where his sweet Phoebus he may safely land.

Meanwhile Arion with his music rare
Pays his dear pilot his delightful fare,
And heaving eyes to heaven,—the haven of pity,—
To his sweet harp he tunes this sacred ditty:
  "O Thou Almighty, who mankind to wrack
Of thousand seas one sea whilom didst make,
And yet didst save from th'universal doom
One sacred household, that in time to come,
From age to age, should sing Thy glorious praise,—
Look down, O Lord, from Thy supernal rays!
Look, look, alas, upon a wretched man
Half tombed already in the ocean!
O be my steersman and vouchsafe to guide
The sternless boat and bitless horse I ride,
So that, escaping winds' and waters' wrath,
I once again may tread my native path;
And henceforth, here with solemn vows I sacre
Unto thy glory, O my God and Maker,
For this great favor's high memorial,
My heart and art, my voice, hand, harp and all."
  Herewith the seas their roaring rage restrain,
The cloudy welkin waxes clear again,
And all the winds do suddenly convert
Their mouths to ears to hear his wondrous art.
The dolphin then, descrying land at last,
Storms with himself for having made such haste,
And wished Laconia thousand leagues from thence,
The while t'enjoy the music's excellence.
But to his own delight preferring far
The unhoped safety of the minstrel rare,
Sets him ashore and, (which most strange may seem,)
Where life he first saw, life still smiles to him. . . .
  While busy poring downward in the deep
I sing of fishes that, there, quarter keep.
See how the fowls are from my fancy fled,
And their high praises quite out of my head!
Their flight out-flies me, and my muse almost
The better half of this bright day hath lost.
But cheer ye, birds; your shadows, as ye pass,

Seeming to flutter on the water's face,
Make me remember, by their nimble turns
Both what my duty and your due concerns.
  But first, I pray, for meed of all my toil,
In bringing you into this happy isle,
Vouchsafe to waken with your various notes
The senseless senses of those drowsy sots
Whose eyelids, laden with a weight of lead,
Shall fall asleep while these my rimes are read.
But if they could not close their wakeful eyes
Among the water's silent colonies,
How can they sleep among the birds, whose sound
Through heaven and earth and ocean doth resound?
  The heavenly phoenix first began to frame
The earthly phoenix, and adorned the same
With such a plume that Phoebus, circuiting
From Fez to Cairo, sees no fairer thing.
Such form, such feathers, and such fate he gave her
That fruitful Nature breedeth nothing braver;
Two sparkling eyes; upon her crown a crest
Of starry sprigs more splendent than the rest;
A golden down about her dainty neck;
Her breast deep purple, and a scarlet back;
Her wings and train of feathers, mixed fine,
Of orient azure and incarnadine.[8]
  He did appoint her fate to be her fere,
And Death's cold kisses to restore her here
To life again, which never shall expire
Until as she, the world consume in fire.
For, having passed under divers climes
A thousand winters and a thousand primes,
Worn out with years, wishing her endless end,
To shining flames she doth her life commend;
Dies to revive, and goes into her grave

---

[8] I do not know whether this is the first instance of the use of "incarnadine" in English, or not. In Shakespeare's Macbeth it appears as a verb, but Macbeth was first printed long after the original publication of the Divine Weeks.

To rise again, more beautiful and brave.
   Perched, therefore, upon a branch of palm,
With incense, cassia, spikenard, myrrh and balm,
By break of day she builds in narrow room
Her urn, her nest, her cradle and her tomb;
Where, while she sits all gladly-sad, expecting
Some flame, against her fragrant heap reflecting,
To burn her sacred bones to seedful cinders,
Wherein her age, but not her life, she renders,
The Phrygian Skinker,[9] with his lavish ewer,
Drowns not the fields with shower after shower;
The shining Coachman with his icy snow
Dares not the forests of Phoenicia strow;
Auster presumes not Libyan shores to pass
With his moist wings; and graybeard Boreas
As the most boisterous and rebellious slave,
Is prisoned close in th'hyperborean cave;
For Nature now, propitious to her end,
T'her living death a helping hand doth lend;
And stopping all those mouths, doth mildly stead
Her funerals, her fruitful birth, and bed.
And Sol himself, glancing his golden eyes
On th'odoriferous couch wherein she lies,
Kindles the spice, and by degrees consumes
Th'immortal phoenix, both her flesh and plumes.
   But instantly out of her ashes springs
A worm, an egg then, then a bird with wings,
Just like the first, rather the same indeed,
Which, re-engendered of its selfly seed,
By nobly dying a new date begins,
And where she loseth, there her life she wins,
Endless by'r end, eternal by her tomb,
While, by a prosperous death, she doth become,
Among the cinders of her sacred fire,
Her own self's heir, nurse, nursling, dam and sire;
Teaching us all in Adam here to die,
That we in Christ may live eternally.

9The rain-bringing zodiacal sign, Aquarius.

The phoenix, cutting th'unfrequented air,
Forthwith is followed by a thousand pair
Of wings in th'instant by th'Almighty wrought,
With divers size, color and motion fraught.

The scent-strong swallow sweepeth to and fro
As swift as shafts fly from a Turkish bow
When, use and art and strength confed'rated,
The skillful archer draws them to a head.
Flying she sings, and singing seeketh[10] where
She, more with cunning than with cost, may rear
Her round front palace in a place secure
Whose plat may serve in rarest architecture.
Her little beak she loads with brittle straws,
Her wings with water, and with earth her claws,
Whereof she mortar makes, and therewithal
Aptly she builds her semicircle wall.

The pretty lark, climbing the welkin clear,
Chants with a cheer, "Here peer I near my dear!"
Then stooping thence, seeming her fall to rue,
"Adieu," she saith, "adieu, dear dear, adieu."
The spink, the linnet and the goldfinch fill
All the fresh air with their sweet warbles' thrill.

But these are nothing to the nightingale,
Breathing so sweetly from a breast so small
So many tunes whose harmony excels
Our voice, our viols, and all music else.
Good Lord, how oft in a green, oaken grove,
In the cool shadow have I stood and strove
To marry mine immortal lays to theirs,[11]
Rapt with the joy of their delicious airs!

10"And singing, startle the dull night."—L'Allegro. "And singing
still dost soar, and soaring ever singest."—Shelley's "To a Skylark."
"They ceasing sung; they singing, ceased still."—Eden (post) note 16.
11"Soft Lydian airs, Married to immortal verse."—L'Allegro. The
marriage of verse and music is a favorite rite with Sylvester, who tells
that in Eden the birds were "marrying their sweet tunes to the angels'
lays," while in a later poem, (The Law,) the Israelites are described
as "marrying all their voices to timbrels," etc., in "The Woodman's
Bear," "to the music choice Of those nimble joints she marries The
echo of her angel voice" and in the "Paradox," the poet pictures himself as "to sweet harmony Marrying my simple voice."

And yet, methinks, in a thick thorn I hear
A nightingale that warbles sweetly clear.
One while she bears the bass, anon the tenor,
Anon the treble and the counter-tenor;
Then all at once, as it were, challenging
The rarest voices with herself to sing.
Thence thirty paces, mid the leafy sprays,
Another nightingale repeats her lays
Just note for note, and adds some strain at last
That she hath conned all the winter past.
The first replies and descants thereupon
With divine warbles of division,
Redoubling quavers, and so, turn by turn,
Alternately, they sing away the morn;
So that the conquest in this curious strife
Doth often cost the one her voice and life.

Then the glad victor all the rest admire,
And after count her mistress of the choir.
At break of day, in a delicious song
She sets the gamut to a hundred young;
And whenas fit for higher tunes she sees them,
Then learnedly she harder lessons gi'es them,
Which, strain by strain, they studiously recite,
And strive to follow all her rules aright.   .   .   .

The ravening kite, whose train doth well supply
A rudder's place; the falcon, mounting high,
The merlin, lanner, and the gentle tercel,
Th'osprey and saker, with a nimble farcel
Follow the phœnix from the clouds almost,
At once discovering many an unknown coast.

In the swift ranks of these fell rovers flies
The Indian griffin with the glistering eyes,
Beak eagle-like, back sable, sanguine breast,
White, swan-like wings, fierce talons, always pressed
For bloody battles; for with these he tears
Boars, lions, horses, tigers, bulls and bears.
With these our grandam's[12] fruitful paunch he pulls,

---

[12]"Our grandam" is as heretofore the earth. Eve assumes the position later. See Sir T. Browne's "Pseudodoxia," III, 11.

Whence many an ingot of pure gold he culls
To floor his proud nest, builded strong and deep
On a high rock, better his thefts to keep.
With these he guards against an army bold
The hollow mines where first he findeth gold,
And wroth that men upon his right should rove.
Or thievish hands usurp his treasure trove,
  O ever may'st thou fight so, valiant fowl,
For this dire bane of our seduced soul;
And with thee may the Dardan ants[13] so ward
That gold committed to their careful guard
That henceforth hopeless man's frail mind may rest her
From seeking that which doth its master master.
O odious poison, for the which we dive
To Pluto's dark den; for the which we rive
Our mother Earth, and not contented with
Th'abundant gifts she outward offereth,
With sacrilegious tools we rudely rend her,
And ransack deeply in her bosom tender,
While underground we live in hourly fear
That the frail mines shall overwhelm us there.
For which beyond rich Taprobane we roll
Through thousand seas to seek another pole,
And maugre winds' and waters' enmity,
We every day new, unknown worlds descry;
For which, alas, the brother fells his brother,
The sire his son, the son his sire and mother,
The man his wife, the wife her wedded fere,
The friend his friend. O what sell we not here
Sithence to satiate our gold-thirsty gall,
We sell ourselves, our very souls and all?
  Near these the crow his greedy wings displays,
The long-lived raven, th'infamous bird that lays
His bastard eggs within the nest of other
To have them hatched by an unkindly mother;

13Fabled insects of the East Indies, the tales of whose exploits
were probably founded upon observations of the white ants (or ter-
mites) of the tropics.

The screech-owl, used in falling towers to lodge,[14]
Th'unlucky night-raven, and thou lazy madge,
That, fearing light, still seekest where to hide;
The hate and scorn of all the birds beside.
But, gentle muse, tell me what fowls are those
That even now from flaggy fens arose.
'Tis th'hungry heron, the greedy cormorant,
The coot and curlew which the moors do haunt,
The nimble teal, the mallard strong in flight,
The didapper, the plover and the snite,
The silver swan that, dying, singeth best,
And the kingfisher which so builds her nest
By the seaside in midst of winter season,
That man, in whom shines the bright lamp of reason,
Cannot devise, with all the wit he has,
The little building how to raise or raze.
So long as there his quiet couch he keeps
Sicilian sea exceeding calmly sleeps,
For Æolus, fearing to drown the brood,
Keeps home awhile, and troubles not the flood.
The pirate, dwelling always in his bark,
In's calendar his building days doth mark,
And the rich merchant resolutely ventures,
So soon as th'halcyon in his broodbed enters.
Meanwhile the langa, skimming as it were
The ocean's surface, seeketh everywhere
The stupid whale, and slipping in by art
In his vast mouth, she feeds upon his heart.
New Spain[15] cucujo in his forehead brings
Two burning lamps, two underneath his wings,
Whose shining rays serve oft in darkest night
Th'embroiderer's hand in royal works to light,
Th'ingenious turner, with a wakeful eye

---

[14]"From yonder ivy-mantled tower The moping owl does to the moon complain."—Gray.

[15]America. The statement appears to be an exaggeration of what was actually seen of fireflies. The cucujus itself is a Brazilian beetle of a character, according to entomologists, not strikingly different from that of allied European species.

To polish fair his purest ivory,
The usurer to count his glistering treasures,
The learned scribe to limn his golden measures.
   But note we now, towards the rich Moluccas,
Those passing strange and wondrous birds, mamucas,[16]—
Wondrous indeed, if sea or earth or sky
Saw ever wonder go, or swim, or fly.
None knows their nest; none knows the dam that breeds
      them;
Foodless they live, for only the air feeds them;
Wingless they fly, and yet their flight extends,
Till with their flight their unknown life's date ends.
   The stork, still eyeing her dear Thessaly,
The pelican comforteth cheerfully;—
Praiseworthy payer, which pure examples yield
Of faithful father and officious child.
One 'quites in time her parent's love exceeding,
From whom she had her birth and tender breeding;
Not only brooding under her warm breast
Their age-chilled bodies, bedrid in the nest,
Nor only bearing them upon her back
Through th'empty air, when their own wings they lack,
But also sparing—this let children note,—
Her daintiest food from her own hungry throat,
To feed at home her feeble parents, held
From foraging with heavy gyves of eld.
   The other, kindly, for her tender brood
Tears her own bowels, trilleth out her blood
To heal her young, and in a wondrous sort
Unto her children doth her life transport;
For, finding them by some fell serpent slain,
She rends her breast and doth upon them rain
Her vital humor; whence, recovering heat
They by her death another life do get.   .   .   .
   Thus dost thou print, O Parent of this all,
In every breast of brutest animal
A kind instinct which makes them dread no less

16Birds of Paradise.

Their children's danger than their own decease;
That so each kind may last immortally,
Though th'individuals pass successively.[17]
So fights a lion, not for glory then,
But for his dear whelps, taken from his den
By hunters fell.   He fiercely roareth out;
He wounds; he kills.   Amid the thickest rout
He rushes in, dreadless of spears and darts,
Swords, shafts and staves, though hurt in thousand parts,
And brave, resolved, till his last breath lack
Never gives over, nor an inch gives back.
Wrath salves his wounds; and lastly, to conclude,
When, overlaid with night and multitude,
He needs must die, dying he more bemoans
Than his own death his captive little ones.
So for their young our mastiff curs will fight,
Eagerly bark, bristle their backs and bite.
So in the deep the dogfish for her fry
Lucina's throes a thousand times will try;
For seeing that the subtle fisher follows them,
Again alive into herself she swallows them,
And when the peril's past she brings them hence
As from the cabins of a safe defence;
And, thousand lives to their dear parent owing,
As sound as ever in the seas are rowing.
So doth a hen make of her wings a targe
To shield her chickens that she hath in charge;
And so the sparrow, with her angry bill,
Defends her brood from such as would them ill.
    I hear the crane, if I mistake not, cry,
Who, forming in the clouds a forked Y,
By the brave orders practised under her,
Instructeth soldiers in the art of war.
For when her troops of wandering cranes forsake
Frost-firmed Strymon, and in autumn take
Truce with the northern dwarfs, to seek adventure
In southern climates for a milder winter,

---

[17]Identical with a sentiment expressed in Locksley Hall.

Afront each band a forward captain flies,
Whose pointed bill cuts passage through the skies;
Two skillful sergeants keep the ranks aright,
And hasten with their voice their tardy flight;
And when the honey of care-charming sleep
Sweetly begins through all their veins to creep,
One keeps the watch, and ever careful-most,
Walks many a round about the sleeping host,
Still holding in his claw a stony clod
Whose fall may wake him if he hap to nod.
Another doth as much,—a third,—a fourth,—
Until by turns the night be turned forth.

There the fair peacock, beautifully brave,
Proud, portly, strutting, stalking, stately, grave,
Whirling his starry train, in pomp displays
His glorious eyes to Phoebus' golden rays.
Close by his side stands the courageous cock,
Crest-people's king, the peasant's trusty clock,
True morning watch, Aurora's trumpeter,
The lion's terror, true astronomer,
Who daily riseth when the sun doth rise,
And when Sol setteth, then to roost he hies.

There, I perceive, amid the flowery plain
The mighty ostrich, striving oft in vain
To mount among the flying multitude,
(Although with feathers, not with flight endowed;)
Whose greedy stomach steely gads digests,
Whose crisped train adorns triumphant crests.

Thou happy witness of my happy watches,
My book, blush not nor think it thee dismatches
To bear about upon the paper tables
Flies, butterflies, gnats, bees, and all the rabbles
Of other insects endless to rehearse,
Limned with the pencil of my varied verse;
Since these are also His wise workmanships
Whose fame no obscure work did e'er eclipse,
And since in these He shows us every hour
More wondrous proofs of His almighty power
Than in huge whales or hideous elephants,

Or whatsoever other monster haunts
In stormless seas, raising a storm about.
While in the sea another sea they spout.[18]
    For if old times admire Callicrates
For ivory emmets, and Mermecides
For framing of a winged ship so small
That with her wings a bee could hide it all,—
Though th'artful fruits of all their curious pain
Fit for no use were, but inventions vain,—·
Admire we then th'all-wise Omnipotence
Which doth within so narrow space dispense
So stiff a sting, so stout and valiant heart,
So loud a voice, so prudent wit and art.
    For where's the state beneath the firmament
That doth excel the bees for government?
No, no; bright Phoebus, whose eternal race
Once every day about the earth doth pass,
Sees here no city that in rites and laws,
For equity, near to their justice draws.
Not that which, flying from the furious Hun,[19]
In th'Adrian sea another world begun.
Their well ruled state my soul so much admires
That, durst I loose the rein of my desires,
I gladly could digress from my design
To sing awhile their sacred discipline.
But if, of all whose skillful pencils dare
To counterfeit th'Almighty's models rare,
None durst yet finish that fair piece, wherein
Learned Apelles drew love's wanton queen,—
Shall I presume Hymettus' mount to climb
And sing the bees' praise in my humble rime,
Which Latin bards' inimitable prince
Hath warbled twice about the banks of Mince?[20]

---

[18]See note on Regiomontanus, in "Religio Medici."
[19]In Campbell's "Hohenlinden" we read "furious Frank and fiery Hun," but the line is evidently inspired by a recollection of that of the above text, notwithstanding the transposition, which is of questionable desirability.
[20]The Mincio, upon which river Mantua is situated.

Yet I may not that little worm pass by,
Of fly turned worm, and of a worm turned fly;
Two births, two deaths, here Nature hath assigned her,
Leaving a posthume—dead-live—seed behind her,
Which soon transforms the fresh and tender leaves
On Thisbe's pale tree to those slender sleaves,
On oval clews, of soft, smooth, silken flakes
Which more for us than for herself she makes.

O precious fleece, which only did adorn
The sacred forms of princes heretoforn!
But our proud age, with prodigal abuse
Hath so profaned th'old honorable use,
That shifters now who scarce have bread to eat
Disdain plain silk, unless it be beset
With one of those dear metals, whose desire
Burns greedy souls with an unending fire.

Thou last, not least; brave eagle, no contempt
Made me so long thy story hence exempt,   .   .   .
For well I know thou holdest worthily
That place among the airy flocks that fly
As doth the dragon or the cockatrice
Among the baneful, creeping companies,
The noble lion among savage beasts,
And gentle dolphin 'mong the diving guests.
I know thy course; I know thy constant sight
Can fix'dly gaze 'gainst heaven's greatest light;
But as the phœnix on my front doth glister
Thou shalt the finials of my frame illuster.

On Thracian shore of the same stormy stream
Which did inherit both the bones and name
Of Phryxus' sister,[21]—and not far from whence
The love-blind Hero's hapless diligence
Instead of love's lamp, lighted death's cold brand
To waft Leander's naked limbs to land,—
There dwelt a maid as noble and as rich
And fair as Hero, but more chaste by much;
For her steel breast still blunted all the darts

---

[21]Helle, after whom the Hellespont was named.

Of Paphos' archer, and eschewed his arts.
  One day this damsel, through a forest thick
Hunting, among her friends that sport did seek,
Unto a steep rock's thorny, thrummed top
Where one would almost fear to clamber up,
Two tender eaglets in a nest espies,
Which sat, trying against the sun their eyes,
Whose callow backs and bodies round about
With soft, short quills began to bristle out;
Who, yawning wide, with empty gorge did gape
For wonted fees out of their parents' rape.
Of the two fowls the fairest up she takes
Into her bosom, and great haste she makes
Down from the rock, and shivering yet for fear,
Trips home as fast as her light feet can bear;
Even as a wolf that, hunting for a prey,
And having stolen at last a lamb away,
Flies with down hanging head, and leereth back,
Whether the mastiff doth pursue his track.
  In time this eaglet was so thoroughly manned
That from the quarry to her mistress' hand
At the first call 'twould come, and fawn upon her,
And bill, and bow in sign of love and honor.
On th'other side the maiden makes as much
Of her dear bird, stroking with gentle touch
Her wings and train, and with a wanton voice
It wantonly doth cherish and rejoice;
And, pretty foundling, she doth prize it higher
Than her own beauties, which all else admire.
  But, as fell fates mingle our single joys
With bitter gall of infinite annoys,
An extreme fever vexed the virgin's bones,
By one disease to cause two deaths at once,
Consumed her flesh and wanly did displace
The rose-mixed lilies in her lovely face.   . . .
But oft the eagle, striving with her fit,
Would fly abroad to seek some dainty bit
For her dear mistress, and with nimble wing
Some rail or quail or partridge would she bring,

Paying with food the food received so oft
From those fair, ivory, virgin fingers soft,
During her nonage, ere she durst essay
To cleave the sky, and for herself to prey.
   The fever now with spiteful fits had spent
The blood and marrow of this innocent
And Life resigned to cruel Death her right,
Who three days after doth the eagle cite.   . . .
O'er the dear corpse sometimes her wings she hovers,
Sometimes the dead breast with her breast she covers;
Sometimes her neck doth the pale neck embrace;
Sometimes she kisses the cold lips and face;
And with sad murmurs she lamenteth so
That her strange moan augments the parents' woe. . . .
   But lo, the while, about the lightsome door
Of th'hapless house a mournful troop that bore
Black on their backs and tapers in their fists,
Tears on their cheeks and sorrow in their breasts,
Who, taking up the sacred load at last,
Whose happy soul already heaven embraced,
With shrill sad cries march toward the fatal pile
With solemn pace; the silly bird the while
Following far off.   . . . .
No sooner had the ceremonial flame
Embraced the body of her tender dame,
But suddenly, distilling all with blood,
Down soused[22] the eagle on the blazing wood;
Nor boots the flamen with his sacred wand
A hundred times to beat her from her stand;
For to the midst still of the pile she plies,
And singing sweet her lady's obsequies
Then burns herself, and blendeth happily
Her bones with hers she loved so tenderly.   . . .

22"Descends in open view
The bird of Jove, and sousing on his prey,
With crooked talons bears the boy away."—Dryden.

THE SIXTH DAY

Of all the beasts which Thou this day didst build
To haunt the hills, the forest and the field,
I see, as viceroy of the brutish band,
The elephant the vanguard doth command;
Worthy that office, whether we regard
His towered back where many soldiers ward,
Or else his prudence, wherewithal he seems
To obscure the wits of human kind sometimes.
As studious scholar he self-rumineth
His lessons given; his king he honoreth;
Adores the moon; moved with a strange desire
He feels the sweet flames of th'Idalian[1] fire,
And, pierced with glance of a kind, cruel eye,
For human beauty seems to sigh and die.
Yea, if the Grecians do not misrecite,
With's crooked trumpet he doth sometimes write.
But his huge strength nor subtle wit cannot
Defend him from the sly rhinocerot
Who never, with blind fury led, doth venture
Upon his foe but, ere the lists he enter,
Against a rock he whetteth round about
The dangerous pike upon his armed snout;
Then buckling close, doth not at random hack
On the hard cuirass on his enemy's back,
But under's belly cunningly finds skin

---

[1]Idalium in Cyprus was sacred to Venus Aphrodite who was therefore sometimes called "Idalia."

Where—and but there—his sharpened blade will in.
  The scaly dragon, being else too low
For th'elephant, up a thick tree doth go,
So closely ambushed almost every day
To watch the carrycastle in his way;
Who, once approaching, straight his stand he leaves
And round about him he so closely cleaves
With writhing body that his enemy,
The stinging knots unable to untie,
Hastes to some tree or to some rock, whereon
To rush and rub off his detested zone,
The fell embraces of whose dismal clasp
Have almost brought him to his latest gasp.
  Then suddenly the dragon slips his hold
From th'elephant, and sliding down, doth fold
About his forelegs, fettered in such order
That, stocked there, he now can stir no furder.
While th'elephant, but to no purpose strives
With winding trunk t'undo his wounding gyves,
His furious foe thrusts in his nose; his nose,
Then head and all, and therewithal doth close
His breathing-passage; but his victory
He joys not long; for his huge enemy,
Down falling dead, doth with his weighty fall
Crush him to death that caused his death withal. . . .
Near th'elephant comes th'horned hirable,[2]
Stream-troubling camel and strong-necked bull,
The lazy-paced, yet laborious ass,
The quick, proud courser which the rest doth pass
For apt address, Mars and his master loving,
After his hand with ready lightness moving.   . . .
In a fresh troop the fearful hare I note,
Th'oblivious coney and the browsing goat,
The slothful swine, the golden-fleeced sheep,
The light-foot hart, which every year doth weep,
As a sad recluse, for his branched head
That in the springtime he before hath shed.

---

[2]The giraffe. Adopted from Du Bartas's original text.

O what a sport to see a herd of them
Take soil in summer in some spacious stream!
One swims before, another on his chine
Nigh half upright, doth with his breast incline;
On that another, and so all do ride
Each after other; and still when their guide
Grows to be weary and can lead no more,
He that was hindmost comes and swims before.
Like as in cities where one magistrate
Bears not the burden of the common state,
But having passed his year, he doth discharge
On others' shoulders his sweet, bitter charge.
But of all beasts none steadeth man so much
As doth the dog; his diligence is such.
A faithful guard, a watchful sentinel,
A painful purveyor that with perfect smell
Provides great princes many a dainty mess,—
A friend till death, a helper in distress,
Dread of the wolf, fear of the fearful thief,
Fierce combatant and of all hunters chief.
There skips the squirrel, seeming weather-wise[3]
Without beholding heaven's twinkling eyes;
For, knowing well which way the wind will change,
He shifts the portal of his little grange;
The wanton weasel's there, the wily fox,
The witty monkey that man's action mocks,
The sweat-sweet civet, dearly fetched from far
For courtiers nice, past Indian Tarnassar. . . .
There the rough hedge-hog, who to shun his thrall
Shrinks up himself as round as any ball,
And fast'ning his slow feet under his chin,
On's thistly bristles rolls him quickly in.
But th'eye of Heaven beholdeth naught more strange
Than the chameleon who, with various change,
Receives the color that each object gives,
And, foodless else, of th'air alonely lives. . . .

---

[3] This word is still in good colloquial use in the northern United States.

O who is he that would not be astound
To be as I am, here environed round
With cruel'st creatures, which for mastery
Have vowed against us endless enmity?
Phoebus would faint, Alcides' self would dread,
Although the first dread Python conquered,
And th'other vanquished th'Erymanthian boar,
The Nemean lion and a many more.
What strength of arm or artful stratagem
From Nile's fell rover could deliver them,
Who runs and rows, warring by land and water
'Gainst men and fishes, subject to his slaughter?
Or from the furious dragon which alone
Set on a Roman army, whereupon
Stout Regulus as many engines spent
As to the ground would Carthage walls have rent?

What shot-free corslet, or what counsel crafty
'Gainst th'angry aspic could assure them safety,
Who, faithful husband, over hill and plain
Pursues the man that his dear fere hath slain,
Whom he can find among the thickest throng
And in an instant 'venge him of his wrong?   ·
What shield of Ajax could avoid their death
By th'basilisk whose pestilential breath
Doth pierce firm marble, and whose baneful eye
Wounds with a glance so that the soundest die?

Lord, if so be Thou for mankind didst rear
This, rich, round mansion, glorious everywhere,
Alas, why didst Thou on this day create
These harmful beasts which but exasperate
Our thorny life?   O wert Thou pleased to form
Th'enameled scorpion and the viper-worm
The horned cerastes, th'Alexandrian skink,[4]

---

[4]The "Index to the Hardest Words", appended to the Divine Weeks
in all the old editions, says that Cerastes is "a serpent of sundry
colors, with hornes like a Ramme," and the Skink is "a land crocodile."
What the drynas or the dipsas may be is not stated. It may have
been a recollection of this catalogue that inspired Milton's "Perverse,
all monstrous, all prodigious things," etc. (Par. Lost II, 625.) In

Th'adder and drynas, full of odious stink,
The eft, snake and dipsas, causing deadly thirst,
Why hast Thou armed them with a rage so curst?
  Pardon, good Lord, pardon me! 'twas our pride,
Not Thou, that troubled first our happy tide,
And in the childhood of the world did bring
Th'amphisboena her baneful double sting.
Before that Adam did revolt from Thee,
And, curious, tasted of the sacred tree,
He lived king of Eden, and his brow
Was never blanched with pallid fear as now;
The fiercest beasts would at his word or beck,
Bow to his yoke their self-obedient neck
As now the ready horse is at command
To the good rider's spur, or word, or wand,
And doth not wildly his own will perform,
But his that rules him with a steady arm.
Yea, as forgetful of so foul offense,
Thou leftst him yet sufficient wisdom, whence
He might subdue and to his service stoop
The stubborn'st herds of all the savage troop.
Of all the creatures through the welkin gliding,
Walking on earth or through the waters sliding,
Thou'st armed some with poison, some with paws,
Some with sharp antlers, some with gripping claws,
Some with keen tushes,[5] some with crooked beaks,
Some with thick cuirass, some with scaly necks;
But mad'st man naked; and for weapons fit
Thou gav'st him nothing but a pregnant wit
Which rusts and dulls, except it subject find
Worthy its worth, whereon itself to grind,
And, as it were,[6] with envious armies great

---

the second part of this work—Adam; The Furies—occurs the following
line:—"A confused host of strange chimeras vain." which somewhat
resembles the concluding line of the foregoing quotation.
  [5]Much more commonly heard than "tusks" in the rural districts
of the northern states.
  [6]The phrase, "as it were", was occasionally used long before this
writing.

Be round about besieged and beset.
　　For what boots Milo's brawny shoulders broad
And sinewy arms, if but a common load
He always bears?　What bays or olive boughs,
Parsley or pine, shall crown his warlike brows,
Except some other Milo, entering lists,
Courageously his boasted strength resists?
In deepest perils shineth wisdom's prime,
Through thousand deaths true valor seeks to climb.
Well knowing conquest yields but little honor
If bloody danger does not wait upon her.
　　O gracious Father, Thou'st not only lent
Prudence to man, the perils to prevent,
Wherewith these foes threaten his feeble life,
But for his sake hast set at mutual strife
Serpents with serpents, and hast made them foes
Which, unprovoked, felly them oppose.　.　.　.
Thou mak'st th'ichneumon whom the Memphs adore
To rid of poisons Nile's manured shore,
Although, indeed, he doth not conquer them
So much by strength as subtle stratagem.
As he that, urged with deep indignity,
By a proud challenge doth his foe defy,
Premeditates his posture and his play,
And arms himself so complete every way,
With wary hand guided by watchful eye,
And ready foot to traverse skillfully,
That the defendant, in the heat of fight,
Finds no part open where his blade can light.
　　So Pharaoh's rat, ere he begin the fray
'Gainst the blind aspic, with a cleaving clay
Upon his coat he wraps an earthen cake
Which afterwards the sun's hot beams do bake,
Armed with this plaster, th'aspic he approacheth
And in his throat his crooked tooth he broacheth,
While th'other bootless tries to pierce and prick
Through the hard temper of his armor thick;
Yet knowing himself too weak, for all his wile,
Alone to match the scaly crocodile,

He with the wren his ruin doth conspire,
The wren, who seeing, pressed with sleep's desire,
Nile's poisonous pirate press the slimy shore,
Comes suddenly and hopping him before,
Into his mouth he skips, his teeth he pickles,
Cleanseth his palate, and his throat so tickles,
That, charmed with pleasure, the dull serpent gapes
Wider and wider with his ugly chaps.
Then like a shaft th'ichneumon instantly
Into the tyrant's greedy gorge doth fly,
And feeds upon that glutton for whose riot
All Nile's far margins could scarce furnish diet.   .   .   .

Already howls the waste-fold wolf, the boar
Whets foamy fangs, the hungry bear doth roar,
The cat-faced ounce that doth me much dismay,
With grumbling horror threatens my decay;
The lightfoot tiger and the leopard,
Foaming with fury, do besiege me hard;
Then th'unicorn, th'hyena tearing tombs,
Swift mantichor, and Nubian cephus comes,[7]
Of which last three, each hath, as here they stand,
Man's voice, man's visage, and man's foot and hand.
I fear the beast, bred in the bloody coast,
Of cannibals, which thousand times almost,
Re-whelps her whelps, and in her tender womb
She doth as oft her living brood retomb.[8]

But O what monster's this that bids me battle,
On whose rough back an host of pikes doth rattle,
Who stringless shoots so many arrows out,
Whose thorny sides are hedged round about
With stiff, steel-pointed quills, and all his parts
Bristled with bodkins, armed with awls and darts,

---

[7]The "Index" does not throw light on these animals of which the translator had perhaps never heard. In the French text they appear as "le vite mantichore et le ceph Nubien." The former seems to refer to an animal mentioned by Ctesias as compounded of lion, porcupine and scorpion, but with human head, while the latter is probably taken from some story of anthropoid apes.

[8]No doubt founded upon reports of marsupials of one kind or another.

Which ay fierce darting seems still fresh to spring,
And to his aid still new supplies to bring.
O fortunate, shaft never wanting, bowman,
Who, as thou fliest canst hit thy following foeman,
And never missest,—or but very narrow,—
Th'intended mark of thy self's kindred arrow!
Who, still self-furnished, needest borrow never
Diana's shaft nor yet Apollo's quiver,
Nor bowstring fetch from Carian Alaband,[9]
Nor bow from Peru, but hast all at hand
Of thine own growth; for in thy hide do grow
The string, thy shafts, thy quiver and thy bow.
But, courage now! here comes the valiant beast,
The noble lion, king of all the rest;
Who, bravely minded, is as mild to those
That yield to him as fierce unto his foes;
To humble suitors neither stern nor stateful,
To benefactors never found ungrateful.

   I call to memory that same Roman thrall
Who, to escape from his mechanical
And cruel master, that for lucre used him
Not as a man, but as a beast abused him,
Fled through the desert, and with travel tired,
At length within a mossy cave retired;
But there no sooner 'gan the drowsy wretch
On the soft grass his weary limbs to stretch,
But, coming swift into the cave, he seeth
A ramping lion, gnashing of his teeth.

   A thief, to shameful execution sent
By justice for his fault's just punishment,
Feeling his eyes' clout, and his elbows' cord,
Waiting for nothing but the fatal sword,
Dies ere his death, he looks so certainly
Without delay in that dread place to die.
Even so the slave, seeing no means to shun
By flight or fight his feared destruction,

9Alabanda was a town south of the Meander river in Caria, Asia Minor.   It is now called Arabissar.

Having no way to fly nor arms to fight,
But sighs and tears, prayers and woful plight,
Embraceth death; abiding for a stoun,
Pale, cold and senseless, in a deadly swoun,
At last again his courage 'gan to gather,
When he perceived no rage, but pity rather,
In his new host, who, with mild looks and meek,
Seemed, as it were, succour of him to seek,
Showing him oft one of his paws, wherein
A festering thorn for a long time had been;
Then, though still fearful, did the slave draw nigher,
And from his foot he lightly snatched the briar,
And wringing gently with his hand the wound,
Caused the hot pus to run upon the ground.
  Thenceforth the lion seeks for booty best
Through hill and dale to cheer his new come guest,
His new physician, who for all his cost
Soon leaves his lodging and his dreadful host,
And once more wanders through the wilderness
Whither his froward fortune would address,
Until, re-ta'en, his fell lord brought him home,
For spectacle unto imperial Rome,
To be, according to their barbarous laws,
Bloodily torn with greedy lion's paws.   .   .   .
  O'er all the beasts that filled the Martian field
With blood and slaughter, one was most beheld,—
One valiant lion, whose victorious fights
Had conquered hundreds of those guilty wights
Whose feeble skirmish had but striven in vain
To 'scape by combat their deserved pain.
That very beast, with faint and fearful feet
This runagate at last is forced to meet;
And being entered in the bloody list,
The lion roused and ruffled up his crest,
Shortened his body, sharpened his grim eye,
And staring wide he roared hideously.
Then often swindging[10] with his sinewy train

---

[10]"Swindges the scaly horror of his folded tail."—Milton's Ode on
the Nativity.

Sometimes his sides, sometimes the dusty plain,
He whets his rage and strongly rampeth on
Against his foe, who nigh already gone
To drink of Lethe, lifteth to the pole
Religious vows,—not for his life, but soul.
    After the beast had marched some twenty pace,
He sudden stopped; and viewing well the face
Of his pale foe, remembered, rapt with joy,
That this was he that eased his annoy;
Wherefore, converted from his hateful wildness,
From pride to pity, and from rage to mildness,
On his bleak face he both his eyes doth fix,
Fawning for homage, and his lean hands licks.
The slave, thus knowing and thus being known,
Lifts to the heavens his front, now hoary grown,
And now no more fearing his tearing paws,
He strokes the lion and his poll he claws,
And shows by proof that "A good turn at need,
At first or last shall be assured of meed."
    There's under sun, as Delphi's god did show,
No better knowledge than ourselves to know.
There is no theme more plentiful to scan
Than is the glorious, goodly frame of man.
For in man's self is fire, air, earth and sea.
Man's, in a word, the world's epitome,
Or little map; which here my muse doth try
By the grand pattern to exemplify.
    A witty mason doth not, with rare art,
Into a palace Parian stone convert,
Ceil it with gold, and to the firmament
Raise the proud turrets of his battlement,
And, to be brief, in every part of it
Beauty to use, use unto beauty fit,
To th'end the screech-owl and night raven should
In those fair walls their habitation hold;
But rather for some wise and wealthy prince,
Able to judge of his art's excellence.   .   .   .
    Now, of all creatures which His word did make,
Man was the last that living breath did take.

Not that he was the least, or that God durst
Not undertake so noble a work at first;
Rather because He should have made in vain
So great a prince without o'er whom to reign.
A wise man never brings his bidden guest
Into his parlor till his room be dressed,
Garnished with lights, and tables neatly spread
Be with full dishes well nigh furnished.
So our great God who, bounteous, ever keeps
Here open court, and th'ever boundless deeps
Of sweetest nectar on us still distils
By twenty times ten thousand sundry quills,
Would not our grandsire to His board invite
Ere He with arras His fair house had dight,
And under starry state-cloths placed His plates,
Filled with a thousand sugared delicates.

All th'admirable creatures made beforn,
Which heaven and earth and ocean do adorn,
Are but essays, compared in every part
To this divinest masterpiece of art.
Therefore the supreme, peerless Architect,
When of mere nothing He did first erect
Heaven, earth, air and seas, at once His thought,
His word and deed all in one instant wrought.
But when He would His own Self's type create,—
Th'honor of nature, earth's sole potentate,—
As if He would a council hold, He citeth
His sacred power, His prudence He inviteth,
Summons His love, His justice He adjourns,
Calleth His goodness, and His grace returns,
To—as it were—consult about the birth
And building of a second God—of earth,—
And each a part with liberal hand to bring
Some excellence unto so rare a thing.

Or rather He consults with's only Son,
His own true portrait, what proportion,
What gifts, what grace, what soul He should bestow
Upon His viceroy of this realm below.
When th'other things God fashioned in their kind,

The sea t'abound in fishes He assigned,
The earth in flocks; but having man in hand,
His very Self He seemed to command.
He, both at once, both life and body lent
To other things, but when in man He meant
In mortal limbs immortal life to place,
He seemed to pause, as in a weighty case;
And so at sundry moments finished
The soul and body of earth's glorious head.
   Admired Spirit, Architect divine,
Perfect and peerless in all works of Thine,
So my rude hand on this rough table guide,
To paint the prince of all Thy works beside,
That grave spectators in his face may spy
Apparent marks of Thy divinity.
   Almighty Father! as of watery matter
It pleased Thee make the people of the water,
So of an earthy substance mad'st Thou all
The slimy burghers of this earthly ball,
To th'end each creature might, as consequent,
Part sympathize with his own element;
Therefore to form Thine earthly emperor
Thou tookest earth, and by Thy sacred power
So tempered it that of the very same
Dead, shapeless lump, didst Adam's body frame.
Yet not his face down to the earthward bending,
Like beasts that but regard their belly, ending
Forever all; but toward the azure sky's
Bright golden lamps, lifting his lonely eyes,
That through their nerves his better part might look
Still to that place from whence her birth she took.
   Also Thou plantedst th'intellectual power
In th'highest stage of all this stately bower,
That thence it might, as from a citadel,
Command the members that too oft rebel
Against his rule; and that our reason there
Keeping continual garrison as it were,
Might avarice, envy and pride subdue,
Lust, gluttony, wrath, sloth and all their crew

Of factious commons that still strive to gain
The golden scepter from their sovereign.
   Th'eyes, body's guides, are set for sentinel
In noblest place of all this citadel,
To spy far off that no mishap befall
At unawares the sacred animal.
In forming these, Thy hand, so famous held,
Seemeth almost to have itself excelled;
Them not transpiercing, lest our eyes should be
As theirs that heaven through hollow canes do see,
Yet see small circuit of the welkin bright,
The cane's strict compass doth so clasp their sight;
And lest so many open holes disgrace
The goodly form of th'earthly monarch's face.
   These lovely lamps, whose sweet sparks lively turning
With sudden glance set coldest hearts a-burning,
These windows of the soul,[11] these starry twins,
These Cupid's quivers, have so tender skins
Through which, as through a pair of shining glasses
Their radiant point of piercing splendor passes,
That they would soon be quenched and put out
But that the Lord hath bulwarked them about,
By seating so their wondrous orb, betwix
The front, the nose, and the vermilion cheeks. . . .
And as a pent-house[12] doth preserve a wall
From rain and hail and other storms that fall,
The twinkling lids, with their quick trembling hairs
Defend the eyes from thousand dangerous fears.
   Who fain would see how much a human face
A comely nose doth beautify and grace,
Behold Zopyrus who cut off his nose
For's prince's sake, to circumvent his foes.
The nose no less for use than beauty makes;
For as a conduit it both gives and takes

11"The window of my heart, mine eyes," Love's Labor's Lost V, 2, 848;
"The windows of mine eyes," Rich. III, V, 3, 116. See also Cymbeline
II, 2, 22, Romeo and Juliet, IV, 1, 100.
  12Shakespeare derived his "pent-house lids" in Macbeth from this
passage.

Our living breath.   It's as a pipe put up
Whereby the moist brain's spongy bone doth sup
Sweet smelling fumes.   It serveth as a gutter
To rid the system of superfluous matter
As by the skull-seams and the pory skin
Evaporate that which is light and thin,—
As through black chimneys flees the bitter smoke
Which, but so vented, would the household choke.
And since that Time doth with his secret file
Fret and diminish each thing every while;
And whatsoever here begins and ends
Wears every hour, and itself's substance spends,
Th'Almighty made the mouth to recompense
The stomach's pension and the time's expense,
Even as the green trees by their roots resume
Sap, for the sap that hourly they consume,
And placed it so that always, by the way,
By scent of meats the nose might take essay,
The watchful eye might true distinction make
'Twixt herbs and weeds, betwixt an eel and snake,
And then th'impartial tongue might, at the last,
Censure[13] their goodness by their savory taste.
     Two equal ranks of orient pearls impale
The open throat, which, queen-like, grinding small
Th'imperfect food, soon to the stomach send it
(Our master cook whose due concoctions mend it,)
But lest the teeth, naked and bare to light,
Should in the face present a ghastly sight,
With wondrous art over that pale do meet
Two moving leaves of coral, soft and sweet.   .   .   .
     O mouth, by thee the rudest wits have learned
The noble arts which but the wise discerned.
By thee we kindle in the coldest spirits
Heroic flames, effecting glorious merits.
By thee we wipe the tears of woful eyes;[14]

13"Censure" is equivalent with "judge."
14An edition of this part of the Divine Weeks was published in 1598,
and perhaps other editions before that. The authorized edition of
the English Bible was first printed in 1611, but I am not able to

By thee we stop the stubborn mutinies
Of our rebellious flesh, whose restless treason
Strives to dethrone and to disscepter reason.
By thee our souls with heaven have conversation;
By thee we calm th'Almighty's indignation,
When faithful sighs from our souls' center fly
About the bright throne of His majesty.
By thee we warble to the King of Kings;
Our tongue's the bow, our teeth the trembling strings,
Our hollow nostrils with their double vent
The hollow body of the instrument;
Our soul's the sweet musician that plays
So divine lessons and so heavenly lays,
As in deep passion of pure burning zeal,
Jove's forked lightnings from his fingers steal.
  But O what member hath more marvels in't
Than th'ear's round-winding, double labyrinth?
The body's scouts, of sounds the censurers,
Doors of the soul, and faithful messengers
Of divine treasures, when our gracious Lord
Sends us th'embassage of His sacred word.
And since all sound seems always to ascend,
God placed the ears where they might best attend,
As in two turrets on the building's top,
Snailing their hollow entries so aslope
That while the voice about those windings wanders
The sound might lengthen in the bowed meanders;
As from a trumpet wind hath longer life
Or from a sackbut, than from flute or fife;
Or as a noise extendeth far and wide
In winding vales or by the crooked side
Of crawling rivers, or with broken trouble
Between the teeth of hollow rocks doth double;
And that no sudden sound, with violence

---

inform myself at present whether the biblical allusions in Isaiah XXV,
8, and Revelations VII, 17; XXI, 4, to the wiping of tearful eyes was
expressed in like manner in the earlier bibles. The original French
of Sylvester's line is, "Par toi nous essuyons des plus tristes les yeux."
Milton's line in Lycidas, "And wipe the tears forever from his eyes,"
should not be overlooked in the examination.

Piercing direct the organs of this sense,
Should stun the brain,—but through these mazy holes
Convey the voice more softly to our souls.   . . .
    But is't not time now, in his inner parts
To see th'Almighty's admirable arts?
First with my lancet shall I make incision
To see the cells of the twin brain's division,—
The treasurer of arts, the source of sense,
The seat of reason, and the fountain, whence
Our sinews flow, whom nature's providence
Armed with a helm whose double linings fence
The brain's cold moisture from its bony armor
Whose hardness else might hap to bruise or harm her,—
A register, where with a secret touch
The studious daily some rare knowledge couch.
    O how shall I on learned leaf forth set
That curious maze, that admirable net,
Through whose fine folds the spirit doth rise and fall,
Making its powers of vital, animal;
Even as the blood and spirits, wandering
Through the preparing vessel's crooked ring,
Are in their winding course concoct and wrought,
And by degrees to fruitful seed are brought?
    Shall I the heart's unequal sides explain,
Which equal poise doth equally sustain?
Whereof one's filled with blood; in th'other bides
The vital spirit which through the body slides,
Whose restless panting by the constant pulse
Doth witness health,—or if that take repulse
And shift the dance and wonted pace it went,
It show's that nature's wronged by accident.
    Or shall I cleave the lungs, whose motions light
Our inward heat do temper day and night?
As summer gales, waving with gentle puffs
The smiling meadows' green and gaudy tuffs;[15]
Light, spongy fans, that ever take and give

---

[15]"Tuff" is the earlier and more appropriate form of "tuft" which
in the French from which it is taken is "touffe".

Th'ethereal air whereby we breathe and live;
Bellows whose blast, breathing by certain pauses,
A pleasant sound through our speech-organs causes.
   Or shall I rip the stomach's hollowness?
That ready cook, concocting every mess,
Which in short time it cunningly converts
Into pure liquor, fit to feed the parts,
And then the same doth faithfully deliver
Into the port-vein, passing to the liver,
Who turns it soon to blood, and thence again
Through branching pipes of the great, hollow vein,
Through all the members doth it duly scatter
Much like a fountain whose divided water
Itself dispersing in a hundred brooks
Bathes some fair garden with her winding crooks.
For as these brooks, thus branching round about,
Make here the pink, there th'aconite to sprout,
Here the sweet plum tree, the sharp mulb'ry there,
Here the low vine and there the lofty pear,   . . .
Even so the blood bred of good nourishment
By divers pipes to all the body sent,
Turns here to bones, there changes into nerves,
Here is made marrow, there for muscles serves,
Here skin becomes, there crooking veins, there flesh,
To make our limbs more forceful and more fresh.
   But now we list no nearer view to take
Of th'inward parts which God did secret make,
Nor pull in pieces all the human frame.
That work were fitter for those men of fame,
Those skillful sons of Esculapius,
Hippocrates, or deep Herophilus,
Or th'eloquent and artificial writ (wit?)
Of Galen, that renowned Pergamite.
Sufficeth me in some sort to express
By this essay the sacred mightiness
Not of Japhetus' witty-feigned son,
But of the true Prometheus, that begun,
And finished with inimitable art
The famous image I have sung in part.

Now this more peerless, learned Imager,
Life to His lovely picture to confer,
Did not extract out of the elements
A certain secret chemic quintessence;
But breathing, sent as from the lively spring
Of His divineness some small riverling,
Itself dispersing into every pipe
Of the frail engine of His earthen type.
Not that His own self's essence blest He brake,
Or did His triple unity partake,
Unto His work; but without self's expense,
Inspired it richly with rare excellence,
And by His power so spread His rays thereon
That even yet appears a portion
Of that pure luster of celestial light
Wherewith at first it was adorned and dight.
This Adam's spirit did from that Spirit derive
That made the world; yet did not thence deprive
Of God's self-substance any part at all,
As in the course of nature doth befall,
That from the essence of an earthly father
An earthly son essential parts doth gather;
Or as in springtime from one sappy twig
There sprouts another consubstantial sprig.
In brief it's but a breath. Now, though the breath
Out of our stomach's concave issueth,
Yet of our substance it transporteth naught,
Only it seemeth to be simply fraught,
And to retain the purer qualities
Of th'inward place whence it derived is.
Inspired by this breath, this breath desire
I to describe. Whoso doth not admire
Its spirit is sprightless, and his sense is past
Who hath no sense of that admired blast.
Yet wot I well that as the eye perceives
All but itself, even so our soul conceives
All save her own self's essence; but the end
Of her own greatness cannot comprehend. . . .
The boisterous wind that rends with roaring blasts

The lofty pines, and to the welkin casts
Millions of mountains from the watery world,
And proudest turrets to the ground hath whirled;
The pleasing fume that fragrant roses yield
When wanton Zephyr, sighing on the field,
Enamels[16] all, and to delight the eye
The earth puts on her richest livery;
Th'accorded discords that are sweetly sent
From th'ivory ribs of some rare instrument,
Cannot be seen; but he may well be thought
Devoid of sense who holds these things for naught.
    Although our soul's pure substance to our sight
Be not subjected, yet her motion light
And rich discourse sufficient proofs do give
That we've more soul than to suffice to live,—
A soul divine, pure, sacred, admirable,
Immortal, endless, simple, impalpable   .   .   .
And whether brain or heart do lodge the soul—
O Seneca, where, where couldst thou enroll
Those many hundred words in prose or verse,
Which at first hearing thou couldst back rehearse?
Whence could great Cyrus that great table shut
Wherein the pictures and the names were put
Of all the soldiers that by thousands wandered
After the fortunes of his famous standard?
In what deep vessel did th'ambassador
Of Pyrrhus—whom the Delphian oracler
Deluded by his double-meaning measures,—
Into what cisterns did he pour those treasures
Of learned store, which, after, for his use
In time and place he could so fit produce?
    The memory is the eyes' true register,
The peasants' book, Time's wealthy treasurer,
Keeping record of acts and accidents

16"O'er the smooth enameled green."—Milton's Arcades, Song II.
Sylvester also has "Ver's enameled tapestry" in the first section of
Adam, "The enameled meads" in the third section and in two or three
of the later poems the same metaphor.

Whatever, subject unto human sense,
Since first the Lord the world's foundations laid,
Or Phoebus first his golden locks displayed,
And his pale sister from his beaming light
Borrowed her splendor to adorn the night.
So that our reason, searching curiously
Through all the rolls of a good memory,
And fastening closely with a Gordian knot
To past events what present times allot,
Foresees the future, and becomes more sage,
More happily to lead our later age.
　And though our soul live as imprisoned here
In our frail flesh, or buried as it were
In a dark tomb; yet at one flight she fllies
From Calpe to Imaus, from earth to skies,
Much swifter than the chariot of the sun,
Which in a day about the world doth run.
For sometimes, leaving these base, slimy heaps,
With cheerful spring above the clouds she leaps,
Glides through the air, and there essays to know
Th'originals of wind and hail and snow,
Of lightning, thunder, blazing stars, and storms
Of rain and ice, and strange exhaled forms.
By th'air's steep stairs she boldly climbs aloft
To the world's chambers. Heaven she visits oft,
Stage after stage. She marketh all the spheres,
And all th'harmonious, various course of theirs.
With sure account and certain compasses
She counts the stars, and metes their distances
And differing paces, and, as if she found
No subject fair enough in all this round,
She mounts above the world's extremest wall,
Far, far beyond all things corporeal,
And there beholds her Maker face to face,—
His frowns of justice and His smiles of grace,
The faithful zeal, the chaste and sober port
And sacred pomp of the celestial court.[17]

---

[17]In Milton's "Vacation Exercise" is an evident paraphrase of this,

What can be hard to a sloth-shunning spirit,
Spurred with desire of fame's eternal merit?
Look, if thou canst, from east to occident,
From Iceland to the Moors' dark continent,
And thou shalt naught perfectly fair behold,
But pen or pencil, graving tool or mould
Hath so resembled that scarce can our eye
The counterfeit from the true thing descry.   .   .   .

The art of man not only can compact
Features and forms that life and motion lack,
But also fill the air with painted shoals
Of flying creatures, artificial fowls.
The Tarentines' valiant and learned lord,
Archytas, made a wooden dove, that soared
About the welkin, by th'accorded slights
And counterpoise of sundry little weights.
Why should I not that wooden eagle mention,
A learned German's late, admired invention,
Which, mounting from his fist that framed her,
Flew far to meet an Almain emperor,
And having met him, with her nimble train
And weary wings turning about again,
Followed him close unto the castle gate
Of Nuremburg; whom all the shows of state,
Streets hung with arras, arches curious built,
Loud thundering cannons, columns richly gilt,
Gray-headed senate, and youths' gallantise
Graced not so much as only this device.

Once as this artist more with mirth than meat
Feasted some friends that he esteemed great,

---

beginning—

    "Such where the deep-transported mind may soar
    Above the whirling poles, and at Heaven's door
    Look in, and see each blissful deity," etc.
  Sylvester's translation of Du Bartas's "Urania" also has the following stanza:

    "I am Urania," then aloud said she,
    "Who human-kind above the poles transport,
    Teaching their hands to touch, and eyes to see
    All th' intercourse of the celestial court."

From under's hand an iron fly flew out,
Which, having flown a perfect roundabout,
With weary wings returned to her master,
And, as with judgment, on his arm she placed her.
O divine wit, that in the narrow womb
Of a small fly could find sufficient room
For all those springs, wheels, counterpoise and chains
Which stood instead of life and spurs and reins!
Yea, you yourselves, ye bright celestial orbs,
Although no stop your restless dance disturbs,
Nor stays your course; yet can ye not escape
The hands of man that are men but in shape.
   A Persian monarch, not content well-nigh
With the earth's bounds to bound his empery,
To reign in heaven raised not with bold defiance
(Like braving Nimrod, or the boisterous giants,)
Another Babel, or a heap of hills;
But without moving from the earth, he builds
A heaven of glass, so huge that thereupon
Sometimes erecting his ambitious throne,
Beneath his proud feet, like a god, he saw
The shining lamps of th'other heaven to draw
Down to the deep, and thence again advance
Like glorious brides their golden radiance.
Yet had that heaven no wondrous excellence
Save greatness, worthy of so great a prince.
   But who would think that mortal hands could mould
New heavens, new stars, whose whirling courses should
With constant windings, through contrary ways,
Mark the true mounds[18] of years and months and days?
Yet 'tis a story that hath oft been heard
And by grave witness hundred times averred,
That that profound Briareus[19] who of yore—

---

[18] Although it seems to the present editor that "rounds" ought to take the place of this word, the fact that it appears in the above shape in all the Sylvestrian editions of the 17th century has decided the question adversely to any substitution.
[19] Archimedes.

(As himself armed with thousand hands or more,)
Maintained so long the Syracusan towers
'Gainst great Marcellus and his Roman powers,
Who fired his foe's fleet with a wondrous glass,
Who, hugest vessels that did ever pass
The Tyrrhene seas, turned only with his hand
From shore to sea, and from the sea to land,—
Framed a sphere where every wandering light
Of lower heavens, and th'upper tapers bright,
Whose glistering flames the firmament adorn,
Did of themselves with ruled motion turn.
    Nor may we smother, or forget ungrately
That heaven of silver that was sent but lately
From Ferdinando as a famous work
Unto Byzantium to the supreme Turk;
Wherein a spirit still moving to and fro
Made all the engine orderly to go,
And though our sphere did always slowly slide,
And, opposite, the other swiftly glide,
Yet still their stars kept all their courses even
With the true courses of the stars in heaven.
The sun, there shifting in the zodiac
His shining houses, never did forsake
His 'pointed path. There in a month his sister
Fulfilled her course, and changing oft her luster
And form of face,—now larger, lesser soon,—
Followed the changes of the other moon.
    O complete creature! who the starry spheres
Canst make to move; who 'bove the heavenly Bears
Extend'st thy power; who guidest with thy hand
The day's bright chariot and the nightly brand;
This curious lust to imitate the best
And fairest works of the Almightiest,
By rare effects bears record of thy lineage
And high descent; and that His sacred image
Was in thy soul engraven when first His spirit,
The spring of life, did in thy limbs inspire it.
    For as His beauties are past all compare,
So is thy soul all beautiful and fair.

As He's immortal and is never idle,
Thy soul's immortal and can brook no bridle
Of sloth to curb her busy intellect.
He ponders all; thou weighest each effect;
And thy mature and settled sapience
Hath some alliance with His providence.
He works by reason, thou by rule.   He's glory
Of th'heavenly stages, thou of th'earthly story.
He's great High Priest; thou His great vicar here.
He's Sovereign Prince and thou His viceroy dear.

For soon as ever He had framed thee,
Into thy hands he put this monarchy;
Made all the creatures know thee for their lord,
And come before thee of their own accord,
And gave thee power as master to impose
Fit, senseful names unto the host that rows
In watery regions, and the wandering herds
Of forest people, and the painted[20] birds.
O too, too happy, had that fall of thine
Not canceled so the character divine.

But since our soul's now sin-obscured light
Shines through the lantern of our flesh so bright;
What sacred splendor will this star send forth
When it shall shine without this veil of earth?
The soul, here lodged, is like a man that dwells
In an ill air, annoyed with noisome smells;
In an old house, open to wind and weather,—
Never in health; not half an hour together;
Or almost like a spider, who, confined
In her web's center, stirred with every wind,
Moves in an instant if a buzzing fly
Stirs but a thread of her lawn canopy.

You that have seen within this ample table
Among so many models admirable,
Th'admired beauties of the king of creatures,

---

[20]Painted, as in Shakespeare's Love's Labor's Lost (V, 1,) the meadows are painted.

Come, come and see the woman's rapting features,
Without whom here man were but half a man,—
But a wild wolf,—but a barbarian,
Brute, rageful, fierce, moody, melancholic,
Hating the light, whom naught but naught could like;
Born solely for himself, devoid of sense,
Of heart, of love, of life, of excellence.
God, therefore, not to seem less liberal
To man than else to every animal,
For perfect pattern of a holy love
To Adam's half another half He gave,
Ta'en from his side, to bind through every age
With kinder bonds the sacred marriage.
   Even as a surgeon, minding off to cut[21]
Some cureless limb, before in use he put
His violent engines on the vicious member,
Bringeth his patient in a senseless slumber,
And painless then, guided by use and art,
To save the whole saws off th'infected part;
So God empaled our grandsire's lively look,
Through all his bones a deadly chil'ness struck,
Sealed up his sparkling eyes with iron bands,
Led down his feet almost to Lethe's sands;
In brief, so numbed his soul's and body's sense
That without pain opening his side, from thence
He took a rib which rarely He refined,
And thereof made the mother of mankind.
Graving so lifelike on the living bone
All Adam's beauties, that but hardly, one
Could have the lover from his love descried,
Or known the bridegroom from his gentle bride,
Saving that she had a more smiling eye,
A smoother chin, a cheek of purer dye,
A fainter voice, a more enticing face,
A deeper tress, a more delightful grace.   .   .   .
   Now, after this profound and pleasing trance.

---

[21] See article "Anaesthesia," Enc. Brit., 9th edition, vol. 1.

No sooner Adam's ravished eyes did glance
On the rare beauties of his new come half,
But in his heart he 'gan to leap and laugh,
Kissing her kindly, calling her his life,
His love, his stay, his rest, his weal, his wife,
His other self, his help, him to refresh,
Bone of his bone, flesh of his very flesh.   .   .   .
    O blessed bond!   O happy marriage,
Which does the match 'twixt Christ and us presage!
O chastest friendship, whose rare flames impart .
Two souls in one, two hearts into one heart!
O holy knot, in Eden instituted,—
Not in this earth, with blood and wrongs polluted,
Profaned with mischiefs the pre-scene of hell
To cursed creatures that 'gainst heaven rebel,—
O sacred covenant, which the sinless Son
Of a pure virgin, when He first begun
To publish proofs of His dread power divine
By turning water into perfect wine
At lesser Cana, in a wondrous manner
Did with His presence sanctify and honor.
    By thy dear favor, after our decease
We leave behind our living images,
Change war to peace, in kindred multiply,
And in our children live eternally.
By it we quench the wild and wanton fires
That in our souls the Paphian shot inspires,
And, taught by Thee a love more firm, and fitter,
We find the mel more sweet, the gall less bitter,
Which here by turns heap up our human life
Even now with joys, anon with jars and strife.
    This done, the Lord commands the happy pair
With chaste embraces to replenish fair
Th'unpeopled world; that, while the world endures,
Here might succeed their living portraitures.
He had imposed the like precept before
On th'ireful droves that in the deserts war,
The feathered flocks, the fruitful spawning legions
That live within the liquid crystal regions.

Thenceforth, therefore, bears bears engendered,
The dolphins dolphins, vultures vultures bred,
Men, men; and nature, with a changeless course
Still brought forth issue like their ancestors;
Though since, indeed, as, when the fire has mixed them,
The yellow gold and silver pale, betwixt them
Another metal, like to neither make,
Which yet of either's riches doth partake,—
So, oft, two creatures of a differing kind,
Against the common course through all assigned,
Confounding their lust-burning seeds together,
Beget an elf not like in all to either,
But surely bearing mongrel marks apparent
Of mingled members, ta'en from either parent.
   God, not contented to each kind to give
And to infuse the virtue generative,
Made by His wisdom many creatures breed
Of lifeless bodies, growing without seed.
So the cold humor breeds the salamander,
Who in effect, like to her birth's commander,
Pregnant with hundred winters, with her touch
Quencheth the fire, though glowing ne'er so much.
So of the fire, in burning furnace springs
The fly, pyrausta, with the flaming wings.
Without the fire it dies; within, it joys;
Living in that which other life destroys.
   So slow Bootes underneath him sees
In th'icy isles those goslings hatched of trees,
Whose fruitful leaves, falling into the water,
Are turned, they say, to living fowls soon after.
So rotten sides of broken ships do change
To barnacles.   O transformation strange!
'Twas first a green tree; then a gallant hull;
Lately a mushroom; now a flying gull.

In Sec. 15 of Part One of Sir Thomas Browne's Religio Medici
may be found several allusions to events of this "Day", and especially to the artificial fly and eagle credited to Regiomontanus.

THE SEVENTH DAY

The cunning painter that with curious care,
Limning a landscape, various, rich and rare,
Hath set a-work, in all and every part,
Invention, judgment, nature, use and art;
And hath at length, t'immortalize his name,
With weary pencil perfected the same;
Forgets his pains, and inly filled with glee,
Still on his picture gazeth greedily.   .   .   .
So th'Architect whose glorious workmanships
My cloudy muse doth but too much eclipse,
Having with painless pains and careless care,
In these six days finished the table fair
And infinite, of th'universal ball,
Resteth this day t'admire Himself in all;
And for a season eyeing nothing else,
Joys in His work since all His work excels.
(If my dull, stutting,[1] frozen eloquence
May dare conjecture of His high intents).
   One while[2] He sees how th'ample sea doth take
The liquid homage of each other lake,
And how, again, the heavens exhale from it
Abundant vapors for our benefit.
And yet it swells not for those tribute streams,
Nor yet it shrinks not for those boiling beams.
There sees He th'ocean-people's plenteous broods,
And shifting courses of the ebbs and floods,

1"Stutt" is the older form of stutter.
2"One while" is a phrase often heard in the northern American
states, and perhaps elsewhere.

Which, with inconstant glances night and day,
The lower planet's forked front doth sway.
Anon upon the flowery plains He looks,
Laced about with snaking silver brooks.
Now He delights to see four brethren's strife
Cause the world's peace, and keep the world in life;
Anon to see the whirling spheres to roll
In restless dances about either pole,
Whereby their cressets, carried divers ways,
Now visit us, anon th'antipodes.
It glads Him now to note how th'orb of flame
Which girds this globe doth not enfire the frame;
How th'air's glib-gliding, firmless body bears
Such store of fowls, hailstorms, and floods of tears;
How th'heavy water, pronest to descend,
Twixt air and earth is able to depend;[3]
And how the dull earth's propless, massy ball
Stands steady still, just in the midst of all.
Anon His nose is pleased with fragrant scents
Of balm, and basil, myrrh and frankincense,
Thyme, spikenard, hyssop, savory, cinnamon,
Pink, violet, rose, and clove-carnation.
Anon His ear's charmed with the melody
Of winged concerts' curious harmony;
For though each bird, guided with artless art,
After his kind observe a song apart,
Yet the sole burden of their several lays
Is nothing but the Heaven-King's glorious praise.
  In brief, th'Almighty's eye and nose and ear,
In all His works doth naught see, smell or hear,
But shows His greatness, savors of His grace,
And sounds His glory over every place.
But above all, man's many beauteous features
Detain the Lord more than all other creatures.
Man's His own minion.   Man's His sacred type,
And for man's sake He loves His workmanship.
  Not that I mean to feign an idle God,

---

[3]To remain suspended.

That lusks in heaven and never looks abroad;
That crowns not virtue and corrects not vice,
Blind to our service, deaf unto our sighs;
A pagan idol, void of power and piety.
A sleeping dormouse matches such a deity!
For though, alas, sometimes I cannot shun
But some profane thoughts in my mind will run,
I never think on God, but I conceive,—
Whence cordial comforts Christian souls receive,—
In God, care, counsel, justice, mercy, might,
To punish wrong and patronize the right;
Since man, but image of th'Almightiest,
Without these gifts is not a man, but beast.
Fond Epicure,[4] thou rather slept'st, thyself,
When thou didst forge thee such a sleep-sick elf
For life's pure fount; or vainly fraudulent
Not shunning th'atheist's sin, but punishment,
Imaginedst a god so perfectless,
In works defying whom thy words profess.
     God is not sitting, like some earthly state,
In proud theater, Him to recreate
With curious objects of His ears and eyes,
Without disposing of the comedies,
Content to've made, by His great word, to move
So many radiant stars as shine above,
And on each thing with His own hand to draw
The sacred text of an eternal law;
Then, bosoming His hand, to let them slide[5]

---

[4]Follower of Epicurus, whose philosophy gave no credit to any supernatural power for activity in the affairs of men.
[5]"Let them (or it) slide" has been until very lately a common expression among descendants of New Englanders, and may still survive, as it appears in Gail Hamilton's "Gala Days", page 6, where she
says "Then I should let the book slide," apparently in the same sense
as used at the beginning of Shakespeare's Taming of the Shrew, where
Christopher Sly cries, "Let the world slide." His "Sessa " in the
same sentence seems to be an exclamation identical with Sylvester's
"Sasa," used as a war cry in the section called "The Vocation" of the
part, "Abraham," in the Divine Weeks series. The "let slide" of the
text is not a translation from the French, the original couplet being
          "Tenant sa dextre au sein, abandonne leur bride,
          Pour laisser courir ou cete loi les guide."

With reins at will, whither that law shall guide;
Like one that having lately forced some lake
Through a new channel a new course to take
Takes no more care thenceforth to those effects,
But lets the stream run where his ditch directs.

The Lord, our God, wants neither diligence
Nor love, nor care, nor power, nor providence.
He proved His power by making all of naught;
His diligence by ruling all He wrought;
His care by ending it in six days' space;
His love by building it for Adam's race;
His providence, maugre time's wasteful rages,
Preserving it so many years and ages.
For O how often had this goodly ball
By its own greatness caused its proper fall,—
How often had this world deceased, except
God's mighty arms had it upheld and kept!

God is the soul, the life, the strength, the sinew
That quickens, moves, and makes this frame continue.
God's the mainspring that maketh every way
All the small wheels of this great engine play.
God's the strong Atlas, whose unshrinking shoulders
Have been and are heaven's heavy globe's upholders.

God makes the fountains run continually,
The days the nights succeed unceasingly;
The seasons in their season He doth bring,—
Summer and autumn, winter and the spring;
God makes earth·fruitful, and He makes the earth's
Large loins not yet faint for so many births.
God makes the sun and stars (though wondrous hot,)
That yet their heat themselves inflameth not,
And that their sparkling beams prevent[6] not so
With woful flames the last great day of woe.
And that, as moved with a contrary wrest,
They turn at once both north and east and west.

---

[6] The word "prevent" is here used in its earlier and more literal
meaning of "come before."

Heaven's constant course His heat doth never break;
The floating water waiteth at His beck;
Air's at His call, the fire at His command,
The earth is His, and there is nothing fand
In all these kingdoms, but is moved each hour
With secret touch of His eternal power.
God is the judge who keeps continual sessions
In every place, to punish all transgressions;
Who, void of ignorance and avarice,
Not won with bribes, nor wrested with device,
Sans fear or favor, hate or partial zeal,
Pronounceth judgments that are past appeal.
Himself is witness, judge and jury too,
Well knowing what we all speak, think or do,
He sounds the deepest of the doublest heart,
Searcheth the reins, and sifteth every part.
He sees all secrets, and His lynx-like eye,
Ere it be thought, doth every thought descry.
His sentence given never returns in vain;
For all the heaven, earth, air and sea contain
Serve Him as sergeants, and the winged legions
That soar above the bright, star-spangled[7] regions,
Are ever pressed for powerful ministers,
And lastly for His executioners.
Satan, assisted with th'infernal band,
Stands ready still to finish His command.
God, to be brief, is a good Artisan
That to His purpose aptly manage can
Good or bad tools; and for just punishment
He arms our sins us sinners to torment;
And to prevent th'ungodly's plot, sometime
He makes His foes, will-nill they, fight for Him.
Yet true it is that human things seem slide
Unbridledly with so uncertain tide,
That in the ocean of events so many,

---

[7]This is the second instance of Sylvester's use of "star-spangled", which later became such a distinctively American adjective. It is not a literal translation from the French in either instance.

Sometimes God's judgments are scarce seen of any.
Rather it seems that giddy fortune guideth
All that beneath the silver moon betideth.
Yet art Thou ever just, O God, though I
Cannot, alas, Thy judgment's depth descry.
My wit's too shallow for the least design
Of Thy dread counsels, sacred and divine,
And Thy least secret secrets I confess
Too deep for us, without Thy spirit's address.
Yet oftentimes what seemeth at first sight
Unjust to us, and past our reason quite,
Thou mak'st us, Lord, acknowledge in due season
To have been done with equity and reason.

So, suffering th'Hebrew tribes to sell their brother,
Thy eternal justice Thou didst seem to smother;
But Joseph, when through such rare hap it chanced
Him from a slave to be so high advanced
To rule the land where Nilus' fertile flood
Dry heaven's defects endeavors to make good,
Learned that his envious brothers' treacherous drift
Him to the stern[8] of Memphian state had lift
That he might there provide relief and room
For Abraham's seed, against the time to come.

When Thy strong arm that plagues the reprobate
The world, and Sodom, did exterminate
With flood and flame,—because there lived then
Some small remains of good and righteous men,
Thou seemed'st unjust; but when Thou saved'st Lot
From fire, from water Noah and his boat,
'Twas plainly seen, Thy justice stands propitious
To th'innocent, and smiteth but the vicious.

He willful winks against the shining sun
That sees not Pharaoh as a means begun
For th'Hebrews' good, and that his hardened heart
Smoothed the passage for their soon depart;
To th'end the Lord, when tyrants will not yield,
Might for His glory find the larger field.

8Referring to a ship and its guidance.

Who sees not also that th'unjust decree
Of a proud judge, and Judas' treachery,
The people's fury, and the prelates' gall
Served all as organs to repair the fall
Of Eden's old prince, whose luxurious pride
Made on his seed his sin forever abide?
  Th'Almighty's care doth diversely disperse
O'er all the parts of all this universe,
But more precisely, His wide wings protect
The race of Adam chiefly—His elect.
For ay He watcheth for His children choice,
That lift to Him their hearts, their hands and voice;
For them He buildeth th'ay-turning heaven's theater;
For them He made the fire, air, earth and water.
He counts their hairs; their steps He measureth,
Handles their hands and speaketh with their breath,
Dwells in their hearts, and plants His regiments
Of watchful angels round about their tents.
  But here what hear I? Faithless, godless men,
I marvel not that you impugn my pen;
But O it grieves me, and I am amazed
That those whose faith, like glittering stars, hath blazed
Even in our darkest nights, should so object
Against a doctrine of so sweet effect,
Because, alas, with weeping eyes they see
Th'ungodliest in most prosperity,—
Clothed in purple, crowned with diadems,
Handling bright scepters, hoarding gold and gems,
Crouched to, and courted with all kind affection,
As privileged by the heavens' affection,
So that their goods, their honors, their delights,
Excel their hopes,—exceed their appetites,—
And opposite, the godly in the storms
Of this world's sea tossed in continual harms.
On earth less rest than Euripus[9] they find,
God's heavy rods still hanging, them behind;

---

[9]The strait between Euboea and Boeotia, where the tide was said
to ebb and flow seven times a day.

Them shame and blame, trouble and loss pursues
As shadows bodies, and as night the dews.
   Peace, peace, dear friends! I hope to cancel quite
This profane thought from your unsettled sp'rit.
Know then that God, to the end He be not thought
A powerless judge, here plagueth many a fault,
And many a fault leaves here unpunished,
That men may also His last judgment dread.
On th'other side, note that the cross becomes
A ladder leading to heaven's glorious rooms;
A royal path, the heavenly Milky Way,
Which doth the saints to God's high court convey.
   O see you not how that a father grave,
Curbing his son much shorter than his slave,
Doth th'one but rare, the other rife reprove,
Th'one but for lucre, th'other all for love?
As skillful 'querry that commands the stable
Of some great prince or person honorable,
Gives oftest to that horse the teaching spur
Which he finds fittest for the use of war.
A painful[10] schoolmaster, that hath in hand
To institute the flower of all the land,
Gives longest lessons unto those where Heaven
The ablest wits and aptest wills hath given;
And a wise chieftain never trusts the weight[11]
Of th'execution of a brave exploit,
But unto those whom he most honoreth
For often proof of their firm force and faith.
Such sends he first t'assault his eager foes;
Such 'gainst the cannon on a breach bestows;
Such he commands naked to scale a fort,
And with small numbers to regain a port.   . . .

---

[10]Painstaking.
[11]This word is spelled "waight" in the old editions. Judging from colloquial New England use in the first half of the nineteenth century, the diphthong "oi" was pronounced in King James's reign among the Puritans like our present long i. It is therefore, from the rhyme in this couplet, possible that the "aigh" combination was pronounced in like manner by our ancestors.

A good physician, that art's excellence
Can help with practice and experience,
Applies discreetly all his recipes
Unto the nature of each fell disease,
Curing this patient with a bitter potion,
That with strict diet, th'other with a lotion,
And sometime cutteth off a leg or arm,
To save if possible the rest from harm.
Even so the Lord, according to th'ill humors
That vex His saintliest with foul, tainting tumors,
Sends sometimes exile, sometimes lingering languor,
Sometimes dishonor, sometimes pining hunger,
Sometimes long lawsuits, sometimes loss of good,
Sometimes a child's death, sometimes widowhood,—
But ay He holdeth, for the good of His,
In one hand rods, in th'other, remedies.

The soldier, slugging long at home in peace,
His wonted courage quickly doth decrease.
The rust doth fret the blade hanged up at rest;
The moth doth eat the garment in the chest;
The standing water spoils with putrefaction,
And virtue hath no virtue but in action.

All that is fairest in the world we find
Subject to travail. So with storms and wind
Th'air still is tossed; the fire and water tend—
This still to mount, that ever to descend;
The spirit is sprightless if it can't discourse;
Heaven's no more heaven, if once it cease its course.

The valiant knight is known by many scars,
But he that steals home woundless from the wars
Is held a coward, void of valor's proof,
That for death's fear hath fled, or held aloof.

The Lord, therefore, to give humanity
Rare precedents of dauntless constancy,
And crown His dear sons with victorious laurels,
Won from a thousand foes in glorious quarrels,
Pours down more evils on their hapless head
Than erst Pandora's odious box did shed,
Yet strengthening still their hearts with such a plaster,

That though the flesh stoop, still the spirit is master.
 But wrongly I these evil call.
Sole vice is ill; sole virtue good; and all
Besides the same is selfly, simply, had
And held indifferent; neither good nor bad.
Let envious Fortune all her forces wage
Against a constant man; her fullest rage
Can never change his godly resolution,
Though heaven itself should threaten him confusion.[12]
A constant man is like the sea, whose breast
Lies ever open unto every guest,
Yet all the waters that it drink cannot
Make it to change its qualities a jot.   . . .
 Though then the Lord's deep wisdom to this day
Work in the world's mysterious, certain sway,
Yet must we credit that His hand composed
All in six days, and that He then reposed;
By His example giving us behest
On the seventh day, for evermore, to rest.
For God remembered that He made not man
Of stone or steel, or brass Corinthian,
But lodged our soul in a frail, earthen mass,
Thinner than water, brittler than glass.
He knows our life is by naught sooner spent
Than having ever mind and body bent.
 A field, left lay for some few years, will yield
The richer crop, when it again is tilled.
A river, stopped by a sluice a space,
Runs, after, rougher and a swifter pace.
A bow, a while unbent, will after cast
Its shafts the farther, and them fix more fast.
A soldier that a season still hath lain,
Comes with more fury to the field again.
Even so this body, when, to gather breath,
One day in seven to rest it sojourneth,
It re-collects its powers, and with more cheer

---

[12]The lover of Horace is here reminded of the 22d ode of his first book.

Falls the next morrow to its new career.
But the chief end this precept aims at is
To quench in us the coals of covetise
That while we rest from all profaner arts,
God's spirit may work in our retired hearts;
That we, down treading earthly cogitations,
May raise our thought to heavenly meditations;
Following good archers' guise, who shut one eye
That they the better may their mark espy.
For by th'Almighty this great, holy day
Was not ordained to dance and mask and play,
To slug in sloth and languish in delights,
And loose the reins to raging appetites,—
To turn God's feasts to filthy Lupercals,
To frantic orgies and fond Saturnals,
To dazzle eyes with pride's vain-glorious splendor,
To serve strange gods, or our ambition tender,
As th'irreligion of loose times hath since
Changed the prime church's chaster innocence.
God would that men should, in a certain place,
This day assemble as before His face,
Lending an humble and attentive ear
To learn His great name's dear, dread, loving fear,
He would that there the faithful pastor should
The Scripture's marrow from its bones unfold,
That we might touch with fingers, as it were,
The sacred secrets that are hidden there.
For though the reading of those holy lines
In private houses somewhat move our minds,
Doubtless the doctrine preached doth deeper pierce,
Proves more effectual, and more weight it bears.
He would that there in holy psalms we sing
Loud praise and thanks to our immortal King
For all the liberal bounties He bestow'th
On us and ours, in soul and body both.
He would that there we should confess His Christ,
Our only Saviour, Prophet, Prince and Priest,
Solemnizing. with sober preparation
His blessed seals of reconciliation;

And in His name beg boldly what we need,
After His will, and be assured to speed,
Since in th'exchequer of His clemency
All goods of fortune, soul and body, lie.
  He would this Sabbath should a figure be
Of the blest Sabbath of eternity;
But th'one, as legal, heeds but outward things,—
Th'other to rest both soul and body brings.
Th'one but a day endures; the other's date
Eternity shall not exterminate.
Shadows the one, th'other doth truth include;
This stands in freedom,—that in servitude;
With cloudy cares th'one's muffled up some whiles;
The other's face is full of pleasing smiles.
For never grief, nor fear of any fit
Of the least care shall dare come near to it.
'Tis the grand jubilee,—the feast of feasts,
Sabbath of Sabbaths, endless rest of rests,
Which with the prophets and apostles zealous,
The constant martyrs and our Christian fellows,
God's faithful servants and His chosen sheep,
In heaven we hope within short time to keep.
  He would this day our soul, sequestered
From busy thoughts of worldly cares, should read
In heaven's bowed arches, and the elements,
His boundless bounty, power and providence,
That every part may, as a master, teach
Th'illiterate, rules past a vulgar reach.[13]
  Come, reader, sit, come sit thee down by me;
Think with my thoughts, and see what I do see.
Hear this dumb doctor; study in this book,
Where day and night thou may'st at pleasure look;
And thereby learn uprightly how to live;
For every part doth special lessons give,

---

[13]One who reads this passage, (remembering that the whole poem
was more widely read and more generally accepted in the England of
the early 17th century as an orthodox religious guide than any other
work whatever,) may easily see how the New England "Sabbath"
came to be what it was two centuries ago.

Even from the gilt studs[14] of the firmament
To the base center of our element.
    Seest thou those stars we wrongly "wandering" call?
Through divers ways they dance about this ball,
Yet evermore their manifold career
Follows the course of the first-moving sphere.
This teacheth thee that, though thine own desires
Be opposite to what Heaven's will requires,
Thou must still strive to follow, all thy days,
God, the first Mover, in His holy ways.
    Vain puff of wind, whom vaunting pride bewitches
For body's beauty or mind's richer riches;
The moon, whose splendor from her brother springs,
May by example make thee veil thy wings;
For thou, no less than the pale Queen of Night[15]
Borrow'st all thy goodness from the Prince of Light.
Wilt thou from orb to orb, to earth descend?
Behold the fire which God did round extend;
As, near to heaven, the same is clear and pure,
Ours here below, sad, smoky and obscure,
So while thy soul doth with the heavens converse,
It's sure and safe from every thought perverse;
And though thou won[16] here in this world of sin,
Thou art as happy as heaven's angels bin.
But if thy mind be always fixed, all,
On the foul dunghill of this darksome vale,
It will partake in the contagious smells
Of th'unclean house wherein it droops and dwells.

---

[14]Near the beginning of the Fifth Day the stars are spoken of as "glistering studs". In Comus, V. 734, Milton speaks of what would happen if all the world should suddenly become temperate in eating, drinking and clothing; how surfeits would prevail, "and the unsought diamonds Would so emblaze the foreheads of the deep, And so bestud with stars, that they below Would . . . come at last To gaze upon the sun with unshamed brows."

[15]The title "Queen of Night" is used by Sylvester both here and in the Fourth Day without the authority of Du Bartas.

[16]From the Anglo Saxon "wunian", to dwell; cognate with the German "wohnen", and still surviving in Scotch dialect. The agricultural phrase "to get wonted", is the most conspicuous derivative from it in general use.

If envious Fortune be thy bitter foe,
And day and night do toss thee to and fro,[17]
Remember, th'air corrupteth soon, except
With sundry winds it be oft swindged[18] and swept.
    The sea,—which sometimes down to hell is driven
And sometimes heaves a frothy mount to heaven,
Yet never breaks the bounds of her precinct
Wherein the Lord her boisterous arms hath linked,—
Instructeth thee that neither tyrant's rage,
Ambition's winds, nor golden vassalage
Of avarice, nor any love, nor fear
From God's command should make thee shrink a hair.
    The earth,—which never all at once doth move,
Though her rich orb received from above
No firmer base, her burden to sustent,
Than slippery props of softest element,—
By her example doth propose to thee
A needful lesson of true constancy.
Nay, there is naught in our dear mother found
But pithily some virtue doth propound.
O let the noble, wise, rich, valiant,
Be as the base, poor, faint and ignorant;
And looking on the fields when Autumn shears,
There let them learn, among the bearded ears,
Which still the fuller of the flowery grain,
Bow down the more their humble heads again,
And ay the lighter and the less their store,
They lift aloft their chaffy crests the more.   . . .
    Thou, thou that prancest after honor's prize,
While by the way thy strength and stomach dies,
Remember honor is like cinnamon,
Which nature mounds with many a million
Of thorny pricks, that none may dangerless
Approach the plant; much less the fruit possess.

17"To and fro" is familiar enough now, but it is noticeably absent from Shakespeare's works, except in the doubtful passages of King Henry VI.
18See note on "Swindge" in Day 6, ante.

Canst thou the secret sympathy behold
Betwixt the bright sun and the marigold,[19]
And not consider that we must no less
Follow in life the sun of righteousness?
  O earth, the treasures of thy hollow breast
Are no less fruitful teachers than the rest;
For, as the lime doth burn and break in water,
And swell and smoke, crackle and skip and scatter,
Waking that fire whose dull heat sleeping was
Under the cold crust of a chalky mass;
He that, to march amid the Christian host,
Yields his heart's kingdom to the Holy Ghost,
And for brave service under Christ his banner
Looks to be crowned with his Chief Champion's honor,
Must in affliction wake his zeal, which oft
In calmer times sleeps too securely soft.
  And opposite, as the rich diamond
The fire and steel both stoutly doth withstand,
So the true Christian should, till life expire,
Contemn proud tyrants' raging sword and fire.
Or if fell rigor with some ruthless smart
A little shake the sinews of his heart,
He must be like the richest mineral,
Whose ingots bend but never break at all,
Nor in thy furnace suffer any loss
Of weight but lees,—not of the gold, but dross.
  The precious stone that bears the rainbow's name[20]
Receives the bright face of Sol's burnished flame,
And by reflection, after, it displays
On the next object all those pointed rays;
So whoso hath from the empyreal pole,
Within the center of his happy soul
Received from splendor of the beams divine,
Must to his neighbor make the same to shine;

---

[19]"Le blond soleil et le blonde Clytie," in the original. The British corn-marigold may be more disposed to keep its face toward the sun than the flower known as the marigold in America.
[20]The old marginal note says here "The stone, Iris."

Not burying talents which our God hath given
To be employed in a rich trade for Heaven,
That, in his church, he may receive his gold
With thirty, sixty and an hundred fold.

As iron, touched by th'adamant's effect,
To the north pole doth ever point direct,
So the soul, touched by the secret power
Of a true, lively faith, looks every hour
To the bright lamp which serves for cynosure[21]
To all that sail upon the sea obscure.

These precedents, from lifeless things collected,
Breed good effects in spirits well affected;
But lessons taken fresh from things that live,
A livelier touch unto all sorts do give.

Up, up, ye princes! Prince and people rise,
And run to school among the honey-flies.
There shall you learn that an eternal law
Subjects the subject under princes' awe.
There shall you learn that a courageous king
To vex his humble vassals hath no sting.

The Persian prince that princely did conclude
So severe laws against ingratitude,
Knew that the merlin, having kept her warm
With a live lark, remits it without harm,
And lest her friend-bird she should after slay,
She takes her flight a quite contrary way.

Fathers, if you desire your children sage[22]
Should by their blessings bless your crooked age,
Train them betimes unto true virtue's lore
By awe, example, and instruction more.
So the old eagle flutters in and out
To teach his young to follow him about.
If his example cannot timely bring
His backward birds to use their feeble wing,

---

[21]The word, "cynosure", does not occur in Shakespeare's dramas
or poems. Milton uses it in Comus and in L'Allegro.
[22]The French "sage" is taken over here instead of being translated.
It signifies, of good disposition, rather than wise.

He leaves them there some days unfed, whereby
Sharp hunger may at length constrain them fly.
If that prevail not then he beats them, both
With beak and wings, to stir their fearful sloth.
    You that to haste your hated spouse's end
Black, deadly poison in his dish do blend,
O can ye see with unrelenting eyes
The turtle-dove? Since, when her husband dies,
Dies all her joy; for never loves she more
But on dry boughs doth her dead spouse deplore.
    Thou, whom the freedom of a foolish tongue
Brings oft in danger from thy neighbor's wrong,
Directly set a hatch before thy door,
As the wise wild geese, when they over-soar
Sicilian mounts, within their bills do bear
A pebble stone both day and night, for fear
Lest ravenous eagles of the north descry
Their army's pillage by their cackling cry. . . .
    O why embrace not we with charity
The living, and the dead with piety?
Giving these succor, sepulture to those,
Even as the dolphins do themselves expose
For their live fellows, and beneath the waves
Cover their dead ones under sandy graves.
    You children whom, beyond hope, Heaven's benignity
Hath heaped with wealth, and lifted up to dignity,
Do not forget your parents, but behold
The careful kids, who, when their parents old
With heavy gyves eld's trembling fever stops
And fetters fast upon the mountain tops,
As good purveyors, bring them home to browse
The tenderest tops of all the tenderest boughs,
And sip—self thirstless—of the river's brink
Which in their mouths they bring them home to drink.
    For household rules, read not the learned writs
Of the Stagyrian,—glory of good wits,—
Nor his whom, for his honey-steeped style
They proverbized "the Attic Muse" erewhile,
Since the single spider teacheth every one

The husband's and the housewife's function;
For, for their food, the valiant male doth roam;
The cunning female tends her work at home.
Out of her bowels wool and yarn she spitteth
And all that else her learned labors fitteth;
Her weight's the spindle that doth twist the twine,
Which her small fingers draw so even and fine;
Still at the center she her warp begins,
Then round at length her little thread she spins
At equal distance to their compass leaves;
Then neat and nimbly her new web she weaves,
With her fine shuttle circularly drawn
Through all the circuit of her open lawn;
Open, lest else the ungentle winds should tear
Her cypress tent, weaker than any hair,
And that the foolish fly might easier get
Within the meshes of her curious net;
Which he no sooner doth begin to shake
But straight the male doth to the center make
That he may conquer more securely there
The humming creature, hampered in his snare.

You kings that bear the sword of just hostility,
Pursue the proud and pardon true humility,
Like noble lions that do never show
Their strength and stomach on a yielding foe,
But rather through the stoutest things do forage,
'Mid thousand deaths, to show their dauntless courage.

Thou sluggard, if thou list to learn thy part,
Go, learn the emmet's and the urchin's art.
In summer one, in autumn th'other takes
The season's fruits, and thence provision makes,
Each in his lodging laying up a hoard
Against cold winter which doth naught afford.

But, reader, we resemble one that winds
From Saba, Bandan, and the wealthy Inds
Through threatening seas and dangers manifold,
To seek far off for incense, spice and gold;
Since we, not loosing from our proper strand,
Find all wherein a happy life doth stand,

And our own bodies' self-contained motions
Give the most gross a hundred goodly notions.
  You pastors, princes, and ye chiefs of war,
Do not your sermons, laws and orders mar,
Lest your examples' baneful leprosies
Infect your flocks, subjects and companies.
Beware your evil make not others so
Since no part's sound if ill the head doth grow.
  Do not, you peers, thorow self-partial zeal,
With light-brained counsels vex your commonweal,
But, as both eyes do but one thing behold,
Let each his country's common good uphold.
  You that for others travail day and night,
With much hard labor and small benefit,
Behold the teeth, which toll-free grind the food,
From whence themselves do reap more grief than good.
  Even as the heart hath not a moment's rest,
But night and day moves in our panting breast,
That by its beating it may still impart
Its lively spirits about to every part;
So those to whom God doth His flock betake
Ought always study, always work and wake,
To breathe, by doctrine and good conversation,
The quick'ning spirit in their congregation.
  And as the stomach, from the wholesome food
Divides the grosser part, not being good,
They ought from false the true to separate,—
Error from faith, and cockle from the wheat,
To have the best received for nourishment,
The bad cast forth as filthy excrement.
  If bat or blade do threaten sudden harm
To belly, breast or leg or head or arm,
With dreadless power the hand doth ward the blow
Taking itself its brethren's bleeding woe;
Then mid the shock of sacrilegious arms,
That fill the world with blood and boisterous storms,
Shall we not lend our helping hands to others
Whom faith hath made more near and dear than
    brothers?

Nor can I see where, underneath the sky,
A man may find a juster policy
Or truer image of a calm estate
Exempt from faction, discord and debate,
Than in th'harmonious order that maintains
Our body's life, through members' mutual pains;
Where one no sooner feels the least offense
But all the rest have of the same a sense.
The foot strives not to smell, the nose to walk,
The tongue to combat, nor the hand to talk;
But without troubling of their commonweal
With mutinies, they voluntary deal,
Each in his office and heaven-appointed place,
Be't vile or honorable, lofty or base.
But stay, my muse!   What, wilt thou still repeat
The map of man which thou hast drawn so late?[23]
If twice or thrice one and the same we bring
'Tis tedious, however sweet we sing.
Therefore, Ashore! Mates, let our anchor fall!
Here blows no wind!   Here are we welcome all.
Besides, consider and conceive, I pray,
We've rowed sufficient,—for a Sabbath day.

.

.

---

[23]This couplet is re-written by the present editor, though without
change of meaning. As it appears in former editions it is obscure
as well as of awkward construction.

PART II.—THE STORY OF ADAM

EDEN

Great God, which hast this world's birth made me see,
Unfold his[1] cradle; show his infancy.
Walk Thou my spirit through all the flowering alleys
Of that sweet garden where, through winding valleys,
Four lively floods crawled.   Tell me what misdeed
Banished both Edens Adam and his seed.
Tell who, immortal, mortalizing, brought us
The balm from heaven which hope and health hath
        wrought us.
Grant me the story of Thy church to sing
And gests[2] of kings, let me this total bring
From Thy first Sabbath to its fatal tomb;
My style extending to the day of doom.
    Lord, I acknowledge and confess before,—
This ocean hath no bottom nor no shore;

---

[1]The form, "it's" occurs several times in the course of Sylvester's versified writings. In transcribing I have eliminated the apostrophe, and have also written "its" in a number of instances where the original has "his". In the case of the above lines it has seemed that the personification of the world by allusions to its birth, etc., makes the use of the old possessive preferable.

[2]"Gests"; deeds. There is something in the rhythm of this couplet which recalls the demand of Richard II to his followers to "sit on the ground and tell sad stories of the death of kings."

But sacred Pilot, Thou canst safely steer
My venturous pinnace to her wished pier,
Where once arrived, all dropping wet, I will
Extol thy favors and my vows fulfill.
    And gracious Guide,[3] which dost all grace infuse,
Since it hath pleased Thee task my hardy muse
With these high themes, that through mine artless pen
This holy lamp may light my countrymen,
Ah! teach my hand; touch mine unlearned lips;
Lest, as the earth's gross body doth eclipse
Bright Cynthia's beams when it is interposed
'Twixt her and Phœbus, so mine ill-disposed,
Dark, gloomy ignorance obscure the rays
Of this divine sun of these learned days.
O furnish me with an unvulgar style,
That I by this may wean our wanton isle
From Ovid's heirs[4] and their unhallowed spell,
Here charming senses, chaining souls in hell.
Let this provoke our modern wits to sacre
Their wondrous gifts to honor Thee, their Maker,
That our mysterious elfin oracle,[5]
Deep, moral, grave, invention's miracle,—
My dear, sweet Daniel, sharp, conceited, brief,
Civil, sententious, for pure accents chief,—
And, our new Naso[6] that so passionates
Th' heroic sighs of love-sick potentates

---

[3]The interpolations of the translator were formerly printed in italics. This one, extending to "mine elder story", will be found of interest as providing a view of English literature at the close of the 16th century.
[4]Ovid's heirs were probably represented by the earlier poems of Shakespeare, then very popular, and by productions of lesser writers in a similar vein.
[5]The "Elfin Oracle" was Edmund Spenser, whose Faerie Queene was published by the printer of the Divine Weeks. Samuel Daniel, mentioned in the same sentence, was a voluminous versifier, some of whose works are still read.
[6]Michael Drayton is now best known by his "Poly-Olbion", a versified encyclopedic gazetteer of England. At the beginning of the 17th century, however, his fame rested principally upon a volume issued by him in 1593 containing imitations of Ovid's narrative and descriptive works.

May change their subject, and advance their wings
Up to these higher and more holy things;
And if, sufficient rich in self-invention,
They scorn to live, as I, of stranger's pension,[7]
Let them devise new weeks, new works, new ways
To celebrate the supreme Prince of praise.
And let not me, good Lord, be like the lead
Which to some city from some conduit-head
Brings wholesome water, yet self-wanting sense,
Itself receives no drop of comfort thence;
But rather as the thorough seasoned butt,
Wherein the tears of death-pressed grapes are put,
Retains, long after all the wine is spent,
Within itself the liquor's lively scent,
Let me still savor of these sacred sweets[8]
Till death fold up mine earth in earthen sheets;
Lest my young lays, now prone to teach Thy glory
To Brutus' heirs,[9] blush at mine elder story.

God, supreme Lord, committed not alone
T'our father Adam this inferior throne
Ranging beneath his rule the scaly nation
That in the ocean have their habitation,
Those that in horror of the deserts lurk
And those that, capering in the welkin, work,
But also chose him for a happy seat
A climate temperate both for cold and heat,
Which dainty Flora paveth sumptuously
With flowery Ver's enameled tapestry,
Pomona pranks[10] with fruits whose taste excels,
And Zephyr fills with musk and amber smells;
Where God himself as gardener treads the alleys,

---

[7]The translator here speaks of himself as living on the liberality of the French author, the "pension" consisting of the material first put into shape by Du Bartas, and later taken into a constructive possession by Sylvester for his own profit.

[8]In Thomas Moore's song the cask of wine becomes a vase of roses, but the figure of speech is essentially the same as that above.

[9]Brutus was the fabled founder of the British nation as it existed before the coming of the Saxons.

[10]See note 17, Day 2, ante.

With trees and corn covers the hills and valleys,
Summons sweet sleep with noise of hundred brooks,
And sun-proof arbors makes in sundry nooks.
He plants, He prunes, He pares, He trimmeth round
Th'evergreen beauties of a fruitful ground.
Here, there, the course of th'holy lakes He leads;
With thousand dyes he mottles all the meads.[11]

 Ye pagan poets that audaciously
Have sought to dark the ever-memory
Of God's great works, from henceforth still be dumb
Your fabled praises of Elysium,
Which by this goodly model you have wrought
Through deaf tradition that your fathers taught;
For the Almighty made His blissful bowers
Better indeed than you have feigned yours.

 For should I say that still with smiling face
Th'all-clasping heavens beheld this happy place,
That honey sweet from hollow rocks did drain,
That fostering milk flowed up and down the plain,
That sweet as roses smelt th'ill-favored rue,
That in all soils, all seasons, all things grew,
That still there dangled on the selfsame treen
A thousand fruits nor over ripe nor green,
That eagrest[12] fruits and bitterest herbs did mock
Madeira sugars and the apricock,
Yielding more wholesome food than all the messes
That now taste-curious, wanton plenty dresses,[13]
Disguising in a thousand costly dishes
The various stores of dainty fowls and fishes
Which far and near we seek by land and seas
More hunger to provoke than to appease.
Or should I say each morning on the ground
Not common dew but manna did abound,

11Milton's "meadows trim with daisies pied" in L'Allegro, may easily
have been suggested by this line.
12"Eagrest" signifies sharpest, the meaning being similar in Hamlet's
allusion to "a nipping and an eager air."
13Compare Milton's "messes Which the neat-handed Phyllis dresses,"
in L'Allegro.

That never gutter-gorging, dirty muds
Defiled the crystal of smooth-sliding[14] floods,
Whose waters passed in pleasant taste the drink
That now in Candia decks Cerathus' brink,
That shady groves of noble palmtree sprays,
Of amorous myrtles and immortal bays
Never unleaved,[15] but evermore their new,
Self-arching arms in thousand arbors grew
Where thousand sorts of birds both night and day
Did bill and woo, and hop about and play,
And marrying their sweet tunes to th'angels' lays
Sung Adam's bliss and their great Maker's praise.
For then the crows', night ravens', and owlets' noise
Was like the nightingale's sweet-tuned voice,
And nightingales sung like divine Arion,
Like Thracian Orpheus, Linus and Amphion.

Th'air's daughter, Echo, haunting, woods among,
A blab that will not, cannot keep her tongue;
Who never asks but only answers all;
Who lets not any her in vain to call;
She bore her part and full of curious skill
They ceasing sung; they singing ceased still.[16]
There music reigned and ever on the plain
A sweet sound raised the dead-live voice again.

If there I say the sun, the seasons' stinter.
Made no hot summer nor no hoary winter,
But lovely Ver kept still in lively luster
The fragrant valleys, smiling meads and pasture,
That boisterous Adam's body did not shrink
For northern winds, nor for the southern wink;
But Zephyr did sweet, musky sighs afford,
Which, breathing through the garden of the Lord,
Gave bodies vigor, verdure to the field,
That verdure flowers, those flowers sweet savor yield;
The day did gladly lend his sister night,

14"Smooth sliding Mincius,"—Lycidas.
15"Myrtles brown, with ivy never sere."—Lycidas.
16See note 10, Day 5, ante.

For half her moisture, half his shining light.
That never hail did harvest prejudice,
That never frost nor snow nor slippery ice
The fields en-aged, nor any stormy stour
Dismounted mountains, nor no violent shower
Poverished the land which frankly did produce
All fruitful vapors for delight and use.
I think I lie not; rather I confess
My stammering muse's poor unlearnedness.
If in two words thou wilt her praise comprise,
Say 'twas the type of th'upper paradise,
Where Adam had, O wondrous strange, discourse
With God himself, with angels intercourse.

Yet, over-curious, question not the site
Where God did plant his garden of delight;
Whether beneath the Equinoctial line,
Or on a mountain near Latona's shine;
Nigh Babylon, or in the radiant East;
Humbly content thee that thou know'st at least
That that rare, plenteous, pleasant, happy thing,
Whereof th'Almighty made our grandsire king,
Was a choice soil through which did, rolling, slide
Swift Gihon, Pison and rich Tigris' tide,
And that fair stream whose silver waves do kiss
The monarch towers of proud Semiramis.

Now if that, roaming round above the earth,
Thou find no place that answers now in worth
This beauteous place, nor country that can show
Where now-a-days those noted floods do flow,
Include not all within this close,[17] confined,
That laboring Neptune's liquid belt doth bind;
A certain place it was, now sought in vain,
Where set by grace, for sin removed again
Our elders were; whereof the Thunder-Darter
Made a bright sword the gate, an angel porter.

Nor think that Moses paints fantastic-wise

17A noun; enclosure.

A mystic tale of feigned paradise.
('Twas a true garden, happy plenty's horn,
And seat of graces;) lest thou make, forlorn,
An ideal Adam's food fantastical,
His sin supposed, his pain poetical,
Such allegories serve for shelter fit
To curious idiots of erroneous wit;
And chiefly then when reading histories,
Seeking the spirit they the body lese.
    But if thou list to guess by likelihood,
Think that the wreakful, nature-drowning flood
Spared not this beauteous place which foremost saw
The first foul breach of God's eternal law.
Think that the most part of the plants it pulled,
And of the sweetest flowers the spirits dulled,
Spoiled the fair gardens, made the fat fields lean,
And changed perchance the rivers' channel clean;
And think that time, whose slippery wheel doth play
In human causes with inconstant sway,
Who exiles, alters, and disguises words,
Hath now transformed the names of all these fords;
For as through sin we lost that place, I fear
Forgetful we have lost the knowledge where
'Twas situate, and of the sugared dainties
Wherewith God fed us in those sacred plenties.
    Now of the trees wherewith th'immortal Power
Adorned the quarters of that blissful bower;
All served the mouth, save two sustained the mind;
All served for food, save two for seals assigned.
    God gave the first for honorable style,
"The tree of life",—true name, alas the while!—
Not for th'effect it had, but should have kept,
If man from duty never had misstept;
For as the air of those fresh dales and hills
Preserved him from epidemic ills,
This fruit had ever calmed all insurrections,
All civil quarrels of the cross complexions;
Had barred the passage of twice childish age,
And evermore excluded all the rage

Of painful griefs, whose swift-slow, posting-pace
At first or last our dying life doth chase.
 Strong counterbane, O sacred plant divine!
What metal, stone, stalk, fruit, flower, root or rine,[18]
Shall I presume in these rude rhymes to suit
Unto thy wondrous world-adorning fruit?
The rarest simples that our fields present us
Heal but one hurt, and healing, too, torment us,
And with the torment lingering our relief,
Our bags of gold void, ere our bulks of grief.
But thy rare fruit's hid power, admired most,
Salveth all sores sans pain, delay, or cost;;
Or rather man from yawning death to stay,
Thou didst not cure but keep all ills away.
 O holy, peerless, rich preservative!
Whether wert thou the strange restorative
That suddenly did age with youth repair,
And made old Aeson[19] younger than his heir,
Or holy nectar that in heavenly bowers
Eternally self-pouring Hebe pours,
Or blest ambrosia, gods' immortal fare;
Or else the rich fruit of the garden rare
Where for three ladies, as assured guard
A fire-armed dragon day and night did ward;
Or precious Moly[20] which Jove's pursuivan,
Wing-footed Hermes, brought to th'Ithacan;
Or else Nepenthe, enemy to sadness,
Repelling sorrows and repealing gladness?
Or mummie, or elixir that excels
Save men and angels every creature else?
No, none of these; these are but forgeries,
But toys, but tales, but dreams, deceits, and lies.
But thou art true, although our shallow sense
May honor more than sound thine excellence.

18"Rine" is an old spelling of "rind", and correctly indicates the pronunciation of the word by a majority of descendants of the Pilgrims.
19See note 13, Day 2, ante.
20"That Moly that Hermes once to wise Ulysses gave."—Comus.

The tree of knowledge th'other tree behight.
Not that it selfly had such special might
As men's dull wits could whet and sharpen so,
That in a moment they might all things know.
'Twas a sure pledge, a sacred sign and seal,
Which being ta'en, should to light man reveal
What odds there is between still peace and strife,
God's wrath and love, dread death and dearest life,
Solace and sorrow, guile and innocence,
Rebellious pride and humble obedience.
  For God had not deprived that primer season
The sacred lamp and light of learned reason.
Mankind was then a thousandfold more wise
Than now; blind error had not bleared his eyes
With mists which make th'Athenian sage suppose
That naught he knows save this,—that naught he
    knows.
That even light Pyrrhon's wavering fantasies
'Reave him the skill his un-skill to agnize.
And the Abderite[21] within a well obscure
As deep, as dark, the truth of things immure.
  He, happy, knew the good by th'use of it;
He knew the bad but not by proof as yet;
But as they say of great Hippocrates,
Who, though his limbs were numbed with no excess,
Nor stopped his throat, nor vexed his fantasy,
Knew the cold cramp, th'angine, and lunacy,
And hundred else pains, whence in lusty flower,
He lived exempt a hundred years and four.
Or like the pure, heaven-prompted prophets rather,
Whose sight so clearly future things did gather,
Because the world's soul, in their soul ensealed
The holy stamp of secrets most concealed.
  But our now-knowledge hath for tedious train
A drooping life and over-racked brain,

---

[21]Democritus is probably meant. He was an adherent of the atomic theory of Leucippus, which bore considerable resemblance to the nebular theory of stellar origins.

A face forlorn, a sad and sullen fashion,
A restless toil, and care's self-pining passion.
Knowledge was then even the soul's soul for light,
The spirit's calm port and lantern shining bright
To straight-stepped feet, clear knowledge not confused,
Not sour, but sweet; not gotten, but infused,
  Now heaven's eternal, all-foreseeing King,
Who never rashly ordereth anything,
Thought good that man, having yet spirits sound-stated,
Should dwell elsewhere than where he was created,
That he might know he did not hold this place
By nature's right, but by mere gift and grace;
That he should never taste fruits unpermitted,
But keep the sacred pledge to him committed,
And dress that park which God, without all term,
On these conditions gave him as in farm.
  God would that, void of painful labor, he
Should live in Eden; but not idlely,
For idleness pure innocence subverts,
Defiles our body and our soul perverts.
Yea, soberest men it makes delicious;[22]
To virtue dull, to vice ingenious.[23]
But that first travel had no sympathy
With our since-travail's wretched cruelty,
Distilling sweat and panting, wanting wind,
Which was a scourge for Adam's sin assigned.
  For Eden's earth was then so fertile fat,
That he made only sweet essays in that
Of skillful industry, and naked wrought,
More for delight than for the gain he sought.
In brief it was a pleasant exercise,
A labor liked, a pain much like the guise
Of cunning dancers, who, although they skip,
Run, caper, vault, traverse and turn, and trip
From morn till even, at night again full merry
Renew their dance, of dancing never weary.

---

[22]Giving oneself up to the search for pleasure.
[23]"Ingenious" here means of the same genus or race.

Or else of hunters, that with happy luck
Rousing betimes some often breathed buck
Or goodly stag, their yelping hounds uncouple,
Wind loud their horns, their whoops and hallos double,
Spur on and spare not, following their desire,
Themselves unweary though their hackneys tire.
But, for in th'end of all their jollity
There's found much stiffness, sweat and vanity,
I rather match it to the pleasing pain
Of angels pure, who ever sloth disdain,
Or to the sun's calm course, who painless, ay
About the welkin posteth night and day.

Doubtless when Adam saw our common air,
He did admire the mansion rich and fair
Of his successors; for frost keenly cold
The shady locks of forests had not polled;[24]
Heaven had not thundered on our heads as yet,
Nor given the earth her sad divorce's writ.

But, when he once had entered paradise,
The remnant world he justly did despise,
Much like a boor, far in the country born,
Who, never having seen but kine and corn,
Oxen and sheep, and homely hamlets thatched,
Which, fond, he counts as kingdoms hardly matched,
When afterward he happens to behold[25]
Our wealthy London's wonders manifold,
The silly peasant thinks himself to be
In a new world; and gazing greedily,
One while he, artless, all the arts admires,
Then the fair temples and their topless spires,
Their firm foundations and the massive pride
Of all their sacred ornaments beside,
Anon he wonders at the differing graces,
Tongues, gests, attires; the fashions and the faces
Of busy-buzzing swarms which still he meets,
Ebbing and flowing over all the streets;

---

[24]"Polled" is also used by Keats in the sense of "pruned".
[25]This and the following twenty-one lines are added by Sylvester.

Then at the signs, the shops, the weights, the measures,
The handicrafts, the rumors, trades and treasures;
But of all sights none seems him yet more strange
Than the rare, beauteous, stately, rich Exchange.
Another while he marvels at the Thames,
Which seems to bear huge mountains on her streams;
Then at the fair-built bridge, which he doth judge
More like a tradeful city than a bridge,
And glancing thence along the northern shore,
That princely prospect doth amaze him more.

For in that garden man delighted so
That, rapt, he wist not if he waked or no;
If he beheld a true thing or a fable,
Or earth or heaven; all more than admirable;
For such excess his ecstasy was small,
Not having spirit enough to muse withal.
He wished him hundredfold redoubled senses,
The more to taste so rare, sweet excellences,
Not knowing whether nose, or ears, or eyes,
Smelt, heard or saw more savors, sounds, or dyes.

But Adam's best and supreme delectation
Was the often haunt and holy conversation
His soul and body had so many ways
With God, who lightened Eden with His rays.
For spirits by faith religiously refined
'Twixt God and man retain a middle kind,
And, umpires, mortal to th'immortal join,
And th'infinite in narrow clay confine.

Sometimes by you, O you all-feigning dreams,
We gain this good, but not when Bacchus' steams
And glutton vapors overflow the brain,
And drown our spirits, presenting fancies vain;
Nor when pale phlegm, or saffron-colored choler,
In feeble stomachs belch with diverse dolor,
And print upon our understandings' tables,
That, water-wracks; this other flameful fables;
Nor when the spirit of lies our spirits deceives,
And guileful visions in our fancy leaves;
Nor when the pencil of cares overdeep

Our day-bred thoughts depainteth in our sleep;
But when no more the soul's chief faculties
Are 'spersed, to serve the body many ways,
When all self-uned, free from day's disturber,
Through such sweet trance she finds a quiet harbor,
Where, some in riddles, some more plain expressed,
She sees things future in th'Almighty's breast.
And yet, far higher is this holy fit,
When not from flesh, but from flesh-cares acquit,
The wakeful soul itself assembling so,
All selfly dies, while that the body though
Lies motionless, for sanctified wholly,
It takes th'impression of God's signet solely,
And in His sacred, crystal map doth see
Heaven's oracles, and angels' glorious glee
Made more than spirit.[26]   Now, morrow, yesterday,
To it all one are; all as present ay;
And though it seem not, when the dream's expired,
Like that it was, yet is it much admired
Of rarest men, and shines among them bright,
Like glistering stars through gloomy shades of night.
But above all, that's the divinest trance,
When the soul's eye beholds God's countenance;
When mouth to mouth familiarly He deals,
And in our face His dread, sweet face He seals;
As when St. Paul on his dear Master's wings
Was rapt, alive, up to th'eternal things,
And he that whilom for the chosen flock
Made walls of waters, waters of a rock.
O sacred flight! sweet rape! love's sovereign bliss!
Which very love's dear lips dost make us kiss!
Hymen, of manna and of mel compact,
Which for a time dost heaven with earth contract;
Fire, that in limbeck of pure thoughts divine
Dost purge our thoughts, and our dull earth refine,

---

[26]It appears from this that what the revivalist preachers of a century ago described as "the power" was not unknown in France two centuries earlier. A good description of the "holy fits" may be read in Mrs. Trollope's "Domestic Manners of the Americans."

And mounting us to heaven, un-moving hence,
Man in a trice in God dost quintessence.
O mad'st thou man divine in habitude,
As for a space,—O sweetest solitude,
Thy bliss were equal with that happy rest
Which after death shall make us ever blest.
   Now I believe that in this latter guise
Man did converse in pleasant paradise
With heaven's great Architect, and happy, there
His body saw, (or body, as it were,)
Gloriously compact with the blessed legions
That reign above the azure, spangled regions.
   "Adam," quoth He, "the beauties manifold
That in this Eden here thou dost behold,
Are all thine only; enter, sacred race;
Come, take possession of this wealthy place.
The earth's sole glory take, dear son, to thee.
This farm's demesnes leave the chief right to me,
And th'only rent that of it I reserve is
One tree's fair fruit, to show thy suit and service.
Be thou the liege and I Lord paramount;
I'll not exact hard fines as men shall wont,
For sign of homage and for seal of faith;
Of all the profits this possessions hath,
I only ask one tree, whose fruit I will
For sacrament shall stand, of good and ill.
Take all the rest, I bid thee; but I vow
By th'unnamed Name whereto all knees do bow,
And by the keen darts of my kindled ire,
More fiercely burning than consuming fire,
That, of the fruit of knowledge if thou feed,
Death, dreadful death, shall plague thee and thy seed.
If, then, the happy state thou hold'st of me,
My holy mildness nor high majesty,—
If faith nor honor curb thy bold ambition,
Yet weigh thyself and thy own seed's condition."
   "Most mighty Lord," quoth Adam, "here I tender
All thanks I can, not all I should Thee render,
For all Thy liberal favors, far surmounting

My heart's conceit; much more my tongue's recounting.
At Thy command I would with boisterous shock
Go, run myself against the hardest rock,
Or cast me headlong from some mountain steep
Down to the whirling bottom of the deep;
Yea, at Thy beck I would not spare the life
Of my dear Phoenix, sister-daughter-wife;
Obeying Thee, I find the things impossible,
Cruel, and painful; pleasant, kind, and possible.
    "But since Thy first law doth more grace afford
Unto the subject than the sovereign lord,—
Since, bounteous Prince, on me and my descent
Thou dost impose no other tax nor rent,
But one sole precept of most just condition,—
No precept neither, but a prohibition,—
And since, good God, of all the fruits in Eden
There's but one apple that I am forbidden,
Even only that which bitter death doth threat,
Better, perhaps, to look on than to eat,
I honor in my soul and humbly kiss
Thy just edict as Author of my bliss,
Which once transgressed deserves the rigor rather
Of sharpest judge than mildness of a father.
    "The firmament shall retrograde its course,
Swift Euphrates go hide him in his source,
Firm mountains skip like lambs beneath the deep,
Eagles shall dive, whales in the air shall keep,
Ere I presume with fingers' ends to touch,—
Much less with lips,—the fruit forbade so much."
    Thus yet in league with heaven and earth he lives,
Enjoying all the goods th'Almighty gives,
And, yet not treading sin's false mazy measures,
Sails on smooth surges of a sea of pleasures.
    Here, underneath a fragrant hedge, reposes
Full of all kinds of sweet, all-colored roses,[27]

---

[27]Comparison of this description of Eden with that in the fourth book of Par. Lost, verses 215-287 will bring many parallel passages to light.

Which one would think the angels daily dress
In true love-knots, triangles, lozenges.
    Anon he walketh in a level lane
On either side beset with shady plane
Whose arched boughs for frieze and cornice bear
Thick groves to shield from future change of air.
Then in a path impaled in pleasant wise
With sharp, sweet, orange, lemon, citron trees,
Whose leafy twigs that intricately tangle
Seem painted walls whereon true fruits do dangle.
    Now in a plenteous orchard, planted rare
With un-graft trees in checker, round and square,
Whose goodly fruits so on his will do wait,
That plucking one, another's ready straight,
And having tasted all with due satiety,
Finds all one goodness, but in taste variety.
    Anon he stalketh with an easy stride
By some clear river's lily paved side,
Whose sands pure gold, whose pebbles precious gems,
And liquid silver all the curling streams,
Whose chiding murmur, mazing in and out,
With crystal cisterns moats a mead about,
And th'artless bridges, overthwart this torrent,
Are rocks self-arched by the eating current,
Or loving palms, whose lusty females, willing
Their marrow-boiling loves to be fulfilling,
And reach their husband-trees on th'other banks,
Bow their stiff backs and serve for passing planks.
    Then in a goodly garden's alleys smooth,
Where prodigue Nature sets abroad her booth
Of richest beauties, where each bed and border
Is like pied posies' diverse dyes and order.
    Now far from noise he creepeth covertly
Into a cave of kindly porphyry,
Which rock-fallen spouts, congealed by colder air,
Seem with smooth antics[28] to have ceiled fair.

---

[28]Probably a phonetic spelling of "antiques" as pronounced by the writer.

There, laid at ease a cubit from the ground,
Upon a jasper fringed with ivy round,
Purfled[29] with veins, thick thrummed with mossy beaver,
He falls asleep fast by[30] a silent river
Whose captive streams, through crooked pipes still
    rushing,
Make sweeter music, with their gentle gushing,
Than now at Tivoli th'hydrantic[31] brawl
Of rich Ferrara's stately cardinal.
Or Ctesibes' rare engines framed there
Whereas they made of Ibis Jupiter.[32]
    Musing anon through crooked walks he wanders
Round winding rings and intricate meanders,
False-guiding paths, doubtful, beguiling strays,
And right-wrong errors of an endless maze;
Not simply hedged with a simple border
Of rosemary cut out with curious order
In satyrs, centaurs, whales and half-men horses,
And thousand other counterfeited corses,
But with true beasts, fast in the ground still sticking,
Feeding on grass and th'airy moisture licking,
Such as those bonarets[33] in Scythia bred
Of slender seeds and with green fodder fed
Although their bodies, noses, mouths and eyes,
Of new yeaned lambs have full the form and guise,
And should be very lambs save that, for foot,
Within the ground they fix a living root,
Which at their navel grows, and dies that day
That they have browsed the neighbor grass away,

29"Purfled" signifies ornamented. "Beaver" seems to refer to the thick cloth so named, and "thrummed" has the general sense of interwoven.

30"Fast by" was not a common phrase in the age of Sylvester and Shakespeare. Milton uses it in the invocation of Par. Lost.

31"Hydrantic" may be a printer's error for hydraulic, but would seem to be formed naturally enough from hydrant. "Brawl" has been explained in a note to Day 1, ante.

32Turned marsh into dry land.

33The "bonaret" may be a kind of orchid of which extravagant accounts were given by travelers. See Par. Lost, VII, 464.

O wondrous virtue of God only good!
The beast hath root; the plant hath flesh and blood;
The nimble plant can turn it to and fro;
The numbed beast can neither stir nor go;
The plant is leafless, branchless, void of fruit;
The beast is lustless, sexless, fireless, mute;
The plant with plants his hungry paunch doth feed;
Th'admired beast is sown a slender seed.

Then up and down a forest thick he paceth,
Which, selfly opening, in his presence 'baseth
Her trembling tresses' never-vading spring,
For humble homage to her mighty king,
Where thousand trees, waving with gentle puffs
Their plumy tops, sweep the celestial roofs;
Yet envying all the massy cerbas'[34] fame
Since fifty paces can but clasp the same.

There springs the shrub, three foot above the grass,
Which fears the keen edge of the curtelace,
Whereof the rich Egyptian so endears
Root, bark, and much, much more, the tears.[35]

There lives the sea-oak in a little shell,
There grows, untilled, the ruddy cochineal,
And there the kermes which on each side arms
With pointed prickles all his precious arms;
Rich trees, and fruitful in those worms of price
Which pressed, yield a crimson-colored juice,
Whence thousand lambs are dyed so deep in grain
That their own mothers know them not again.[36]

There mounts the melt,[37] which serves in Mexico
For weapon, wood, needle, and thread to sew,
Brick, honey, sugar, sucket, balm and wine,
Parchment, perfume, apparel, cord and line.

---

[34]A marginal note in the folios states that the cerbas is "a tree in the Indies fifteen fathoms about."
[35]Perhaps the Acacia Nilotica is indicated.
[36]A common saying now with little change in the words.
[37]Apparently the agave, although here endowed with too many functions.

His wood for fire, his harder leaves are fit
For thousand uses of inventive wit.
   Sometimes thereon they grave their holy things,
Laws, lauds of idols, and the gests of kings;[38]
Sometimes, conjoined by a cunning hand,
Upon their roofs for rows of tile they stand;
Sometimes they twine them into equal threads.
Small ends make needles, greater, arrow-heads;
His upper sap the sting of serpents cures;
His new-sprung bud a rare conserve indures;
His burned stalks with strong fumosities
Of piercing vapors, purge the French disease,
And they extract from liquor of his feet
Sharp vinegar, pure honey, sugar sweet.
   There quakes the plant which, in Pudefetan,
Is called "the shame-faced;" for, ashamed of man
If towards it one do approach too much
It shrinks its boughs to shun our hateful touch,
As if it had a soul, a sense, and sight
Subject to shame, fear, sorrow, and despite.
   And there that tree from off whose trembling top
Both swimming shoals and flying troops do drop.
I mean the tree now in Juturna growing,
Whose leaves, dispersed by Zephyr's wanton blowing,
Are metamorphosed both in form and matter,
On land to fowls, to fishes in the water.[39]
But seest thou not, dear Muse, thou tread'st the same
Too curious path thou dost in others blame;
And striv'st in vain to paint this work so choice,
The which no human spirit nor hand nor voice
Can once conceive, less portray, least express,
All overwhelmed in gulfs so bottomless?

---

[38]See note 2, ante.
[39]"I told them that in our country were trees that bear fruit which become birds flying; and those that fall in the water live, and they that fall on the earth die anon; and they be right good to man's meat."—Sir John Maundeville, ch. XXVI. See also Lupton's "Notable Things," Book VII, sec. 3, and Harrison's "Description of Britain" in Holinshed.

Who matching art with nature, likeneth
Our grounds to Eden, fondly measureth
By painted butterflies th'imperial eagle,
And th'elephant by every little beagle.
   This fear to fail shall serve me for a bridle,
Lest, lacking wings and guide, too busy-idle
And over-bold God's cabinet I climb,
To seek the place and search the very time
When both our parents, or but one, was ta'en
Out of our earth into that fruitful plain;
How long they had that garden in possession
Before their proud and insolent transgression;
What children there they earned[40] and how many,
Of whether sex, or whether none or any,
And how, at least, they should have propagated,
If the sly malice of the serpent hated,
Causing their fall, had not defiled their kin
And unborn seed with leprosy of sin.   . . .
   Whether their seed should with their birth have
      brought
Deep knowledge, reason, understanding, thought,
Since now we see the new fallen, feeble lamb
Yet stained with blood of his distressed dam,
Knows well the wolf, at whose fell sight he shakes,
And right the teat of th'unknown ewe he takes,
And since a dull dunce, which no knowledge can,
Is a dead image and no living man.
Or the thick veil of ignorance's night
Had hooded up their issue's inward sight
Since the much moisture of an infant brain
Receives so many shapes that, overlain,
New dash the old, and the trim commixation
Of confused fancies full of alteration
Makes th'under standing hull, which settle would,
But finds no firm ground for its anchors hold.
   Whether old Adam should have left the place
Unto his sons, they to their after race,

40"Earned" is probably a misprint for "eaned".

Or whether all together at the last
Should gloriously from thence to heaven have passed,—
Search whoso list; who list let vaunt in pride
T'have hit the white, and let him, sage, decide
The many other doubts that vainly rise.
For mine own part I will not seem so wise.
I will not waste my travail and my seed,
To reap an empty straw or fruitless reed.
    Alas, we know what Orion[41] of grief
Rained on the cursed head of the creatures' chief,
After that God against him war proclaimed;
But none can know precisely how, at all,
Our elders lived before their odious fall.
An unknown cipher and deep pit it is
Where Dircean Oedipus[42] his marks would miss,
Since Adam's self, if now he lived anew,
Could scant unwind the knotty, snarled clew
Of double doubts, and questions intricate,
That schools dispute about this pristine state.
    But this sole point I rest resolved in,—
That seeing death's the mere effect of sin,
Man had not dreaded death's all-slaying might,
Had he still stood in innocence upright.
    For as two bellows, blowing turn by turn,
By little and little make cold coals to burn,
And then their fire inflames with glowing heat
An iron bar which, on the anvil beat,
Seems no more iron, but flies almost all
In hissing sparks and quick, bright cinders small,
So the world's soul should in our soul inspire
Th'eternal force of an eternal fire;
And then our soul, as form, breathe in our corse
Her countless numbers and heaven-tuned force,

41"The rainy Hyades" are near the constellation Orion. This is not
the only place where Sylvester plays havoc with the pronunciation
of classical proper names.

42Oedipus did wonderful guessing on the question of the Sphinx, but
why he is called "Dircean" does not clearly appear. Dirce was a queen
of Thebes, killed by being dragged about by a bull, but not related
to Oedipus otherwise, so far as I can ascertain.

Wherewith our bodies' beauties, beautified,
Should, like our deathless soul, have never died.
　Here wot I well some wranglers will presume
To say small fire will by degrees consume
Our humor radical, and howbeit
The differing virtues of those fruits as yet
Had no agreement with the harmful spite
Of the fell, Persian, dangerous aconite,
And notwithstanding that then Adam's taste
Could well have used all without all waste,
Yet could they not restore him every day
Unto his body that which did decay,
Because the food can not, as being strange,
So perfectly in human substance change.
For it resembleth wine wherein too rife
Water is brewed, whereby the pleasant life
Is over-cooled, and so there rests in fine
Naught of the strength, savor, or taste of wine.
Besides, in time the natural faculties
Are tired with toil, and th'humor-enemies,
Our death conspiring, undermine at last
Of our souls' prisons the foundations fast.
　Aye, but the tree of life the strife did stay,
Which th'humors caused in this house of clay
And stopping th'evil, changed (perfect good
In body fed,) the body of the food;
Only the soul's contagious malady
Had force to frustrate this high remedy.
　Immortal, then, and mortal, man was made;
Mortal he lived, and did immortal vade;
For, 'fore th'effects of his rebellious ill,
To die or live was in his power and will;
But since his sin and proud apostasy,
Ah! die he may, but not, alas, not die!
As, after his new birth he shall attain,
Only, a power to never die again.

THE IMPOSTURE

O who shall lend me light and nimble wings
That, passing swallows and the swiftest things,
Even in a moment, boldly daring I
From hell to heaven, from heaven to hell may fly?
O who shall show the countenance and gestures
Of Mercy and Justice, which fair, sacred sisters
With equal poise do ever balance even
Th'unchanging projects of the King of Heaven?
One stern of look, the other mild aspecting,
One pleased with tears, the other blood affecting;
One bears the sword on vengeance unrelenting,
The other pardon brings for the repenting;
One from earth's Eden Adam did dismiss,
The other raised him to a higher bliss.
Who shall direct my pen to paint the story
Of wretched man's forbidden-bit, lost glory?
What spell shall charm th'attentive reader's sense?
What fount shall fill my voice with eloquence,   . . .
Though Adam's doom, in every sermon common,
And founded on the error of a woman,
Weary the vulgar and be deemed a jest
Of the profane, zeal-scoffing atheist?
Ah, Thou, my God, even Thou, my soul refining
In holy Faith's pure furnace, clearly shining,
Shalt make my hap far to surmount my hope,
Instruct my spirit, and give my tongue smooth scope.
Thou, bounteous, in my bold attempts shalt grace me,
And in the ranks of holiest poets place me;
And frankly grant that soaring near the sky
Among our authors eagle-like I fly,—
Or at the least, if Heaven such hap denay,

I may point others Heaven's beauteous way.
    While Adam bathes in these felicities
Hell's prince, sly parent of revolt and lies,
Feels a pestiferous, busy-swarming nest
Of never dying dragons in his breast,
Sucking his blood, tiring upon his lungs,
Pinching his bowels with ten thousand tongues,
His cursed soul still most extremely racking,
So frank in giving torments and in taking;
But above all, hate, pride and envious spite
His hellish life do torture day and night.
For the hate he bears to God, who hath him driven
Justly, forever, from the glittering[1] heaven,
To dwell in darkness of a sulphury cloud,
Though still his brethren's service be allowed,—
The proud desire to have in his subjection
Mankind, enchained in gyves of sin's infection,
And th'envious heart-break to see yet to shine
In Adam's face God's image, all divine,
Which he had lost, and that man might achieve
The glorious bliss his pride did him deprive,—
Grown barbarous tyrants of his treacherous will,
Spur on his course, his rage redoubling still.   .   .   .

    To vent his poison, this notorious tempter—
Mere spirit,—assails not Eve, but doth attempt her
In feigned form; for else the soul divine
Which ruled as queen the little world's design,
So purely kept her vow of chastity,
That he in vain should tempt her constancy.
Therefore he fleshly doth the flesh assay,
Suborning that, its mistress to betray,—
A subtle pander with more 'ticing slights
Than sea hath fish, or heaven hath twinkling lights.

---

[1]The fact that the word "glittering" sometimes appears in the Divine Weeks instead of the usual "glistering" is an indication that the two forms were differentiated as to meaning. "Glister" seemed to be practically a synonym of "shine", while "glitter" had already assumed its present signification.

For, had he been of an ethereal matter,
Of fiery substance or aerial nature,
The needful help of language had he wanted,
Whereby faith's groundwork was to be supplanted,
Since such pure bodies have not teeth nor tongues,
Lips, art'ries, nose, palate, nor panting lungs,
Which, rightly placed, are properly created
True instruments of sounds articulated.
　And furthermore, though from his birth he'd had
Heart-charming cunning, smoothly to persuade,
He feared, malicious, if he careless came
Unmasked, like himself, in his own name,
In deep distrust man, entering, suddenly
Would stop his ears, and his foul presence fly;
As, opposite, taking the shining face
Of sacred angels, full of glorious grace,
He then suspected the Omnipotent
Might think man's fall scarce worthy punishment.
　Much like, therefore, some thief that doth conceive
From travelers both life and goods to reave,
And in the twilight, while the moon doth play
In Thetis' palace, near the king's highway
Himself doth ambush in a bushy thorn,—
Then in a cave,—then in a field of corn,—
Creeps to and fro, and fisketh in and out,
And yet the safety of each place doth doubt,
Till, resolute at last, upon his knee
Taking his level, from a hollow tree,
He swiftly sends his fire-winged messenger,
At his false suit t'arrest the passenger,—
Our freedom's felon, fountain of our sorrow,
Thinks now the beauty of a horse to borrow;
Anon to creep into a heifer's side;
Then in a cock or in a dog to hide;
Then in a nimble hart himself to shroud;
Then in the starred plumes of a peacock proud;
And, lest he miss the mischief to effect,
Oft changeth mind and varies oft aspect.
At last, remembering that, of all the broods

In water, air, plains, mountains, wilds and woods,
The knotty serpent's spotty generation
Are filled with infectious inflammation;
And though they want dogs' teeth, boars' tusks, bears'
  paws,
The vulture's beak, bull's horns, and gryphon's claws,—
Yea, seem so weak as if they had not might
To hurt us once; much less to kill us quite;
Yet many times they treacherously betray us,
And with their breath, look, tongue or train, they flay
  us,—
He crafty cloaks him in a dragon's skin
All bright bespecked, that speaking so within
That hollow sackbut's supple wreathing plies,
The mover might with th'organ sympathize.
For yet the faithless serpent, as they say,
Crawled not with horror groveling on the clay,
Nor to mankind as yet was held for hateful,
Since that's the hire of his offense ungrateful.
    But now, to censure how this change befell,
Our wits come short; our words suffice not well
To utter it; much less our feeble art
Can imitate this sly, malicious part.
    Sometimes meseems, troubling Eve's spirit, the fiend
Made her this speaking fancy apprehend.
For, as in liquid clouds exhaled thickly,
Water and air, as moist, do mingle quickly,
The evil angels slide too easily
As subtile spirits into our phantasy.
    Sometimes meseems she saw—wo-worth the hap!—
No very serpent, but a serpent's shape.
Whether that Satan played the juggler there,
Who tender eyes with charmed tapers blear,
Transforming so by subtile, vapory gleams,
Men's heads to monsters, into eels the beams,
Or whether, devils having bodies light,
Quick, nimble, active, apt to change with slight
In shapes or shows they, guileful, have proposed;
In brief like th'air whereof they are composed.

For, as the air, with scattered clouds bespread,
Is here and there black, yellow, white and red,
Resembling armies, monsters, mountains, dragons,
Rocks, fiery castles, forests, ships and wagons,
And such to us, through glass transparent, clear,
From form to form varying, it doth appear,
So these seducers can grow great or small,
Or round, or square, or straight, or short, or tall,
As fits the passions they are moved by,
And such our soul receives them from our eye.
    Sometimes, that Satan, only for this work,
Feigned him a serpent's shape, wherein to lurk;
For Nature framing our soul's enemies
Of bodies light, and in experience wise,
In malice crafty, curious they assemble
Small elements, which as of kin resemble,
Whereof a mass is made, and thereunto
They soon give growth and lively motion, too.
Not that they be creators; for th'Almighty—
Who first of nothing made vast Amphitrite,[2]
The world's dull center, heaven's ay turning frame,
And whirling air,—sole merits that high name;
Who solely being, being gives to all,
And of all things the seeds substantial
Within their new-born bodies hath enclosed,
To be in time by Nature's hand disposed.   .   .   .
    But to conclude, I think 'twas no conceit,
No feigned idol, nor no juggling slight,
Nor body borrowed for this use's sake,
But the true serpent which the Lord did make
In the beginning.   For his hateful breed
Bears yet the pain of this pernicious deed.
    Yet 'tis a doubt whether the devil did
Govern the dragon, not there selfly hid,
To raise his courage and his tongue direct,
Locally absent, present by effect;

---

[2] In the Homeric poems the name Amphitrite was used as a general
appellation of the sea.

As when the sweet strings of a lute we strike,
Another lute, laid near it, sounds the like—
Nay, the same—note, through secret sympathy,
Untouched receiving life and harmony;
Or as a star which, though far distant, pours
Upon our heads hapless or happy showers.
    Or whether for a time he did abide
Within the doubling serpent's damask hide
Holding a placeless place, as our soul dear
Through the dim lantern of our flesh shines clear,
And, boundless, bounds itself in so strict space
As form in body, not as body in place.
    But this stands sure.   However else it went,
Th'old serpent served as Satan's instrument
To charm in Eden with a strong illusion
Our silly grandam to herself's confusion.
For as an old, rude, rotten, tuneless kit,
If famous Dowland deign to finger it,
Makes sweeter music than the choicest lute
In the gross handling of a clownish brute;
So, while a learned fiend with skillful hand
Doth the dull motions of his mouth command,
These self-dumb creatures' glozing rhetoric
With bashful shame great orators would strike.
So fairy trunks within Epirus' grove,
Moved by the spirit that was inspired by Jove,
With fluent voice, to every one that seeks,
Foretell the fates of light-believing Greeks.
So, all incensed, the pale engastromith,[3]
Ruled by the furious spirit he's haunted with,
Speaks in his womb; so well a workman's skill
Supplies the want of any organ ill.
So the fanatic, lifting up his thought
On Satan's wing, tells with a tongue distraught
Strange oracles, and his sick spirit doth plead
Even of those arts that he did never read.

---

[3]The Greek form of "ventriloquist".

O ruthless murderer of immortal souls!
Alas, to pull us from the happy poles,
And plunge us headlong in thy yawning hell,—
Thy ceaseless frauds and fetches who can tell?
Thou play'st the lion when thou dost engage
Bloodthirsty Nero's barbarous heart with rage,
While, fleshed in murders, butcher-like he paints
The saint-poor world with the dear blood of saints.
Thou play'st the dog, when by the mouth profane
Of some false prophet thou dost belch thy bane,
While from the pulpit barkingly he rings
Bold blasphemies against the King of Kings.
Thou play'st the swine when plunged in pleasures vile
Some epicure doth sober minds defile,
Transforming lewdly, by his loose impiety,
Strict Lacedaemon to a soft society.
Thou play'st the nightingale, or else the swan,
When any famous rhetorician
With captious wit and curious language draws .
Seduced hearers, and subverts the laws.
Thou play'st the fox, when thou dost feign aright
The face and phrase of some deep hypocrite,—
True painted tomb, dead seeming coals but quick,
A scorpion fell whose hidden tail doth prick.
Yet this were little if thy spite audacious
Spared at the least the face of angels gracious,
And if thou didst not, ape-like, imitate
Th'Almighty's works, the wariest wits to mate.
But without numbering all thy subtle baits,
And nimble juggling with a thousand slights,
Timely returning where I first digressed,
I'll only here thy first deceit digest.
The dragon then, man's fortress to surprise,[4]
Follows a captain's martial policies,
Who, ere too near an adverse place he pitch,
The situation marks, and sounds the ditch;

---

[4]Compare Par. Lost, IX, 510 et seq.

With his eyes level the steep wall he metes,
Surveys the flanks, his camp in order sets,
And then approaching, batters sore the side
Which art and nature have least fortified.
So this old soldier, having marked rife
The first born pair's yet danger-dreadless life,
Mounting his cannon, subtly he assaults
The part he finds with evident defaults,—
Namely, poor woman, wavering, weak, unwise,
Light, credulous, news-lover, given to lies.
    "Eve, second honor of this universe,
Is't true, I pray, that jealous God, perverse,
Forbids," quoth he, "both you and all your race[5]
All the fair fruits these silver brooks embrace,
So oft bequeathed you, and by you possessed,
And day and night by your own labor dressed?"
    With th'air of these sweet words the wily snake[6]
A poisoned air inspired, as it spake,
In Eve's frail breast, who thus replies: "O know,
Whate'er thou be,—but thy kind care doth show
A gentle friend,—that all the fruits and flowers[7]
In this earth's heaven are in our hands and powers,
Except alone that goodly fruit divine,
Which in the midst of this green ground doth shine.
But all-good God,—alas, I wot not why,—
Forbade us touch that fruit on pain to die."
She ceased; already brooding in her heart
A curious wish that will her weal subvert.
    As a false lover, that thick snares hath laid
T'entrap the honor of a fair young maid,
When she, though little, yet some heed accords[8]
To his sweet, courting, deep affected words,
Feels that th'awakening of a new desire
Will soon assuage his passion's eager fire;

---

[5] Compare Par. Lost, IX, 532 and 656.
[6] Compare Par. Lost, IX, 625.
[7] Compare Par. Lost, IX, 660.
[8] Compare Par. Lost. IX, 667.

And rapt with joy, upon this point persists,
That parleying city never long resists;
Even so the serpent that doth counterfeit
A guileful call to lure us to his net,
Perceiving Eve his flattering gloss digest,
He follows still, and jocund doth not rest,
Till he hath tried foot, hand and head, and all
Upon the breach of this new-battered wall.
    "No, fair," quoth he, "believe not that the care
God hath, mankind from spoiling death to spare,
Makes Him forbid you on so strict condition
This purest, fairest, rarest fruit's fruition.
A doubtful fear, an envy and a hate
His jealous heart forever cruciate.[9]
Since the suspected virtue of this tree
Shall soon disperse the cloud of idiocy[10]
Which dims your eyes; and, further, make you seem,
Excelling us, even equal gods to Him.
O world's rare glory! reach thy happy hand!
Reach, reach, I say; why dost thou stop or stand?
Begin thy bliss, and do not fear the threat
Of an uncertain godhead, only great
Through self-awed zeal; put on the glistering pall
Of immortality. Do not forestall,
As envious step-dame, thy posterity
The sovereign honor of divinity."
    The parley ended, our ambitious grandam,
Who yet did only eye and heart abandon
Against the Lord, now further doth proceed,
And hand to mouth makes guilty of the deed.
    A novice thief that in a closet spies
A heap of gold that on a table lies,
Pale, fearful, shivering, twice or thrice extends[11]
And twice or thrice withdraws his fingers' ends,

9Compare Par. Lost, IX, 729.
10"Idiocy" and "idiot" in the Divine Weeks always refer to lack of
trained knowledge, and not to lack of intellectual power.
11The punishment for larceny was death.

And yet again returns; the booty takes,
And faintly bold, up in his cloak it makes,
Scarce finds the door; with faltering feet he flies
And still looks back for fear of hue-and-cries.[12]
Even so doth Eve show, by like fearful fashions,
The doubtful combat of contending passions.
She would; she would not; glad; sad; comes and goes,
And long she marts about a match of woes;
But, out, alas! at last she toucheth it
And having touched, tastes the forbidden bit.

Then as a man that from a lofty cliff
Or steepy mountain doth descend too swift,
Stumbling at somewhat, quickly clips[13] a limb
Of his dear kinsman, walking next to him,
And by his headlong fall so brings his friend
To an untimely, sad and sudden end,
Our mother, falling, hales her spouse anon
Down to the gulf of pitchy Acheron.
For, to the wished fruit's beautiful aspect,
Sweet, nectary taste and wonderful effect,
Cunningly adding her quaint, smiling glances,
Her witty speech and pretty countenances,
She so prevails that her blind lord at last
A morsel of the sharp-sweet fruit doth taste.   .   .   .

Now the sad soul hath lost the character
And sacred image that did honor her;
The wretched body, full of shame and sorrow
To see its nakedness, is forced to borrow
A tree's broad leaves, whereof they aprons frame,
From Heaven's fair eye to hide their new found shame.

Alas, fond[14] deathlings, O behold, how clear
The knowledge is that you have bought so dear.
In heavenly things ye are more blind than moles,
In earthly more than owls.   Ye silly souls,
Think ye the sight that through earth's solid centers,
As globes of pure, transparent crystals enters,

12"Hu-on cries" in the quartos and folios.
13See note 18, Day 1, ante.
14Foolish—as in Shakespeare, passim.

Cannot transpierce your leaves, or do ye ween
Covering your shame, so to conceal your sin?
Or that a part thus clouded, all doth lie
Safe from the search of Heaven's all-seeing eye?
Thus yet, man's troubled, dull intelligence
Had of his fault but a confused sense;
As in a dream after much drink, it chances
Disturbed spirits are vexed with raving fancies.
Therefore the Lord, within the garden fair
Moving betimes,—I wot not, I, what air,
But supernatural, whose breath divine
Brings of His presence a most certain sign,—
Awakes their lethargy, and to the quick
Their self-doomed souls doth sharply press and prick,
Now more and more making their pride to fear
The frowning visage of their Judge severe,
To seek new refuge in more secret harbors
Among the dark shades of those tufting arbors.[15]
"Adam!" quoth God, with thundering majesty;
"Where art thou, wretch? What dost thou? Answer
    me,
Thy God and Father, from whose hand thy health
Thou holdst,—thine honor, and all forms of wealth!"
At this sad summons, woeful man resembles
A bearded rush that in a river trembles.
His rosy cheeks are turned to earthy hue;
His fainting body drops an icy dew;
His tear-drowned eyes a night of clouds bedims;
About his ears a buzzing horror swims;
His weakened knees with feebleness are humble;
His faltering feet do hide away and stumble;
He hath not now his free, bold, stately port,
But downcast looks, in fearful, slavish sort.
Now naught of Adam doth in Adam rest;
He feels his senses pained, his soul oppressed,
A confused host of violent passions jar;
His flesh and spirit are in continual war,

---

[15]Compare Par. Lost, X, 100.

And now no more, through conscience[16] of his error,
He sees or hears th'Almighty but with terror;
And loth he answers, as with tongue distraught,
Confessing thus his fear, but not his fault:
   "O Lord! Thy voice, Thy dreadful voice hath made
Me, fearful, hide me in this covert shade;[17]
For, naked as I am, O Most of Might!
I dare not come within Thine awful sight."
   "Naked?" quoth God; "why, faithless renegate,—
Apostate pagan!—who hath told thee that?
Whence springs thy shame?   What makes thee thus to
      run
From shade to shade, my presence thus to shun?
Hast thou not tasted of the learned tree
Whereof, on pain of death, I warned thee?"
   "O righteous God," quoth Adam, "I am free
From this offense.   The wife Thou gavest me
For my companion and my comforter,—
She made me eat the deadly meat with her."
   "And thou," quoth God, "O frail and treacherous
      bride,
Why with thyself hast thou seduced thy guide?"
   "Lord," answers Eve, "the serpent did entice
My simple frailty to this sinful vice."
   Mark here, how He, who fears not who reform
His high decrees,—not subject unto form
Or style of court,—who, all-wise, hath no need
T'examine proof or witness of the deed;
Who, for sustaining of unequal scale
Dreads not the doom of a mercurial,
Ere sentence pass doth publicly convent,[18]
Confront, and hear with ear indifferent[19]
Th'offenders sad; then, with just indignation
Pronounced thus their dreadful condemnation:

16"Conscience" in the sense of "consciousness" is a common Shakespearean use, as in Hamlet's soliloquy on Death.
17See Par. Lost, X, 116.
18"Convent" for convene.
19"Indifferent" has the meaning of "impartial".

"Ah, cursed serpent! which my fingers made
To serve mankind,—thou'st made thyself a blade
Wherein vain man, and his inveigled wife,
Self-parricides, have reft their proper life,—
For this, thy fault, true fountain of all ill,
Thou shalt be hateful 'mong all creatures still.
Groveling in dust, of dust thou ay shalt feed;
I'll kindle war between the woman's seed
And thy fell race; hers on the head shall ding
Thine, thine again hers in the heel shall sting.
 "Rebel to me! unto thy kindred curst!
False to thy husband! to thyself the worst!
Hope not thy fruit so eas'ly to bring forth
As now thou slay'st it.   Henceforth every birth
Shall torture thee with thousand sorts of pain;   .   .   .
Under his yoke thy husband shall thee have,—
Tyrant,—by thee made the arch-tyrant's slave.
 "And thou, disloyal, who hast hearkened more
To a wanton fondling than my sacred lore,—
Henceforth the sweat shall bubble on thy brow;
Thy hands shall blister and thy back shall bow;
Ne'er shalt thou send into thy branched veins
A bit not bought with price of thousand pains;
For the earth feeling, even in her, th'effect
Of the doom thundered 'gainst thy foul defect,
Instead of sweet fruit which she selfly yields
Seedless and artless, over all thy fields,
With thorns and burrs shall bristle up her breast;
In short, thou shalt not taste the sweets of rest
Till ruthless Death, by his extremest pain,
Thy dust-born body turn to dust again."
 Here I conceive that flesh and blood will brangle,
And murmuring reason with th'Almighty wrangle,
Who did our parents with free-will indue,
Though He foresaw that that would be the clew
Should lead their steps into the woful way
Where life is death ten thousand times a day.
Now all that He foresees befalls; and further,
He all events by His free power doth order.

Man taxeth God of an unjust severity,
For plaguing Adam's sin in his posterity,
So that th'old years' renewed generations
Cannot assuage His venging indignations,
Which have no other ground to prosecute[20]
But the mis-eating of a certain fruit.
    O dusty wormling, dar'st thou strive and stand
With heaven's high Monarch?   Wilt thou, wretch,
    demand
Count of His deeds?   Ah, shall the potter make
His clay such fashion as him list to make,
And shall not God, world's Founder, nature's Father,
Dispose of man, His own mere creature, rather?
The supreme King, who, Judge of greatest kings,
By number, weight and measure, sets all things,—
Vice-loathing Lord, pure Justice, Patron strong,
Law's Life, right's Rule,—will He do any wrong?
    Man, holdest thou of God thy frank free-will
But free t'obey His sacred goodness still,—
Freely to follow Him and do His hest,
Not philter-charmed, nor by Busiris[21] pressed.
God arms thee with discourse, but thou, O wretch,
By the keen edge the wound-soul sword dost catch,
Killing thyself, and in thy loins thy line,
O baneful spider, weaving woful twine!
All Heaven's pure flowers thou turnest into poison.
Thy sense 'reaves sense; thy reason robs thy reason;
For thou complainest of God's grace, whose still[22]
Extracts from dross of thine audacious ill
Three unexpected goods; praise for His name;
Bliss for thyself; for Satan endless shame.
Since but for sin Justice and Mercy were
But idle names; and but that thou didst err,

20"Prosecute" has its original signification of "follow".
21Busiris was king of Egypt and a son of Neptune. His habit of inducing strangers to visit his altars where they were offered up as sacrifices was his own undoing when he tried the scheme with Hercules, as that hero promptly slew him.
22"Still" is a noun, subject of the verb, "extracts".

Christ had not come to conquer and to quell,
Upon the cross, Sin, Satan, Death and Hell;
Making thee blessed more since thine offense,
Than in thy primer, happy innocence.
Then, might'st thou die; now, death thou dost not
    doubt;
Now, in the heaven; then didst thou ride without.
In earth thou liv'dst then; now in heaven thou be'st;
Then thou didst hear God's word; now it thou seest.
Then pleasant fruits; now Christ is the repast;
Then might'st thou fall, but now thou standest fast.
    Now Adam's fall was not, indeed, so light
As seems to reason's sin-bleared, owly sight;
But 'twas a chain where all the greatest sins
Were one in other linked fast as twins.
Ingratitude, pride, treason, gluttony,
Too curious skill, thirst, envy, felony,
Too light, too late belief, were the sweet baits
That made him wander from Heaven's holy straits.
    What wouldst thou, father, say unto a son
Of perfect age, to whom, for portion,
Witting and willing, while thyself yet livest,
All thy possessions in the earth thou givest,
And yet th'ungrateful, graceless insolent
In thine own land rebellion doth invent.
Map thou an Adam in thy memory,
By God's own hand made with great majesty,
Not poor nor pined,[23] but at whose command
The rich abundance of the world doth stand;
Not slave to sense, but having freely might
To bridle it, and range it still aright;
No idiot fool, nor drunk with vain opinion,
But God's disciple and His dearest minion,
Who rashly grows, for little—nay for naught,—
His deadly foe that all his good had wrought.
    So may'st thou guess what whip, what rope, what rack,
What fire were fit to punish Adam's lack.

---

[23] "Pine" is in this volume synonymous with "famish".

Then, since man's sin by little and little runs
Endless, through every age from sires to sons;
And still the farther this foul sin-spring flows
It still more muddy, and more filthy grows,
Thou ought'st not marvel if even yet his seed
Feel the just wages of this wicked deed.
For, though the keen sting of concupiscence
Cannot, ere birth, its fell effect commence,
The unborn babe, hid in the mother's womb,
Is sorrow's servant, and sin's servile groom;
As a frail mote, from the first mass extract,
Which Adam baned by his rebellious act.
Sound offspring comes not of a kind infected.
Parts are not fair if totals be defected.   . . .
  While night's black muffler hoodeth up the skies,
The silly blind man misseth not his eyes;
But when the day summons to work again,
Of his unending night he doth complain,
That he goes groping, and his hand, alas,
Is fain to guide his foot and guard his face.
So man that liveth in the womb's obscurity
Knows not nor maketh known his lust's impurity;
Which, for 'tis sown in a too plenteous ground,
Takes root already in the caves profound
Of his infected heart.   With's birth it peers,
And grows in strength as he doth grow in years;
And, waxed a tree, though pruned with thousand cares,
An execrable, deadly fruit it bears.
  Thou seest no wheat can helleborus bring,
Nor barley from the madding morel spring,
And bleating lambs brave lions do not breed,
And leprous parents raise a leprous seed.
Even so our grandsire, living innocent,
Had stocked the whole world with a saint descent,
But suffering sin in Eden him t'invade,
His sons the sons of sin and wrath he made.
For God did seem t'endow with glory and grace
Not the first man so much as all the race;
And after 'reave again those gifts divine,

Not him so much as, in him, all his line.

For, if an odious traitor that conspires
Against a prince, or to his state aspires,
Feel not alone the law's extremity,
But his sons' sons, although sometimes they be
Honest and virtuous, for their father's blame
Are hapless scarred with an eternal shame;
May not th'Eternal, with a righteous terror,
In Adam's issue punish Adam's error?
May He not thrall them under Death's command,
And scar their brows with everlasting brand
Of infamy, who in His stock, accurst,
Have graft worse slips than Adam set at first?

Man's seed then, justly, by a due succession,
Bears the hard penance of his high transgression;
And Adam here, from Eden banished,
As first offender, is first punished.

"Hence!" quoth the Lord; "hence! hence! accursed
     race,
Out of my garden! quick, avoid the place,—
This beauteous place, pride of this universe,—
A house unworthy masters so perverse!"

Those that in quarrel of the strong of strongs,[24]
And just revenge of queen and country's wrongs,
Were witnesses to all the woful plaints,
The sighs and tears, and pitiful complaints
Of braving Spaniards—chiefly brave in word,—
When, by the valiant, heaven-assisted sword
Of Mars-like Essex, England's marshal-earl,
(Then Albion's patron and Eliza's pearl,)
They were expelled from Cad'z, their dearest pleasure,
Losing their town, their honor and their treasure,—
"Wo-worth," said they, "wo-worth[25] our king's ambi-
     tion!

---

[24]These two score lines of Sylvester's interpolation have a value as
being illustrative of the feeling of England towards Spain in the 1590's,
although not material to the subject in hand.

[25]"Wo-worth" is used by Spenser and by the author of Piers Plow-
man's Crede long before. The second syllable is from the Anglo Saxon
"wurdhan", and is the same as the German "werden".

Wo-worth our clergy and their inquisition!
He seeks new kingdoms, and doth lose his old.
They burn for conscience, but their thirst's for gold.
Woe and alas! Woe to the vain bravados
Of Typhon-like 'invincible armados'
Which, like the vaunting monster man of Gath
Have stirred against us little David's wrath.
Wo-worth our sins; wo-worth ourselves, and all
Accursed causes of our sudden fall."
Those well may guess the bitter agonies
And luke-warm rivers, gushing from the eyes,
Of our first parents, out of Eden driven,
Of repeal hopeless, by the hand of Heaven.
  For the Almighty set before the door
Of th'holy park a seraphin who bore
A waving sword, whose body shined bright,
Like flaming comet in the depth of night,—
A body merely metaphysical
Which, differing little from th'One Unical,
Th'Act simply pure, the only being Being,
Approacheth matter. Ne'ertheless, not being
Of matter mixed; or rather is so made
So merely spirit that not the murdering blade
His joined quantity can part in two;
For, pure, it cannot suffer aught, but do.[26]

---

[26]Compare Par. Lost. VI, 330-353.

THE FURIES

This is not th'world! O whither am I brought?
This earth I tread—this hollow hanging vault—
Which days reducing, and renewing nights,
Renews the grief of mine afflicted sprites.
The sea I sail, this troubled air I sip,
Are not the first week's glorious workmanship.
This wretched round is not the goodly globe
Th'Eternal trimmed in so various robe;
Tis but a dungeon and a dreadful cave,—
Of that first world the miserable grave.

All quickening Spirit! great God, that, justly strange,
Judge-turned-Father,[1] wrought'st this wondrous change,
Change and new-mould me, Lord; my hand assist,
That in my muse appear no earthly mist.
Make me thine organ. Give my voice dexterity
Sadly[2] to sing this sad change to posterity.

And, bounteous Giver of each perfect gift,[3]
So tune my voice to his sweet sacred clef,
That in each strain my rude, unready tongue[4]
Be lively echo of his learned song,
And henceforth let our holy music ravish

---

[1] In "Building the World" some effort was made to avoid reproducing the queer compounds and harsh combinations of consonants in which the poet occasionally indulged. In "Adam" the editor has endeavored to give the verses (except as to spelling and punctuation) as nearly as possible in just the shape in which they were written. A few elisions have seemed imperative, but they are very few. In the present instance "Judge-turned Father" means Father turned to Judge.

[2] Meaning seriously; as in the old observation about the English taking their pastimes sadly.

[3] The translator here speaks for himself through two dozen lines.

[4] "Unready" seems to be used in its old sense of "unlearned".

All well-born souls from fancies lewdly lavish;
Of charming sin the deep enchanting sirens,
The snares of virtue, valor-softening hyrens,[5]
That, touched with terror of Thine indignation,
Presented in this woful alteration,
We all may seek, by prayer and true repentance,
To shun the rigor of Thy wrathful sentence.
  But, ere we farther pass, our slender bark
Must here strike topsails to a princely ark,[6]
Which keeps these straits.   He hails us threatfully:
Starboard our helm!   Come underneath his lee!
"Ho! whence your bark?"   "Of Zealland."   "Whither
    bound?"
"For Virtue cape."   "What lading?" "Hope." "This
    sound
You should not pass, save that your voyage tends
To benefit our neighbors and our friends."
"Thanks, kingly captain.   Deign us, then, we pray,
Some skillful pilot through this furious bay,
Or, in this channel, since we are to learn,
Vouchsafe to tow us at your royal stern."
  Ere that our sire, O too, too proudly base,
Turned tail to God and to the fiend his face,
This mighty world did seem an instrument
True strung, well tuned, and handled excellent,
Whose symphony resounded sweetly shrill
Th'Almighty's praise, who played upon it still.
While man served God, the world served him.   The
    live
And lifeless creatures seemed all to strive
To nurse this league, and loving zealously,
These two dear heads embraced mutually

5Corruption of the Greek "Irene", (the name of a favorite of Sultan
Mohammed II) and used to designate a class of women, as "Abigail"
is used to indicate another class.   See 2 King Henry IV, II, 4.
  6Before the accession of James I to the English throne he had posed
as a man of letters, and among other worthless productions had translated The Furies, Urania and a few others of Du Bartas's works, of
which Sylvester thought best to make recognition, and did so in an
awkward fashion in these lines.

In sweet accord, the base with high rejoiced,
The hot with cold, the solid with the moist;
And innocent Astræa did combine
All with the mastick of a love divine.
    For th'hidden love that nowadays doth hold
The steel and loadstone, hydrargire and gold,
Th'amber and straw; that lodgeth in one shell
Pearlfish and sharpling, and unites so well
Sargons[7] and goats, the sparage[8] and the rush,
Th'elm and the vine, th'olive and myrtle bush,
Is but a spark or shadow of that love
Which at the first in everything did move,
Whenas the earth's muses with harmonious sound
To heaven's sweet music humbly did resound.
But Adam, being chief of all the strings
Of this large lute, o'er retched,[9] quickly brings
All out of tune, and now, for melody
Of warbling charms, it yells so hideously
That it affrights fell Enyo,[10] who turmoils
To raise again th'old Chaos' antique broils.
    Heaven, that still smiling on his paramour,[11]
Still in her lap did mel and manna pour,
Now with his hail, his rain, his frost and heat,
Doth parch and pinch, and overwhelm and beat,
And hoars her head with snows, and jealous dashes
Against her brows his fiery lightning flashes.
On th'other side the sullen, envious earth,
From blackest cells of her foul breast, sends forth
A thousand foggy fumes, which, everywhere,
With cloudy mists heaven's crystal front besmear.
    Since that the wolf the trembling sheep pursues,
The crowing cock the lion stout eschews,
The pullein hide them from the puttocks' flight,[12]

---

[7]DuBartas believed the story of a fish called Sargon, which was said to leave the sea to foregather with goats.
[8]The asparagus is indigenous on sea shores.
[9]Stretched too tightly.
[10]Enyo was the Greek goddess corresponding to the Roman Bellona.
[11]Paramour—the earth.
[12]Though pullein and puttock seem strange now, they were familiar English in 1600 for "poultry" and "sparrow-hawk" respectively.

The mastiff's mute at the hyena's sight,—
Yea, who would think it? these fell enmities
Rage in the senseless trunks of plants and trees.
The vine the cole, the cole-wort swine's-bread dreads,
The fern abhors the hollow waving reeds,
The olive and the oak participate
Even to their earth, signs of their ancient hate,
Which suffers not—O dateless discord!—th'one
Live in that ground where th'other first hath grown.
O strange instinct! O deep, immortal rage!
Whose fiery feud no Lethe flood can 'suage.
    The first-moved heaven in 'tself itself still stirring,
Rapts with its course, quicker than wind's swift whir-
    ring,
All th'other spheres, and to Alcides' spires[13]
From Alexander's altars drives their fires.
But mortal Adam, monarch here beneath,
Erring draws all into the paths of death,
And on rough seas, as a blind pilot rash,
Against the rock of heaven's just wrath doth dash
The world's great vessel, sailing erst at ease,
With gentle gales, good guide, on quiet seas.
    For, ere his fall, which way soe'er he rolled
His wondering eyes, God everywhere behold;
In heaven, in earth, in ocean and in air,
He sees and feels and finds Him everywhere.
The world was like a large and sumptuous shop,
Where God His goodly treasures did unwrap,
Or crystal glass, most lively representing
His sacred goodness everywhere frequenting.
    But since his sin, the woeful wretch finds none
Herb, garden, grove, field, fountain, stream or stone,
Beast, mountain, valley, sea-gate, shore or heaven,
But bears his death's doom openly engraven.
In brief, the whole scope this round center hath,
Is true store-house of Heaven's righteous wrath.

13Alexander's altars" were at the foot of the Rhipean mountains,
supposed to be a western branch of the Urals. "Alcides' spires" of
course means the Pillars of Hercules, at Gibraltar.

Rebellious Adam, from his God' revolting,
Finds his erst subjects 'gainst himself insulting;
The tumbling sea, the air with tempests driven,
Thorn-bristled earth, the sad and lowering heaven,
(As from the oath of their allegiance free,)
Revenge on him th'Almighty's injury.
  The stars conjured,[14] through envious influence,
By secret hangmen punish this offense;
The sun with heat, the moon with cold doth vex him,
Th'air with unlooked-for, sudden changes checks him
With fogs and frosts, hails, snows, and sulphury thun-
    ders,
Blasting and storms, and more prodigious wonders.
  Fire fallen from heaven, or else by art incited,
Or by mischance in some rich building lighted,
Or from some mountain's burning bowels thrown,
Replete with sulphur, pitch, and pumice stone,
With sparkling fury spreads, and in few hours
The labor of a thousand years devours.
  The greedy ocean, breaking wonted bounds,
Usurps his herds, his wealthy isles, and towns.
The grieved earth, to ease her as it seems
Of such profane, accursed weight, sometimes
Swallows whole countries, and the airy tops
Of prince-proud towers in her black womb she wraps;
And in despite of him, abhorred and hateful,
She many ways proves barren and ungrateful,
Mocking our hopes, turning our seed-wheat kernel
To burn-grain thistle, and to vapory darnel,
Cockle, wild oats, rough burrs, corn-cumbering tares,—
Short recompense for all our costly cares.
  Yet this were little if she, more malicious,
Fell stepdame, brought us not plants more pernicious;
As sable henbane, morel, making mad,
Cold, poisoning poppy, itching, drowsy, sad;
The stif'ning carpese,[15] th'eye's foe, hemlock stinking,

14Sworn to mutual support; covenanted.
15Carpesium is a southern European shrub.

Limb-numbing, belching; and the sinew-shrinking,
Dead-laughing apium, weeping aconite,
Which, in our vulgar, deadly wolf's bane hight,
The dropsy-breeding, sorrow-bringing sylly,[16]
(Here called flea-wort), Colchis' baneful lily,
(With us wild saffron,) blistering, biting, fell;
Hot napell,[17] making lips and tongue to swell,
Blood-boiling yew, and costive misletoe,
With ice-cold mandrake, and a many mo
Such fatal plants, whose fruit, seed, sap or root,
T'untimely grave do bring our heedless foot.
   Besides, she knows we, brutish, value more
Than lives or honors her rich glittering ore,
That avarice our boundless thought still vexes;
Therefore among her wreakful baits she mixes
Quicksilver, lithargy, and orpiment,
Wherewith our entrails are oft gnawn and rent,
So that sometimes for body and for mind,
Torture and torment in one mind we find.
   What resteth more? The masters skillful most,
With gentle gales driven to their wished coast,
Not with less labor guide their winged wains
On th'azure forehead of the liquid plains;
Nor crafty jugglers can more easily make
Their self-lived puppets, for their lucre's sake,
To skip and scud, and play and prate and prance,
And fight and fall, and trip and turn, and dance;
Then, happy, we did rule the scaly legions
That dumbly dwell in stormy water regions;
Then feathered singers, and the stubborn droves
That haunt the deserts, and the shady groves.
At every word they trembled then for awe,
And every wink then served them as a law,
And, always bent all duty to observe,
Without command stood ready still to serve.
   But now, alas, through our fond parents' fall,
They of our slaves are grown our tyrants all.

16Psylly, or flea-wort, is the inula coryza.
17Napell—the bitter vetch; lathyrus macorrhizus.

Wend we by sea, the dread leviathan
Turns upside down the boiling ocean,
And on the sudden sadly doth entomb
Our floating castles[18] in deep Thetis' womb.
Erst in the welkin like an eagle towering,
And on the water like a dolphin scouring,
Walk we by land, how many loathsome swarms
Of speckled poisons with pestiferous arms
In every corner in close ambush lurk,
With secret bands our sudden banes to work.
Besides the lion and the leopard,
Boar, bear, and wolf, to death pursue us hard,
And jealous vengers of the wrongs divine
In pieces pull their sovereign's sinful line.
The huge thick forests have not bush nor brake,
But hides some hangman, our loathed life to take;
In every hedge and ditch both day and night
We fear our death, of every leaf affright.
Rest we at home, the mastiff fierce in force,
Th'untamed bull, the hot, courageous, horse,
With teeth, with horns and hoofs, besiege us round,
As grieved to see such tyrants tread the ground;
And there's no fly so small but now dares bring
Her little wrath against her quondam king.
  What hideous sights, what horror-boding shows,—
Alas, what yells, what howls, what thundering throes!
O am I not near roaring Phlegethon,
Alecto sad, Meger' and Ctesiphon?
What spells have charmed ye from your dreadful den
Of darkest hell? Monsters, abhorred of men,—
O night's black daughters, grim-faced furies sad,
Stern Pluto's posts, what makes ye here so mad?
O feels not man a world of woeful terrors
Beside your goring wounds and ghastly horrors?
  So soon as God from Eden Adam drave
To live in this earth—rather in this grave—
Where reign a thousand deaths, he summoned up

18An early suggestion of the idea expressed in Campbell's "Mariners of England."

With thundering call the damned crew that sup
Of sulphury Styx and fiery Phlegethon,
Bloody Cocytus, muddy Acheron.
Come, snake-tressed sisters, come, ye dismal elves;
Come now to curse and cruciate yourselves.
Come, leave the horror of your houses pale!
Come, parbreak here your foul, black, baneful gall;
Let lack of work no more from henceforth fear you;
Man by his sin a hundred hells doth rear you.
  This echo made all hell to tremble, troubled,
The drowsy night her deep, dark horrors doubled,
And suddenly Avernus' gulf did swim
With rosin, pitch and brimstone to the brim,
And th'ugly Gorgons and the Sphinxes fell,
Hydras and harpies, 'gan to yawn and yell.[19]
  As the heat, hidden in a vapory cloud,
Striving for issue with strange murmurs loud,
Like guns astuns with round, round-rumbling thunder,
Filling the air with noise, the earth with wonder,
So the three sisters, the three hideous rages,
Raise thousand storms, leaving th'infernal stages.
  Already all roll on their steely cars,
On th'ever-shaking, ninefold, steely bars
Of Stygian bridge and in that fearful cave
They jumble, tumble, rumble, rage and rave.
Then dreadful Hydra and dire Cerberus,
Which on one body beareth, monsterous,
The heads of dragon, dog, ounce, bear and bull,
Wolf, lion, horse, of strength and stomach full;
Lifting his lungs he hisses, barks and brays;
He howls, he yells, he bellows, roars and neighs;
Such a black sant, such a confused sound
From many-headed bodies doth rebound.
  Having attained to our calm haven of light
With swifter course than Boreas' nimble flight,
All fly at man, all at intestine strife,

---

[19]"Gorgons and Hydras and Chimeras dire."—Par. Lost, II, 628.
"Fell" is an adjective, meaning cruel.

Who most may torture his detested life.
Here first comes dearth, the lively form of death,
Still yawning wide with loathsome, sickening breath,
With hollow eyes, with meager cheeks and chin,
With sharp, lean bones piercing her sable skin,
Her empty bowels may be plainly spied
Clean through the wrinkles of her withered hide.
She hath no belly but the belly's seat,
Her knees and knuckles swelling hugely great,
Insatiate Orque that, even at one repast,
Almost all creatures in the world would waste;
Whose greedy gorge dish after dish doth draw,
Seeks meat in meat.   For still her monstrous maw
Voids in devouring, and sometimes she eats
Her own dear babes for lack of other meats.
Nay, more; sometimes, O strangest gluttony,
She eats herself, herself to satisfy,
Lessening herself, herself so to enlarge,
And cruel thus she doth our grandsire charge;
And brings besides from Limbo to assist her
Rage, feebleness and thirst, her ruthless sister.
   Next marches war, the mistress of enormity
Mother of mischief, monster of deformity,
Laws, manners, arts she breaks, she mars, she chases,
Blood, tears, bowers, towers, she spills, swills, burns,
        and razes;
Her brazen feet shake all the earth asunder;
Her mouth's a firebrand, and her voice a thunder;
Her looks are lightnings, every glance a flash,
Her fingers guns that all to powder pash,
Fear and despair, flight and disorder coast[20]
With hasty march before her murderous host,
As burning, waste, rape, wrong, impiety,
Rage, ruin, discord, horror, cruelty,

---

[20]"What horrors round him wait!
Amazement in his van, with Flight combined,
And Sorrow's faded form, and Solitude behind."
Gray, "The Bard", II, 1.
The ninth stanza of Gray's "Elegy" is almost wholly Sylvestrian.

Sack, sacrilege, impunity and pride
Are still stern consorts by her barbarous side,
And poverty, sorrow, and desolation
Follow her army's bloody transmigration.
  Here's th'other fury, or my judgment fails,
Which furiously man's woeful life assails
With thousand cannons, sooner felt than seen,
Where weakest, strongest; fraught with deadly teen,[21]
Blind, crooked, cripple, maimed, deaf and mad,
Cold, burning, blistered, melancholic, sad,—
Many-named poison, minister of death,
Which from us creeps, but to us gallopeth;
Foul, trouble-rest, fantastic, greedy-gut,
Blood-sweating, heart's thief, wretched, filthy slut,
The child of surfeit, and air's temper vicious,
Perilous known, but unknown most pernicious.
  Th'enameled meads in summer cannot show
More grasshoppers above nor frogs below,
Than hellish murmurs hereabout do ring;
Nor never did the pretty little king
Of honey-people, on a sunshine day,
Lead to the field in orderly array
More busy buzzers, when he casteth, witty,
The first foundations of his waxen city,
Than this fierce monster musters in her train,—
Fell soldiers charging poor mankind amain.[22]
  Lo, first a rough and furious regiment
T'assault the fort of Adam's head is sent,.
Reason's best bulwark, and the holy cell
Wherein the soul's most sacred powers dwell.
  A king that aims his neighbor's crown to win,
Before the bruit of open wars begin,
Corrupts his counsel with rich recompenses,
For in good counsel stands the strength of princes.
So this fell fury for forerunners sends
Mania and frenzy to suborn her friends;

---

[21] Injury, vexation.
[22] Shakespeare uses "amain" rather as implying celerity than might.
Milton, like Sylvester, indicates the latter quality.

Whereof th'one drying, th'other over-warming,
The feeble brain, the seat of judgment harming,
Within the soul fantastically they feign
A confused host of strange Chimeras vain:
The karos,[23] th'apoplexy and lethargy,
As forlorn hope assault the enemy
On the same side, but yet with weapons others,
For they freeze up the brain and all its brothers,
Making the live man like a lifeless carcass,
So that again he scapeth from the Parcas.
And now the palsy and the cramp dispose
Their angry darts; this binds and that doth loose
Man's feeble sinews, shutting up the way
Whereby before the vital spirits did play.
    Then, as a man that fronts in single fight
His sudden foe, his ground doth traverse light,
Thrusts, wards, avoids and best advantage spies,
At last to daze his rival's sparkling eyes
He casts his cloak, and then with coward knife
In crimson streams he makes him strain his life.
So sickness, Adam to subdue the better,
Whom thousand gyves already fastly fetter,
Brings to the field the faithless ophthalmy
With scalding blood to blind her enemy,
Darting a thousand thrusts; then she is backed
By the amafrose,[24] and cloudy cataract;
That, gathering up gross humors inwardly
In the optic sinew, clean puts out the eye,—
This other caseth in an envious caul
The crystal humor, shining in the ball.
    This past, in steps that insolent insulter,
The cruel quinsy, leaping like a vulture
At Adam's throat, his hollow weasand swelling
Among the muscles, through thick blood congealing,
Leaving him only this essay for sign
Of's might and malice, to his future line,
Like Hercules that in his infant brows

23"Karos" is a Greek word, meaning drowsiness and headache.
24Amaurosis.

Bore glorious marks of his undaunted prowess,
When, with his hands like steely tongs, he strangled
His spiteful step-dam's dragons, spotty-spangled,
A proof presaging the triumphant spoils
That he achieved by his twelve famous toils.
  The second regiment with deadly darts
Assaulteth fiercely Adam's vital parts.
Already th'asthma, panting, breathing tough,
With humors gross the lifting lungs doth stuff;
The pining phthisic fills them all with pushes,
Whence a slow spout of corsy matter gushes;
A wasting flame, the peripneumony
Within those sponges kindles cruelly;
The spawling empyem', ruthless as the rest,
With foul imposthumes fills his hollow chest;
The pleurisy stabs him with desperate foil
Beneath the ribs where scalding blood doth boil;
Then th'incubus, by some supposed a sprite,
With a thick phlegm doth stop his breath by night.
    Dear Muse, my guide,—dear Truth—that naught
        dissembles,
Name me that champion that with fury trembles,
Who, armed with blazing fire-brands, fiercely flings
At th'army's heart, not at our feeble wings;
·Having for aids, Cough, Headache, Horror, Heat,
Pulse-Beating, Burning, cold-distilling Sweat,
Thirst, Yawning, Yolking, Casting, Shivering, Shaking,
Fantastic Raving and continual Aching,
With many more: O is not this the fury
We call the Fever?   whose inconstant fury
Transforms her ofter than Vertumnus can,
To tertian, quartan, and quotidian,
And second, too; now posting, sometimes pausing,
Even as the matter all these changes causing,
Is rummaged with motions slow or quick
In feeble bodies of the ague-sick.
    A treacherous beast! needs must I know thee best:
For four whole years thou wert my poor heart's guest;
And to this day, in body and in mind
I bear the marks of thy despite unkind;

For yet, besides my veins and bones bereft
Of blood and marrow, through thy secret theft
I feel the virtue of my spirit decayed,
Th'enthusiasm of my muse allayed;
My memory, which had been meetly good,
Is now, alas, much like the fleeting flood,
Whereon, no sooner have we drawn a line
But it is canceled, leaving there no sign.[25]
For the dear fruit of all my care and cost,
My former study, almost all is lost;
And oft in secret have I blushed at
Mine ignorance, like Corvine,[26] who forgat
His proper name; or like George Trapezunce,
Learned in youth, and in old age a dunce;
And thence it grows that, maugre my endeavor,
My numbers still by habit have the fever;
One while with heat of heavenly fire ensouled,—
Shivering anon through faint, unlearned cold.

Now the third regiment, with stormy stours
Sets on the squadron of our natural powers,
Which happily maintain us, duly, both
With needful food and with sufficient growth.
One while the bulimy, then anorexie,[27]
Then the dog-hunger or the bradypepsie,
And child-great pica, of prodigious diet,
In straitest stomachs rage with monstrous riot;
Then on the liver doth the jaundice fall,
Stopping the passage of the choleric gall;
Which then for good blood, scatters all about
Her fiery poison, yellowing all without;
But the sad dropsy freezeth it extreme,
Till all the blood be turned into fleam,[28]
But see, alas, by far more cruel foes,
The slippery bowels thrilled with thousand throes;

---

[25]"Virtues we write in water."—King Henry VIII, III, 2.
[26]Hunyadi Janos was the first Hungarian Corvinus, and was followed by his son Matthias who became king.
[27]Bulimia is an intense craving for food, anorexia a loathing of the same.
[28]An orthographical variant of phlegm.

With prisoned winds, the wringing colic pains them,
The iliac passion with more rigor strains them.   . . .
  The fell fourth regiment is outward tumors,
Begot of vicious, undigested humors;
As phlegmons, oedems, scirrhus, erysipiles,
King's-evils, cankers, cruel gouts and biles,[29]
Wens, ringworms, tetters; these from every part
With thousand pangs brave the besieged heart,
And their blind fury, wanting force and courage
To hurt the fort, the champaign country forage.
O tyrants! sheath your feeble swords again;
For death already thousand times hath slain
Your enemy; and yet your envious rigor
Doth mar his feature and his limbs disfigure,
And with a dull and ragged instrument
His joints and skin are sawed and torn and rent.
Methinks most rightly to a coward crew
Of wolves and foxes I resemble you,
Who in a forest, finding in the sand
The lion dead that did alive command
The land, about whose awful countenance
Melted far off their ice-like arrogance,
Mangle the members of their lifeless prince
With feeble signs of dastard insolence.
  But with the griefs that charge our outward places
Shall I account the loathsome phthiriasis?[30]
O shameful plague! O foul infirmity!
Which makes proud kings fouler than beggars be,
That, wrapt in rags and wrung with vermin sores,
Their itching backs sit shrugging evermore
To swarm with lice that rubbing cannot rid,
Nor often shift of shirts and sheets and beds;
For as in spring stream stream pursueth fresh,

---

[29]Boils were called "biles" by fairly well educated northern Americans within the memory of people still alive. Possibly "'erysipiles" might have been thought to afford an allowable rhyme for the former by some citizens in the early nineteenth century.
[30]Phthiriasis was said to have been the effect of burrowing by certain insects in the human body, and the death of King Herod was attributed to it.

Swarm follows swarm, and their too fruitful flesh
Breeds her own eaters, and till death arrest,
Makes of itself an execrable feast.
   Nor may we think that chance confusedly
Conducts the camp of our third enemy;
For of her soldiers some, as led by reason,
Can make their choice of country, age and season.
So Portugal hath phthisics most of all;
Eber, king's-evils; Arne, the sudden-fall.   .   .   .
After the influence of the heavens all-ruling,
Or country's manners, so soft childhood, puling,
Is wrung with worms begot of crudity,
Is apt to lasks,[31] through much humidity.   .   .   .
To bloody fluxes youth is apt inclining,
Continual fevers, frenzies, phthisic, pining;
And feeble age is seldom times without
Her tedious guests, the palsy and the gout,
Coughs and catarrhs, and so the pestilence,
The quartan ague with her accidents,
The flux, the hip-gout, and the watery tumor
Are bred with us of an autumnal humor.
The itch, the murrain, the Alcides' grief,
In Ver's hot moisture do molest us chief;
The diarrhoea and the burning fever
In summer season do their full endeavor;
And pleurisies, the rotten coughs, and rheums
Wear curled flakes of white celestial plumes
Like sluggish soldiers, keeping garrison
In th'icy bulwarks of the year's gelt son.[32]
   Some, seeming most in multitudes delighting,
Bane one by other not the first acquitting,
As measles, mange, and filthy leprosy,
The plague, small-pox and phthisic malady;
And some, alas, we leave as in succession
Unto our children for a sad possession:
Such are king's-evils, dropsy, gout and stone,
Blood-boiling lepra, and consumption,

---

[31]"Apt to lasks" is "inclined to fluxes."
[32]Winter; because unproductive.

The swelling throat-ache, th'epilepsy sad,
And cruel rupture, paining too, too bad;
For their hid poisons' after-coming harm
Is fast combined unto the parent sperm.
   But O what arms, what shield shall we oppose,
What stratagems, against those treacherous foes,
Those treacherous griefs that our frail art detects,
Not by their cause, but by their sole effects?
Such are the fruitful matrix suffocation,
The falling sickness, and pale swooning passion,
The which, I wot not what strange wind's long pause,
I wot not where, I wot not how doth cause.
   Or who, alas, can 'scape the cruel wile
Of those fell pangs that physic's pains beguile,
Which by being banished from a body, yet
Under new names return again to it;
Or rather, taught the strange metempsychosis
Of the wise Samian, one itself transposes
Into some worse grief, either through the kindred
Of th'humors vicious or the member hindered,
Or through their ignorance or avarice,
That do profess Apollo's exercise.
So melancholy, turned into madness,
Into the palsy, deep affrighted sadness,
Th'ill-habitude into the dropsy chill,
And megrim grows to the comitial ill.[33]
   In brief, poor Adam, in this piteous case,
Is like a stag that, long pursued in chase,
Flying for succor to some neighboring wood,
Sinks on the sudden in the yielding mud,
And sticking fast amid the rotten grounds,
Is overtaken by the eager hounds.
One bites his back, his neck another nips,
One pulls his breast, at's throat another skips,
One tugs his flank, his haunch another tears,
Another lugs him by the bleeding ears,
And last of all the woodman with his knife

---

[33]The epilepsy was sometimes so called, because if a case occurred in the Roman comitia the meeting was adjourned forthwith.

Cuts off his head, and so concludes his life.
Or like a lusty bull, whose horned crest
Awakes fell hornets from their drowsy nest,
Who, buzzing forth, assail him on each side
And pitch their valiant bands about his hide,
With fisking train, with forked head and foot,
Himself, air, earth, he beateth to no boot,
Flying through woods, hills, dales and rolling rivers,
His place of grief, but not his painful grievers,
And in the end, stitched full of stings, he dies,
Or on the ground as dead, at least, he lies.
    For man is laden with ten thousand languors:
All other creatures only feel the angers
Of few diseases, as the gleaning quail
Only the falling sickness doth assail,
The turn-about and murrain trouble cattle,
Madness and quinsy bid the mastiff battle.
Yet each of them can naturally find
What simples cure the sickness of their kind;
Feeling no sooner their disease begin,
But they as soon have ready medicine.
The ram for physic takes strong scenting rue;
The tortoise, slow, cold hemlock doth renew;
The partridge, blackbird and rich painted jay,
Have th'oily liquor of the sacred bay.
The sickly bear the mandrake cures again,
And mountain siler[34] helpeth goats to yean.
    But we know nothing till, by poring still
On books, we get us a sophistic skill,—
A doubtful art, a knowledge still unknown,
Which enters but the hoary heads alone
Of those that, broken with unthankful toil,
Seek others' health, and lose their own the while;
Or rather those,—such are the greatest part,—
That, waxing rich at others' cost and smart,
Grow famous doctors, purchasing promotions,
While churchyards swell because of their vile potions;

---

[34]The siler is a family of umbellifers, to which carrots and parsnips belong.

Who, hangman-like, fearless and shameless too,
Are prayed and paid for murders that they do.
  I speak not of the good, the wise, the learned,
Within whose hearts God's fear is well discerned;
Who to our bodies can again unite
Our parting souls, ready to take their flight;
For these I honor as Heaven's gifts excelling,
Pillars of health, death and disease repelling,—
Th'Almighty's agents, Nature's counsel ors,
And flowering youth's wise, faithful governors.
Yet, if their art can ease some kind of dolors,
They learned it first of Nature's silent scholars;
For from the sea-horse came phlebotomies,
From the wild goat the healing of the eyes,
From stork and hern our clysters laxative;
From bears and lions diets we derive.
  'Gainst man's frail body all these champions stout
Strive, some within and other some without;
Or if that any th'all-fair soul have stricken,
'Tis not directly, but that in that they weaken
Her officers, and spoil the instruments,
Wherewith she works such wondrous precedents.
  But lo, four captains, far more fierce and eager,
That on all sides the spirit itself beleaguer;
Whose constancy they shake, and soon by treason
Draw the blind judgment from the rule of reason.
Opinions issue, which, though self unseen,
Make through the body their fell motions seen.
  Sorrow's first leader of this furious crowd,
Muffled all over in a sable cloud,
Old before age, afflicted night and day,
Her face with wrinkles warped every way;
Creeping in corners, where she sits and vies[35]
Sighs from her heart, tears from her blubbered eyes;
Accompanied by self-consuming Care,
By weeping Pity, Thought, and mad Despair

---

[35]Ben Johnson's "Fox", IV, 2, has the ejaculation, "Now thine eyes
vie tears with the hyena." Perhaps the idea of competition is included
in both examples.

(That bears about her burning coals and cords,
Asps, poisons, pistols, halters, knives and swords,)
Foul, squinting Envy, that self-eating elf,
Through others' leanness fatting up herself,
Joying in mischief, feeding but with languor
And bitter tears her toad-like swelling anger,—
And Jealousy that never sleeps, for fear,
(Suspicion's flea still nibbling in her ear;[36])
That leaves repast and rest, ne'er pined,[37] and blind
With seeking what she would be loth to find.
    The second captain is excessive Joy
Who leaps and tickles, finding th'Appian way
Too straight for her whose senses all possess
All wished pleasures in all plenteousness.
She hath in conduct false, vainglorious vaunting,
Bold, soothing, shameless, loud, injurious taunting.
The winged giant, lofty, staring pride,
That in the clouds her braving crest doth hide,
And many other, like the empty bubbles
That rise when rain the liquid crystal troubles.
    The third is bloodless, heartless, witless Fear,
That like an asp-tree trembles everywhere.
She leads black Terror, and base, clownish Shame
And drowsy Sloth, that counterfeiteth lame,
With snail-like motion measuring the ground,
Having her arms in willing fetters bound.
Foul, sluggish drone, barren but sin to breed,
Diseased beggar, starved with willful need.
    And thou, Desire, whom nor the firmament,
Nor air nor earth nor ocean can content,
Whose looks are hooks, whose belly's bottomless,
Whose hands are gripes to scrape with greediness!
Thou art the fourth, and under thy command
Thou bring'st to field a rough, unruly band.
First, secret, burning, mighty, swoll'n Ambition,
Pent in no limits, pleased with no condition,

---

[36]Possibly the origin of the proverbial "flea in his ear."
[37]Famished. "Surfeit by the eye, and pine the maw."—Venus and Adonis.

Whom Epicurus' many worlds suffice not;
Whose furious thirst of proud aspiring dies not;
Whose hands, transported with fantastic passion,
Bear painted scepters in imagination.

    Then Avarice, all armed in hooking tenters,
And clad in bird-lime, without bridge she ventures
Through fell Charybdis' and false Syrtes' nesse;[38]
The more her wealth the more her wretchedness;
Cruel, respectless, friendless, faithless elf,
That hurts her neighbor, but much more herself,
Whose foul, base fingers in each dunghill pore,
Like Tantalus, starved in the midst of store,
Nor what she hath, but what she wants, she counts,
A well-winged bird that never lofty mounts.

    Then boiling Wrath, stern, cruel, swift and rash,
That like a boar her teeth doth grind and gnash,
Whose hair doth stare like bristled porcupine,[39]
Who sometimes rolls her ghastly, glowing eyen,
And sometimes fixtly on the ground doth glance,
Now bleak, now bloody,[40] in her countenance,
Raving and railing with a hideous sound,
Clapping her hands, stamping against the ground,
Bearing Bocconi fire and sword, to slay
And murder all that her for pity pray,
Baning herself to bane her enemy,
Disdaining death provided others die;
Like falling towers o'erturned by the wind
That break themselves on that they undergrind.

    And then that tyrant, all controlling Love,
Whom here to paint doth little me behoove,
After so many rare Apelleses

---

[38]Syrtes, a dangerous point in the African coast. Nesse signifies land, but is now obsolete except in combinations like Sheerness, Holderness, etc.

[39]Shakespeare's revision of this expression in the Ghost's assurance to Hamlet that he could a tale unfold to make "each particular hair to stand on end like quills upon the fretful porpentine" gives an additional interest to the original. "Stare" is also used by Shakespeare in the Sylvestrian sense. (J. Caesar, IV, 3, 280; Tempest, I, 2, 247.) Cain's horse in "The Handicrafts" "bristles" his mane.

[40]That is, now pale, now purple.

As in this age our Albion nourishes,[41]
And, to be short, thou dost to battle bring
As many soldiers 'gainst the creatures' king,
(Yet not his own,) as in this life mankind
True, very goods, or seeming goods, doth find.

Now if, but like the lightning in the sky,
These sudden passions passed but swiftly by,
The fear were less; but, O, too oft they leave
Keen stings behind in souls that they deceive.
From this foul fountain all these poisons rise—
Rapes, treasons, murders, incests, sodomies,
Blaspheming, bibbing, thieving, false-contracting
Church-chaffering, cheating, bribing and exacting.

Alas, how these (far worse than death) diseases
Exceed each sickness that our body seizes,
Which makes us open war, and by its spite
Gives to the patient many a wholesome light,
Now by the color, or the pulse's beating,
Or by some fit, some sharper dolor threating,
Whereby the leech, near guessing at our grief,
Not seldom finds sure means for our relief.
But, for these ills' reign in our intellect,
(Which only them both can and ought detect,)
They rest unknown, or rather self-concealed,
And soul-sick patients care not to be healed.

Besides we plainly call the fever, fever,
The dropsy, dropsy, over-gilding never
With guileful flourish of a feigned phrase
The cruel languors that our bodies craze,
Whereas our fond self-soothing soul, thus sick,
Rubs her own sore with glossing rhetoric,
Cloaking her vice; and makes the blinded blain[42]
Not fear the touch of reason's cauter vain.

And sure, if ever filthy vice did jet
In sacred virtue's spotless mantle neat,
'Tis in our days more hateful and unhallowed

41This and the two preceding lines original with Sylvester.
42A skin disease. See Exodus IX, 9, and Shakespeare's Timon of Athens, IV, I.

Than when the world the waters wholly swallowed.
I'll spare to speak of foulest sins that spot
Th'infamous beds of men of mighty lot,
Lest I the saints' chaste, tender ears offend,
And seem them more to teach than reprehend.
Who bear upon their French-sick backs about,
Farms, castles, fees, in golden threads cut out,
Whose lavish hand at one primero-rest,
One mask, one tourney, or one pampering feast,
Sends treasures scraped by th'usury and care
Of miser parents, "liberal" counted are.
   Who with a maiden voice and mincing pace,
Quaint looks, curled locks, perfumes and painted face,
Base, coward heart, and wanton, soft array,
Their manhood only by their beard bewray,
Are "cleanly" called. . . .
Who by false bargains and unlawful measures,
Robbing the world, have heaped kingly treasures,
Who cheat the simple, lend for fifty, fifty,
Hundred for hundred, are esteemed "thrifty."
   Who always murder and revenge affect,
Who feed on blood, who never do respect
State, sex, or age, but in all human lives,
In cold blood, bathe their parricidal knives,
Are styled "valiant."   Grant, good Lord, our land
May want such valor, whose self-cruel hand
Fights for our foes, our proper life-blood spills,
Our cities sacks, and our own kindred kills!
Lord, let the lance, the gun, the sword and shield,
Be turned to tools to furrow up the field,
And let us see the spider's busy task
Woven in the belly of the plumed casque.[43]
   But if, brave lands-men, your war thirst be such,
If in your breast sad Enyo boil so much,
What holds you here? Alas! what hope of crowns?
Our fields are flockless, treasureless our towns.[44]

---

[43]Let the helmet be hung up so long that the spiders shall have closed its open side with their webs.
[44]Harried by the soldiers of "The League" on the one hand, and by those of "The Religion" on the other.

Go then, nay, run, renowned martialists!
Refound French Greece, in now Natolian[45] lists,
Hie, hie, to Flanders! free with conquering stroke
Your Belgian brethren from th'Iberian's yoke![46]
To Portugal! People Galician Spain,
And grave your names on Lisbon's gates again.

---

[45]Pertaining to the Levant. The adjuration to "refound French Greece" may have reference to the establishment of Godfrey of Boulillon as king of Jerusalem at the close of the first crusade.

[46]At the time of the composition of these poems the Spanish atrocities in the Low Countries were being carried on in full strength.

THE HANDICRAFTS

Heaven's sacred imp,[1] fair goddess, that renewest
Th'old golden age, and brightly now re-bluest
Our cloudy sky, making our fields to smile;
Hope of the virtuous, horror of the vile,
Virgin unseen in France this many a year,
O blessed Peace, we bid thee welcome here![2]
  Lo, at thy presence, how who late were pressed
To spur their steeds, and couch their staves[3] in rest
For fierce encounter, cast away their spears,
And rapt with joy, them inter-bathe with tears!

---

[1]When James Thomson, in his "Castle of Indolence," wrote of a "generous imp of fame", he was one of the latest to use the word seriously in its original sense. In the time of Sylvester it had no more offensive signification than the word "child", essentially its synonym.

[2]A series of sonnets on "The Miracle of Peace" between Henry III and his cousin of Navarre was translated by Sylvester, the first of which is given below so that it may be seen to what extent it influenced Milton's construction of his sonnet "To the Lord General Cromwell." Sylvester writes:

Henry, triumphant though thou wert in war,
  Though Fate and Fortitude conspired thy glory;
  Though thy least conflicts well deserve a story;
Though Mars's fame by thine be darkened far;
Though from thy cradle, infant conqueror,
  Thy martial proofs have dimmed Alcides' praise,
  And though with garlands of victorious bays
Thy royal temples richly crowned are;
  Yet, matchless prince, naught hast thou wrought so glorious
As this unlook't for, happy peace admired,
  Whereby thyself art of thyself victorious;
For while thou mightst the world's throne have aspired,
  Thou by this peace thy warlike heart hast tamed.
  What greater conquest could there then be named?

[3]Plural of staff, meaning of lances.

Lo, how our merchant vessels to and fro
Freely about our tradeful waters go!
How the grave senate with just, gentle rigor
Resumes its robes, the laws their ancient vigor!
Lo, how oblivion's seas our strifes do drown;
How walls are built that war had thundered down!
Lo, how the shops with busy craftsmen swarm;
How sheep and cattle cover every farm!
Behold the bonfires waving to the skies;
Hark! hark, the cheerful and rechanting cries
Of old and young, singing this joyful ditty:
Io! rejoice! rejoice through town and city!
Let all our air re-echo with the praises
Of th'everlasting, glorious God, who raises
Our ruined state, who giveth us a good
We sought not for, or rather we withstood;
So that to hear and see these consequences
Of wonders strange, we scarce believe our senses.
O, let the king, let Monsieur and the sover'n
That doth Navarra's Spain-wronged scepter govern
Be all by all "their country's fathers" clept.
O, let the honor of their names be kept,
And on brass leaves engraven eternally
In the bright temple of fair memory,
For having quenched so soon so many fires,
Disarmed our arms, appeased the heavenly ires,
Calmed the pale horror of intestine hates,
And dammed up the bi-front fathers' gates.[4]

   Much more let us, dear, world-divided land,[5]
Extol the mercies of Heaven's mighty hand
That while the world war's bloody rage hath rent,
To us so long so happy peace hath lent,
Maugre the malice of th'Italian priest
And Indian Pluto,—prop of Anti-Christ,—

---

[4]Even without the sonnet above transcribed this hymn of praise
might have been sufficient to inspire the immortal line, "Peace hath
her victories no less than War."

[5]Here steps forward the translator with 28 lines of his own, paying
his personal respects to the Pope and to Philip II of Spain.

Whose host, like Pharaoh's threatening Israel,
Our gaping seas have swallowed quick to hell,
Making our isle a holy, safe retreat
For saints exiled in persecution's heat.
Much more let us with true, heart-tuned breath,
Record the praises of Elizabeth,
Our martial Pallas and our mild Astraea,
Of grace and wisdom the divine Idea,
Whose prudent rule with rich, religious rest,
Well near nine lusters[6] hath this kingdom blest.
O pray we Him, that from home plotted dangers,
And bloody threats of proud ambitious strangers,
So many years hath so securely kept her
In just possession of this flowering scepter,
That to His glory and His dear Son's honor,
All happy length of life may wait upon her,
That we, her subjects, whom He blesseth by her,
Psalming His praise may sound the same the higher.
But waiting, Lord, in some more learned lays
To sing Thy glory and my sovereign's praise,
I sing the young world's cradle as a proem
Unto so rare and so divine a poem.
Who, full of wealth and honor's blandishment,
Among great lords his younger years hath spent,
And, quaffing deeply of the court delights,
Used[7] naught but tilts, tourneys, and masks and sights,
If, in his age, his prince's angry doom
With deep disgrace drive him to live at home,
In homely cottage, where continually
The bitter smoke exhales abundantly
From his before-unsorrow-drained brain—
The brackish vapors of a silver rain;
Where usherless both day and night the north,

---

[6]As Elizabeth did not reign quite forty-five years, the date of this interpolation must have been near the time of her decease.

[7]"Use," in the sense of the verb "frequent", occurs several times in Sylvester's poems, but not elsewhere so far as I have learned, except in Milton's Lycidas. One example occurs in some lines on tobacco quoted in the introduction to this volume.

South, east and west winds enter and go forth;
Where round about the low-roofed, broken walls,
Instead of arras hang with spider's cauls,
Where all at once he reacheth as he stands,
With brows the roof, both walls with both his hands;
He weeps and sighs, and shunning comforts ay,
Wisheth pale death a thousand times a day,
And yet, at length falling to work, is glad
To bite a brown crust that the mouse hath had,
And in a dish instead of plate or glass,
Sups oaten drink instead of hippocras;
So, or much like, our rebel elders, driven,
For ay from Eden, earthly type of heav'n,
Lie languishing near Tigris' grassy side,
With numbed limbs and spirits stupefied.

But powerful need, art's ancient dame and keeper,
The early watch clock of the slothful sleeper,
Among the mountains makes them seek their living,
And foaming rivers through the champaign driving.
(For yet the trees with thousand fruits y-fraught
In formal checkers were not fairly brought.
The pear and apple lived dwarf-like there,
With oaks and ashes shadowed everywhere;
And yet, alas, their meanest simple cheer
Our wretched parents bought full hard and dear.)
To get a plum sometimes poor Adam rushes
With thousand wounds among a thousand bushes.
If they desire a medlar for their food,
They must go seek it through a fearful wood;
Or a brown mulberry, then the ragged bramble
With thousand scratches doth their skin bescramble.

Wherefore as yet more led by th'appetite
Of th'hungry belly than the taste's delight,
Living from hand to mouth,[8] soon satisfied
To earn their supper, th'afternoon they plied
Unstored of dinner till the morrow day,
Pleased with an apple or some lesser prey;[9]

---

[8] An expression still common in America, at least.
[9] "Pleased with a rattle, tickled with a straw."—Pope.

Then, taught by Ver, richer in flowers than fruit,
And hoary Winter, of both destitute,
Nuts, filberts, almonds, wisely up they hoard,
The best provisions that the woods afford.
    Touching their garments: For the shining wool
Whence the robe-spinning, precious worms are full,
For gold and silver woven in drapery,
For cloth dipped double in the scarlet dye,
For gems' bright luster, with excessive cost
Of rich embroideries by rare art embossed—
Sometimes they do the far spread gourd unleave,
Sometimes the fig tree of its branch bereave,
Sometimes the plane, sometimes the vine they shear,
Choosing their fairest tresses here and there,
And with their sundry locks thorned each to other, ·
Their tender limbs they hide from Cynthia's brother.[10]
    Sometimes the ivy's climbing stems they strip,
Which lovingly its lively prop doth clip,
And with green lace in artificial order
The wrinkled bark of th'acorn tree doth border,
And with its arms th'oak's slender twigs entwining,
A many branches in one tissue joining
Frames a loose jacket, whose light nimble quaking,
Wagged by the winds, is like the wanton shaking
Of golden spangles that, in stately pride,
Dance on the tresses of a noble bride.
    But while that Adam, waxen diligent,
Wearies his limbs for mutual nourishment,
While craggy mountains, rocks, and thorny plains
And bristly woods be witness of his pains,
Eve, walking forth, about the forests gathers
Speights', parrots', peacocks', ostrich' scattered feathers
And then with wax the smaller plumes she ceres
And sews the greater with a white horse' hairs;
For they as yet did serve her in the stead
Of hemp and tow and flax and silk and thread,
And thereof makes a medley coat, so rare

---

[10]The sun—brother of the moon.

That it resembles Nature's mantle fair,
When in the sun, in pomp all glistering,
She seems with smiles to woo the gaudy spring.
    When by stolen moments this she had contrived,
Leaping for joy, her cheerful looks revived;
Sh'admires her cunning, and incontinent
'Says on herself her manly ornament,
And then through pathless paths she runs apace
To meet her husband, coming from the chase.
    "Sweetheart," quoth she, and then she kisseth him,
"My love, my life, my bliss, my joy, my gem,
My soul's dear soul, take in good part, I pray thee,
This pretty present that I gladly give thee."
"Thanks, my dear all," quoth Adam then for this;
And with three kisses he requites her kiss.
Then on he puts his painted garment new,
And peacock-like, himself doth often view,
Looks on his shadow, and in proud amaze
Admires the hand that had the art to cause
So many several parts to meet in one,
To fashion thus the quaint mandilion.[11]
    But when the winter's keener breath began
To crystallize the Baltic ocean,
To glaze the lakes and bridle up the floods,
And periwig with wool the bald-pate woods,[12]
Our grandsire, shrinking, 'gan to shake and shiver,
His teeth to chatter, and his beard to quiver.
Spying, therefore, a flock of muttons coming
Whose frieze-clad bodies feel not winter's numbing,
He takes the fairest and he knocks it down;
Then by good hap finding upon the down
A sharp, great fish-bone which, long time before,
The roaring flood had cast upon the shore,
He cuts the throat, flays it and spreads the fell;

---

[11]Perhaps from the Italian "mandiglione". Chapman uses the word
in his translation of Homer to designate a soldier's outer garment.
[12]These are the lines which Dryden confessed to have greatly admired when a boy, though afterwards characterizing them as "abominable fustian".

Then dries it, pares it, and he scrapes it well;
Then clothes his wife therewith, and of such hides
Slops,[13] hats and doublets for himself provides.
A vaulted rock, a hollow tree, a cave,
Were the first buildings that them shelter gave;
But finding th'one to be too moist a hold,
Th'other too narrow, th'other over cold,
Like carpenters, within a wood they choose
Sixteen fair trees that never leaves do lose,
Whose equal front in quadran form prospected,
As if of purpose nature them erected.
Their shady boughs first bow they tenderly,
Then interbraid and bind them curiously,
That one would think, that had this arbor seen,
'T had been true ceiling, painted over green.
    After this trial, better yet to fence
Their tender flesh from th'airy violence,
Upon the top of their fit-forked stems
They lay across bare oaken boughs for beams,
Such as dispersed in the woods they find,
Torn off in tempests by the stormy wind.
Then these again with leafy boughs they load;
So covering close their sorry, close abode;
And then they ply from th'eaves unto the ground,
With mud-mixt reeds to wall their mansion round;
All save a hole to th'eastward situate,
Where straight they clap a hurdle for a gate,
Instead of hinges, hanged on a withe
Which, with a sleight, both shuts and openeth.
    Yet fire they lacked; but lo, the winds that whistle
Amid the groves, so oft the laurel jostle
Against the mulberry, that their angry claps
Do kindle fire that burns the neighbor copse.
    When Adam saw a ruddy vapor rise
In glowing streams, astound with fear he flies.
It follows him until a naked plain

---

[13]"Slop" for outer garment, like "fell" for skin, is now obsolete except in a compound or two. Both were in common use formerly, however, and may be found in Shakespeare's plays.

The greedy fury of the flames restrain;
Then back he turns, and coming somewhat nigher
The kindled shrubs, perceiving that the fire
Dries his dank clothes, his color doth refresh,
And unbenumbs his sinews and his flesh,
By th'unburned end a good big[14] brand he takes,
And hieing home, a fire he quickly makes,
And still maintains it till the starry Twins'
Celestial breath another fire begins.
But winter being come again, it grieved him
T'have lost so fondly what so much relieved him,
Trying a thousand ways, since now no more
The jostling trees his damage would restore.
    While elsewhere musing, one day he sat down
Upon a steep rock's craggy, forked crown,
A foaming beast, come toward him, he spies,
Within whose head stood burning coals for eyes;
Then suddenly with boisterous arms he throws
A knobby flint that hummeth as it goes.
Hence flies the beast; th'ill aimed flint-shaft, grounding
Against the rock, and on it oft rebounding,
Shivers to cinders whence there issued
Small sparks of fire, no sooner born than dead.
This happy chance made Adam leap for glee,
And quickly calling his cold company,
In his left hand a shining flint he locks,
Which with another in his right he knocks
So up and down, that from the coldest stone
At every stroke small fiery sparkles shone.
Then with the dry leaves of a withered bay
The which together handsomely they lay;
Then take the falling fire, which like a sun
Shines clear and smokeless, in the leaf begun.
    Eve, kneeling down with hand her head sustaining,
And on the low ground with her elbow leaning,

14"Good big" is still a colloquial phrase among New Englanders to indicate a size somewhat larger than would be understood by "big" alone. "Great long" used by Sylvester in his "Tobacco Battered" is also a survival at American firesides.

Blows with her mouth, and with her gentle blowing
Stirs up the heat that, from the dry leaves glowing,
Kindles the reed, and then that hollow kix[15]
First fires the small, and they the greater sticks.
. And now mankind with fruitful race began
A little corner of the world to man.
First Cain is born, to tillage all addicted,
Then Abel, most to keeping flocks affected;
Abel, desirous still at hand to keep
His milk and cheese, unwilds the gentle sheep,
To make a flock that, when it tame became,
For guard and guide should have a dog and ram.
Cain, more ambitious, gives but little ease
To's boisterous limbs, and, seeing that the peas
And other pulse, beans, lentils, lupins, rice,
Burned in the copses as not held in price,
Some grains he gathers, and with busy toil
Apart he sows them in a better soil,
Which first he rids of stones and thorns and weeds,
Then buries there his dying, living seeds.
  By the next harvest, finding that his pain
On this small plot was not ingrately vain,
To break more ground, that bigger crop may bring,
Without so often weary laboring,
He tames a heifer, and on either side,
On either horn a three-fold twist he tied
Of osier twigs, and for a plough he got
The horn or tooth of some rhinocerot.
  Now one in cattle, th'other rich in grain,
On two steep mountains build they altars twain,
Where, humbly sacred, th'one with zealous cry
Cleaves bright Olympus' starry canopy;
With feigned lips the other loud resounded,
Heart-wanting hymns on self-deserving founded.
Each on his altar offereth to the Lord
The best that either's flocks or fields afford.
    Rein-searching God, thought-sounding Judge, that
      tries

---

[15] Usually written "kex", a hollow stalk.

The will and heart more than the work and guise,
Accepts good Abel's gift, but hates the other
Profane oblation of his furious brother,
Who, feeling deep th'effects of God's displeasure,
Raves, frets and fumes and murmurs out of measure.
   "What boots it, Cain, O wretch, what boots it thee
T'have opened first the fruitful womb," quoth he,
"Of the first mother and, first born, the rather
T'have honored Adam first with name of father?
Unfortunate, what boots thee to be wealthy,
Wise, active, valiant, strongly limbed and healthy,
If this weak girl-boy, in man's shape disguised,
To heaven and earth be dear, and thou despised?
What boots it thee for others, night and day,
In painful toil to wear thyself away,
And, more for others' than thine own relief,
To have devised of all arts the chief,
If this dull infant of thy labor nursed
Shall reap the glory of thy deeds accursed?
Nay, rather quickly rid thee of the fool!
Down with his climbing hill, and timely cool
This kindling flame, and that none overcrowd thee,
Reseize the right that birth and virtue owed thee."
   Ay in his mind this counsel he revolves,
And hundred times to act it he resolves,
And yet as oft relents, stopped worthily
By the pain's horror and sin's tyranny.
But one day, drawing with dissembled love
His harmless brother far into the grove,
Upon the verdure of whose virgin boughs
Bird had not perched, nor never beast did browse,
With both his hands he takes a stone, so huge
That in our age three men could hardly budge,
And just upon his tender brother's crown,
With all his might he cruel casts it down.
   The murdered face lies printed in the mud,
And loud for vengeance cries the martyred blood.
The battered brains fly in the murderer's face;
The sun to shun this tragic sight apace

Turns back his team; th'amazed parricide[16]
Doth all the furies' scourging whips abide;
External terrors and th'internal worm
A thousand kinds of living deaths do form.
All day he hides him, wanders all the night,
Flies his own friends, of his own shade afright,
Scared at a leaf and starting at a sparrow,
And all the world seems for his fear too narrow.
  But for his children, born by three and three,
Produce him nephews,[17] that still multiply
With new increase, who ere their age be rife
Become great-grand-sires in their grand-sire's life.
Staying at length, he chose him out a dwelling,
For woods and floods and air and soil excelling.
  One fells down firs; another of the same
With crossed poles a little lodge doth frame,
Another mounds it with dry walls about,
And leaves a breach for passage in and out;
With turf and furze, some others yet more gross
Their homely sties, instead of walls, enclose;
Some, like the swallow, mud and hay do mix,
And that about their silly cotes they fix;
Some make their roofs with ferns or reeds or rushes,
And some with hides, with oase,[18] with boughs and
    bushes.
  He that still fearful seeketh still defence,
Shortly his hamlet to a town augments,
For with keen coulter having bounded, witty,
The four-faced rampire of his simple city
With stones soon gathered on the neighbor strand,
And clayey mortar ready there at hand,
Well trod and tempered, he immures his fort,
A stately tower erecting on the port,

16As this is the second appearance of the word "parricide" in the
sense of fratricide, it must be surmised that Sylvester's learning is
at fault, though "fratricide" is seen a little further on, perhaps by fav-
or of the printer.
  17"Nephews" formerly meant grandchildren and posterity still further removed.
  18Osiers.

Which awes his own and threats his enemies,
Securing somewhat his pale tyrannies.
  O tiger! think'st thou, hellish fratricide,
Because with stone-heaps thou art fortified,
Prince of some peasants trained in thy tillage,
And silly kingling of a simple village,—
Think'st thou to 'scape the storm of vengeance dread
That hangs already o'er thy hateful head?
No; wert thou, wretch, encamped at thy will
On strongest top of any steepest hill,
Wert thou immured in triple brazen wall,
Having for aid all creatures in this all;
If skin and heart of steel and iron were,
Thy pain thou couldst not, less avoid thy fear,
Which chills thy blood and runs through all thy veins,
Racking thy bones with twenty thousand pains.
  Cain, as they say, by this deep fear disturbed,
Then first of all th'untamed courser curbed,
That while about on others' feet he run,
With dusty speed he might his deathsman shun.
Among a hundred brave, light, lusty horses,
With curious eye marking their comely forces,
He chooseth one for his industrious proof,[19]
With round, high, hollow, smooth, brown, jetty hoof,
With pasterns short, upright but yet in mean,
Dry, sinewy shanks, strong, fleshless knees and lean,
With hart-like legs, broad breast and large behind,
With body large, smooth flanks and double chine,
A crested neck curved like a half bent bow,
Whereon a long, thin curled mane doth flow;
A firm, full tail, touching the lowly ground,
With dock between two fair, fat buttocks drowned;
A pricked ear that rests as little space

---

[19]The resemblance between this description and that of Adon's horse in "Venus and Adonis" is so marked that one can hardly avoid being interested in comparing the two. Both may be taken from an earlier description, but Shakespeare's poem was certainly written before Sylvester's translation, and Du Bartas's original was as certainly published before "Venus and Adonis" saw the light.   See Virgil, Georgics, 3, 75.

As his light foot, a lean, bare, bony face,
Thin jowl and head, but of a middle size,
Full, lively-flaming, quickly rolling eyes;
Great, foaming mouth, hot, fuming nostrils wide,
Of chestnut hair, his forehead starrified,
Three milky feet, a feather on his breast,
Whom seven year old at the next grass he guessed.
  This goodly jennet gently first he wins,
And then to back him actively begins.
Steady and straight he sits, turning his sight
Still to the fore part of his palfrey light.
The chafed horse such thrall ill suffering,
Begins to snuff and snort, and leap and fling;
And flying swift, his fearful rider makes
Like some unskillful lad that undertakes
To hold a ship's helm, while the headlong tide
Carries away the vessel and her guide,
Who, near devoured in the jaws of death,
Pale, fearful, shivering, faint and out of breath,
A thousand times with heaven-directed eyes,
Repents him of so bold an enterprise.
  But sitting fast, less hurt than feared, Cain
Boldens himself and his brave beast again;
Brings him to pace; from pacing to the trot;
From trot to gallop; after runs him hot
In full career, and at his courage smiles,
And sitting still, to run so many miles.
  His pace is fair and free, his trot as light
As tiger's course, as swallow's nimble flight,
And his brave gallop seems as swift to go
As Biscayan darts, or shafts from Russian bow;
But roaring cannon from its smoking throat
Never so speedy spews the thundering shot
That in an army mows whole squadrons down,
And batters bulwarks of a summoned town,
As this light horse scuds, if he do but feel
His bridle slack, and in his side the heel.
Shunning himself, his sinewy strength he stretches;
Flying the earth, the flying air he catches,
Borne whirlwind like; he makes the trampled ground

Shrink under him, and shake with doubling sound.
And when the sight no more pursue him may
In fieldy clouds he vanisheth away.
 The wise-waxed rider, not esteeming best
To take too much now of his lusty beast,
Restrains his fury; then with learned wand
The triple curvet makes him understand.
With skillful voice he gently cheers his pride,
And on his neck his flattering[20] palm doth slide.
He stops him steady, still new breath to take,
And in the same path brings him softly back.
 But th'angry steed, rising and rearing proudly,
Striking the stones, stamping and neighing loudly,
Calls for the combat; plunges, leaps and prances,
Befoams the path; with sparkling eyes he glances,
Champs on his burnished bit, and gloriously
His nimble fetlocks lifteth belly high,
All sidelong jaunts, on either side he jostles,
And's waving crest courageously he bristles,[21]
Making the gazers glad on every side
To give more room unto his portly pride.
 Cain gently strokes him, and now sure in seat,
Ambitiously seeks still some fresher feat;
To be more famous one while trots the ring,
Another while he doth him backward bring;[22]
Then of all four he makes him lightly bound,
And to each hand to manage rightly round;
To stoop, to stop, to caper and to swim,
To dance, to leap, to hold up any limb,
And all so done with time, grace, ordered skill,
As both had but one body and one will.
Th'one for his art no little glory gains,
Th'other through practice by degrees attains

20Caressing.
21Causes to stand erect. See the lines in "The Furies" referred to
by note 29 of that subdivision.
22The use of "while" as a substantive is now infrequent except
colloquially. "Once in a while" is the phrase most commonly heard
with "while" as a noun, but the locution in the text has not wholly
disappeared in America.

Grace in his gallop, in his pace agility,
Lightness of head and in his stop, facility,
Strength in his leap, and steadfast managings,
Aptness in all, and in his course new wings.
The use of horses thus discovered,
Each to his work more cheerly settled,
Each plies his trade, and travels for his age,
Following the paths of painful Tubal sage.
While through a forest Tubal with his yew
And ready quiver did a boar pursue,
A burning mountain from its fiery vein
An iron river rolls along the plain.
The witty huntsman musing, thither hies,
And of the wonder deeply 'gan devise,
And first perceiving that this scalding metal,
Becoming cold, in any shape would settle,
And grow so hard that with its sharpened side
The firmest substance it would soon divide,
He casts a hundred plots, and ere he parts,
He moulds the groundwork of a hundred arts.
Like as a hound, that following loose behind
His pensive master, of a hare doth find;
Leaves whom he loves, upon the scent doth ply,
Figs to and fro, and falls in cheerful cry,
And with uplifted head and nostril wide,
Winding his game, snuffs up the wind, his guide;
A hundred ways he measures vale and hill,
Ears, eyes nor nose, nor foot nor tail are still,
Till in her hot form he hath found the prey
That he so long hath fought for every way.
For now the way to thousand works revealed
Which long shall live, maugre the rage of eld,
Into square creases of unequal sizes,
To turn two iron streamlings he devises;
Cold takes them thence, then off the dross he rakes,
And this a hammer, that an anvil makes;
And adding tongs to these two instruments,
He stores his house with iron implements,
As forks, rakes, hatchets, ploughshares, coulters, staples,

Bolts, hinges, hooks, nails, whittles, spokes and grap-
    ples;
And grown more cunning, hollow things he formeth,
He hatcheth files, and winding vises wormeth;
He shapeth shears, and then a saw indents,
Then beats a blade, and then a lock invents.
    Happy device! we might as well want all
The elements, as this hard mineral.
This to the ploughman for great uses serves;
This for the builder wood and marble carves;
This arms our bodies against adverse force;
This clothes our backs; this rules th'unruly horse;
This makes us dry-shod dance in Neptune's hall;
This brightens gold; this conquers self and all;
Fifth element; of instruments the haft;
The tool of tools and hand of handicraft.
    While, compassed round with smoking Cyclops rude,
Half naked Bronts, and Sterops swarthy hued—
All well near weary—sweating Tubal stands,
Hastening the hot work in their sounding hands,
No time lost Jubal. Th'unfull harmony
Of uneven hammers beating diversely
Wakens the tunes that his sweet, numbery soul
Ere birth, some think, learned of the warbling pole.
    Thereon he harps and ponders in his mind,
And glad and fain some instrument would find,
That in accord those discords might renew,
And th'iron anvil's rattling sound ensue,[23]
And iterate the beating hammer's noise
In milder notes, and with a sweeter voice.
It chanced that, passing by a pond, he found
An open tortoise lying on the ground,
Within the which there nothing else remained
Save three dry sinews, on the shell stiff strained.
This empty house Jubal doth gladly bear;
Strikes on those strings, and lends attentive ear;
And by this mould frames the melodious lute,
That makes woods hearken and the winds be mute,

---

[23]Follow. Often used transitively,

The hills to dance, the heavens to retrograde,
Lions be tame, and tempests quickly vade.
　His art, still waxing, sweetly marrieth
His quavering fingers to his warbling breath.
More little tongues t'his charm-care lute he brings;
More instruments he makes; no echo rings
Mid rocky concaves of the babbling vales
And bubbling rivers, rolled with gentle gales,
But wiry cymbals, rebecks' sinews twined,
Sweet virginals, and cornets' curled wind.
　But Adam guides, through paths but seldom gone,
His other sons to virtue's sacred throne,
And chiefly Seth set in good Abel's place,
Staff of his age, and glory of his race.
Him he instructed in the ways of verity
To worship God in spirit and sincerity,
To honor parents with a reverent awe,
To train his children in religious law,
To love his friends, his country to defend,
And helpful hands to all mankind to lend,
To know heavens' course, and how their constant sways
Divide the year in months, the months in days,
What star brings winter, what is summer's guide,
What sign foul weather, what doth fair betide,
What creature's kind and what is cursed to us,
What plant is wholesome and what venomous,
　No sooner he his lessons cán commence
But Seth hath hit the white of his intents;
Draws rule from rule, and of his short collations
In a short time a perfect art he fashions.
The more he knows the more he craves, as fuel
Kills not a fire but kindles it more cruel.
　While on a day by a clear brook they travel,
Whose gurgling streams frizadoed[24] on the gravel,

---

[24]Frisado is a Spanish word meaning silk plush or woolen goods
of long nap. It might have borne a somewhat different signification
300 years ago. Many Spanish words were adopted about that time, as
armada, barricade, bravado, desperado, grenade, parade, tornado, etc.
Trench says that the scholars and statesmen of Elizabeth's reign
were rarely ignorant of the Spanish language.

He thus bespake: "If that I did not see
The zeal, dear father, that you bear to me,—
How still you watch me with your careful eyen,
How still your voice with prudent discipline
My prentice ear doth oft reverberate,
I should misdoubt to seem importunate,
And should content me to have learned how
The Lord the heavens about this all did bow;
What things have hot, and what have cold effect,
And how my life and manners to direct.
But your mild love my studious heart advances
To ask you further of the various chances
Of future times; what offspring spreading wide
Shall fill this world; what shall the world betide;
How long to last; what magistrates, what kings,
With justice' mace shall govern mortal things?"
    "Son," quoth the sire, "our thought's internal eye
Things past and present may by means descry,
But not the future, if by special grace
It read it not in th'One-Trine's glorious face."
    "Thou, then, that only things to come dost know,
Not by heaven's course nor guess of things below,
Nor coupled points, nor flight of fatal birds,
Nor trembling tripes of sacrificed herds,
But by a clear and certain prescience,
As seer and agent of all accidents,
With whom at once the threefold times do fly,
And but a moment lasts eternity—
O God, behold me, that I may behold
Thy crystal face! O Sun, reflect thy gold
On my pale moon, that now my veiled eyes
Earthward eclipsed, may shine unto the skies!
Ravish me, Lord! O my soul's Life, revive
My spirit apace, that I may see alive
Heaven, ere I die, and make me now, good Lord,
The echo of Thy all-celestial word."
    With sacred fury suddenly he glows;

Not like the Bedlam Bacchanalian froes,[25]
Who dancing, foaming, rolling furious-wise
Under their twinkling lids their torch-like eyes,
With ghastly voice, with visage grisly, grim,
Tossed by the fiend that fiercely tortures them,
Bleaking and blushing, panting, shrieking, swooning,
With wrathless wounds their senseless members wound-
      ing;—
But as th'imperial, airy people's prince,[26]
With stately pinions soaring high from hence,
Cleaves through the clouds, and bravely bold, doth think
With his firm eye to make the sun's eye wink,
So Adam, mounted on the burning wings
Of a seraphic love, leaves earthly things,
Feeds on sweet ether, cleaves the starry spheres,
And on God's face his eyes he fixtly bears;
His brows seem brandished with a sun-like fire,
And his purged body seems a cubit higher.
      Then thus began he: "Th'ever trembling field
Of scaly folk, the arch's starry field
Where th'All-Creator hath disposed well
The sun and moon by turns for sentinel,
The clear cloud-bounding air, the camp assigned
Where angry Auster and the rough north wind,
Meeting in battle, throw down to the soil
The woods that middling stand to part the broil;
The diapry mansions where mankind doth trade;
Were built in six days, and the seventh was made
The sacred Sabbath. So sea, earth, and air
And azure-gilded heaven's pavilions fair,
Shall stand six days, but longer diversely
Than the days bounded by the world's bright eye.

---

[25]Variant orthographically of "frow", having the same origin as
the German "Frau", and earlier the same meaning. By Elizabeth's
time it had come to be a contemptuous term applicable to women of
disreputable character.
      [26]The eagle.

"The first begins with me. The second's morn[27]
Is the first shipwright, who doth first adorn
The hills with vines. That shepherd is the third,
That after God through strange lands leads his herd,
And past man's reason crediting God's word,
His only son slays with a willing sword.
The fourth's another valiant shepherdling,
That for a cannon takes his silly sling,
And to a scepter turns his shepherd's staff;
Great prince, great prophet, poet, psalmograph.
The fifth begins from that sad prince's night
That sees his children murdered in his sight,
And, on the banks of fruitful Euphrates,
Poor Judah led in captive heaviness.
Hoped Messiah shineth in the sixth,
Who, mocked, beat, banished, buried, crucifixt,
For our foul sins, still fleshly innocent,
Hath fully borne the hateful punishment.
The last shall be the very resting day.
Th'air shall be mute, the water's work shall stay,
The earth her store, the stars shall leave their measures,
The sun his shine, and in eternal pleasures
We, plunged in heaven, shall ay solemnize all
Th'eternal Sabbath's endless festival.[28]
    "Alas, what may I of that race presume,
Next th'ireful flame that shall this frame consume,
Whose gut their God, whose lust their law shall be,
Who shall not hear of God nor yet of me,
Since those outrageous that began their birth

---

[27]Du Bartas here explains what he means by his "second week", of which these pages form the conclusion of the first day. His division of the "days" of the second week into fractional parts, however, made so awkward and unintelligible a construction that it has been thought best to ignore the hebdomadal idea altogether in what follows the week of creation.

[28]The foregoing, being interpreted, is to the effect that the titles of the seven parts of the second "week" are to be respectively "Adam", "Noah", "Abraham", "David", "Zedekiah", "Messiah", and "The Eternal Sabbath". Only the four first named were completed when the death of the author occurred in 1590, from wounds received while fighting under Henry IV at the battle of Ivry.

On the holy groundsill of sweet Eden's earth,
And yet the sound of Heaven's dread sentence hear,
And as eyewitness of my exile were,
Seem to despite God. Did it not suffice,
O lustful soul, first to polygamize?
Sufficed it not, O Lamech, to distain
Thy nuptial bed, but that thou must ingrain
In thy great grand-sire's grand-sire's reeking gore
Thy cruel blade; respecting nought before
The prohibition, and the threatening vow
Of Him to whom infernal powers do bow,
Neither His passport's sealed character
Set in the forehead of the murderer?
  "Courage, good Enos, re-advance the standard
Of holy faith by human reason slandered,
And, trodden down, invoke th'immortal Power.
Upon his altars warm blood-offerings pour;
His sacred nose[29] perfume with sacred vapor,
And teend[30] again truth's near extinguished taper.
  "Thy pupil Enoch, selfly dying wholly,
(Earth's ornament,) to God he liveth solely.
Lo, how he labors to endure the light
Which in th'arch-essence shineth glorious bright;
How wrapt from sense and freed from fleshly lets,[31]
Sometimes he climbs the sacred cabinets
Of the divine ideas everlasting,
Having for wings faith, fervent prayer and fasting!
How at some times, though clad in earthly clod,
He, sacred, sees, feels, all enjoys in God;
How at some times, mounting from form to form,[32]
In form of God he happy doth transform.

---

[29]It might be difficult to explain why a sacred nose should not be as awe-inspiring as sacred lips, for instance; but the fact remains that the former is not generally accepted in that way, and the epithet must be relegated to the same shelf with the snowy periwig against which the adult Dryden filed objections that had not occurred to him in earlier years.

[30]Kindle. "Teend" seems to have the same root as "tinder".

[31]Hindrances.

[32]Referring to the forms in schools from one to another of which students are promoted.

Lo, how th'All Fair, as burning all in love,
With His rare beauties not content above,
T'have half, but all, and ever sets the stairs
That lead from hence to heaven His chosen heirs.
Lo, now he climbeth the supernal stories.
Adieu, dear Enoch! In eternal glories
Dwell there with God! Thy body, changed to quality
Of spirit or angel, puts on immortality.
Thine eyes, already now no longer eyes,
But new bright stars, do brandish in the skies.
Thou drinkest deep of the celestial wine;
Thy sabbath's endless. Without veil in fine
Thou seest God face to face, and near unite
To th'one-trine Good, thou liv'st in th'infinite.
"But here the while, new angel, thou dost leave
Fell, wicked folk, whose hands are apt to 'reave,
Whose scorpion tongues delight in sowing strife,
Whose guts are gulfs incestuous all their life.
"O, strange to be believed, the blessed race,
The sacred flock whom God by special grace
Adopts for His,—even they, alas, most shameless,
Do follow sin most beastly, brute, and tameless;
With lustful eyes choosing for wanton spouses
Men's wicked daughters, mingling so the houses
Of Seth and Cain, preferring foolishly
Frail beauty's blaze to virtuous modesty.
From these profane, foul, cursed kisses sprung
A cruel brood, feeding on blood and wrong,
Fell giants, strange of haughty hand and mind,
Plagues of the world and scourges of mankind.
"Then, righteous God, though ever prone to pardon,
Seeing His mildness but their mildness harden,
List[33] plead no longer, but resolves the fall
Of man forthwith, and for man's sake, of all.
Of all, at least, the living creatures gliding
Along the air, or on the earth abiding.
Heaven's crystal windows with one hand he opes,

---

[33] As in the sentence: "They have done unto him whatsoever they listed."—Matthew XVII, 12.

Whence on the world a thousand seas he drops,
With th'other hand he grips, and wringeth forth
The spungy globe of th'execrable earth,
So straitly pressed that it doth straight restore
All liquid floods that it had drunk before.
In every rock new rivers do begin,
And to his aid the snows come tumbling in.
The pines and cedars have but boughs to show,
The shores do shrink, the swelling waters grow.
    "Alas, so many nephews[34] lose I here
Amid these deeps, that, but for mountains near,
Upon the rising of whose ridges lofty
The lusty climb on every side for safety,
I should be seedless; but, alas, the water
Swallows those hills, and all this wide theater
Is all one pond.   O children, whither fly you?
Alas, heaven's wrath pursues you to destroy you!
The stormy waters strangely rage and roar,
Rivers and seas have all one common shore,—
To-wit, a sable, water-laden sky,
Ready to rain new oceans instantly.
    "O sonless father!   O too fruitful haunches!
O wretched root!   O hurtful, hateful branches!
O gulfs unknown!   O dungeons deep and black!
O world's decay!   O universal wrack!
O heavens, O seas, O earth, now earth no more!
O flesh, O blood!"—Here sorrow stopped the door
Of his sad voice; and almost dead for woe,
The prophetizing spirit left him so.[35]

---

[34]See note 17, ante.

[35]It has been shown (note 6, ante) that an interpolation in this section was probably written in 1602 or 1603. Shakespeare's Midsummer Night's Dream was first printed in 1600, unless the late theories of experts that these quartos bear dates anterior to their publication are correct.   But in any event the lament of Pyramus over Thisbe's death which Theseus declared was a "passion would go near to make a man look sad", seems to be in the nature of a parody on the conclusion of Adam's "prophetizing".   The love affair in the Dream which involved the subvention of fairies with their vegetable juice for lovers' eyes, was almost certainly founded upon Sylvester's early poem of "The Woodman's Bear;" (reprinted by The Blue Sky Press, Chicago, 1906) and probably other allusions in the play to the work of the puritan poet might be discovered by close attention.

APPENDIX

EPISTLE TO ROBERT NICOLSON

Though providence all prudent have decreed
To hold me still under the tyrant, Need;
So hard and scant that scarce a breathing while
My care-full life hath had just cause to smile,
Of all the wants I feel, of all the woes—
Witness Heart-Searcher which all secrets knows—
None woundeth deeper my distressful breast
Than want of power to parallel the least
Of thousand favors, of a thousand kinds
Vouchsafed me from many noble minds,
Among which number, neither least nor last
In my memorial is your merit placed;
The constant kindness of whose cordial love
From my best thought shall never aught remove.

For though, alas, my fates no means afford
To quit good turns, my faith shall them record,
And sue with sighs unto th' eternal Throne,
My friends may reap what they have kindly sown;
So that for one they may have seven times seven
In earth of grace, of glory more in heaven.

Hereby in part you may perceive, report
Hath bruited false my fortunes in the court.
The King indeed, whose bounty is renowned,
Now five years since gave me five hundred pound

Of debts long due to our late royal maid[1]
Which never were nor never will be paid,
Because Prince Henry, who devised the plot,
Died suddenly ere anything was got;
Nor could I since have light of anything,
Wherein to seek the favor of the King.

My gracious Prince! O how his name doth pierce
My grieved soul, and sables all my verse!
Henry, my whole and sole Macænas late,
With princely pension did relieve my state;
With princely purpose to have deigned me room
Of grace and gain—his privy chamber-groom.
But he is dead, alas, and with him died
My present help and future hope beside;
So that, with Job, I murmur not, but mourn,
"Naked I came, and naked shall return."

His will be done that can do what He will;
He to us all is all-sufficient still;
For at all times, in all extremest straits
His sacred arm—our secret army—waits
To succor us, and in all various sort,
Our wants, our weakness, to supply, support;
Whereof mine own proofs pass mine own account,
And past examples past all numbers mount.

What shall I then repay His providence,
His goodness, bounty and beneficence,
For all His mercies and for every one,
Beside, beyond, yea, against, hope bestown
On me whose sins might more His wrath incense?

---

[1]Apparently the right to collect indebtedness which the government had been unable to collect for itself. Prince Henry died Nov. 6, 1612, aged 18. He was detested by James, whose ill-will extended beyond the grave.

What can I give my friends for recompense
Of all their favors severally shown—
Unsought, unthought, unknowing, some unknown
To me, the least in my most indigence—
But laud the Author, love His instruments,
Praise Him for all, and pray for all their weal
Whose hearts He moves by faith, with hope and zeal,
To succor Art's poor, humble innocents,
As you on me and mine, heap sweet contents?

So, manifold be multiplied to you
All earthly goods, Heaven's grace, and glory too.
To you and yours so ever I beseech
Th' Eternal grant His treasure truly rich;
And so I rest as ever by desert
Much bound to you and your "Soon Calm in Hart;"[2]
In hearty love, though lacking helpful powers,
Unfeigned, faithful and as thankful, yours.

This messenger, your brother and our friend,
Gave first occasion these few lines to send;
With these few tears that have been lately shed
For two great Henrys, too untimely dead,[3]
A sigh for Sidney and the "Map of Man."
These if you please mildly awhile to scan,
Ere many months (or weeks, I hope) expire,
Except the heavens still envy my desire,
I'll send, or show you, ere the press prevent,

---

[2]This is a favorite anagram with Sylvester of the name of Martha Nicolson, wife of Robert. It would seem to indicate a hasty temper on the part of the lady.
[3]The other was Henry IV of France, assassinated May 14, 1610. Sylvester says elsewhere:
"When great French Henry fates bereft,
His name and fame to ours he loft."
The "tears" are the elegiac leaflets published by Sylvester on the deaths of the prince and Sir William Sidney.

My "Little Bartas" and my "Parliament
Of Royal Virtues," summoned long since,
And now assembled to create a prince
Such as was Henry while he was with us,
And Charles will be, we hope, "Panaretus;"[4]
Of whom no more till face to face we meet,
To view avie our papers, sheet for sheet.

❧

A HEBREW COURTSHIP

(From David—The Magnificence)

HE

O bright-eyed virgin, O how fair thou art!
    O how I love thee, my snow-winged dove!
O how I love thee! Thou hast rapt my heart;
    For thee I die; for thee I live, my love.

SHE

How fair art thou, my dear; how dear to me,
    Dear soul! Awake I faint, I sink, I swoon
At thy dear sight; and when I sleep, for thee
    Within my breast still wakes my sharp, sweet wound.

HE

My love, what odors thy sweet tress it yields!
    What ambergris, what incense breath'st thou out
From purple fillets! and what myrrh distils
    Still from thy fingers, ring'd with gold about!

---

[4]The quotations are of titles of some of Sylvester's productions.

SHE

Sweetheart, how sweet's the odor of thy praise!
    O what sweet airs doth thy sweet air deliver
Unto my burning soul; what honeyed lays
    Flow from thy throat—thy throat a golden river!

HE

Among the flowers, my flower's a rose, a lily;
    A rose, a lily—this a bud, that blown.
This fragrant flower first of all gather will I,
    Smell to it, kiss it, wear it as mine own.

SHE

Among the trees my love's an apple tree
    Thy fruitful stem bears flower and fruit together;
I'll smell thy flower, thy fruit shall nourish me,
    And in thy shadow will I rest forever.

❧

TO THE MILITANT CHRISTIAN

Thou must be valiant, and with dauntless breast
Rush through the thickest, run upon the best
Of braving foes; and on their flight and foil
Rear noble trophies of triumphant spoil.
For this world's prince, dark Limbo's potentate,
Drifts Man's destruction, and with deadly hate
Still strifeful labors, and by all means seeks
To trouble all, and heaven with hell to mix.

SONNET I

There needs no praising of a perfect creature;
There needs no sign to help good wine away;
There needs no candle to commend the day;
 There needs no foil to grace a faultless feature;
Nor needs our friend my fameless pen's obscureness
 To give a luster to its lightsome glass,
 Since the bright substance of the same doth pass
The clearest crystal far, for price and pureness.
 Who list to look in his fair glass shall find
Fair Albion, full of life-prolonging smiles,
Choice queen of beauties and the chief of isles—
 World's wonder and the maze of every mind.
Then who can see such beauties and refrain
To praise the hand that took such happy pain?

SONNET II

Thrice toss these oaken ashes in the air,
And thrice three times tie up this true-love's knot;
 Thrice sit thee down in this enchanted chair,
And murmur soft, "She will," or "She will not."
 Go, burn these poison'd weeds in that blue fire,
This cypress, gathered at a dead man's grave,
 These screech-owls' feathers, and this pricking briar,
That all thy thorny cares an end may have.
 Then come you fairies, dance with me a round;
Dance in this circle, let my love be center,
 Melodiously breathe out a charming sound;
Melt her hard heart that some remorse may enter.
 In vain are all the charms I can devise;
 She hath an art to break them with her eyes.

SONNET III

As in the deadness of the silent night
A dream doth forge strange shadows of delight,
So thy fair image in my fancy wrought,
Presenting wonders to my troubled thought;
    For still, methinks that I do either hear
    Thy voice, as any challenged echo clear—
Thy voice that makes the silver strings contend
How they may best thy most fine fingers bend—
    Or that I see thy feet in measures fall,
    And then I start, as one distraught withal.
I die; revive me, that it may be said
Your beauty can put life into the dead.

SONNET IV

Love, do thy worst; use all thy tyrannies,
    And as thou list, torment and torture me;
    I'll ne'er relent, nor shalt thou ever see
Me cease to serve her ever sacred eyes.
    I know my fault, and knowing I confess it;
Like th' Argive lad I took my flight too high;
But what of that? There's now no remedy,
    Unless, perhaps, propitious Death redress it.
Back, reason, then, thou dost in vain advise me;
    If Death prevent me, then my pain expires,
    And honored Death doth wait on high desires.
I must proceed, whatever end arise me.
    If it were pride at first to undertake it,
    'T were cowardice now faintly to forsake it.

SONNET V

Ev'n as the timely, sweet, heat-tempering showers
 Feed the faint earth and clothe it all with green,
With grain and grass, and plants and fruit and flowers,
 Whereby the beauty of the world is seen;
Ev'n so my tears, tempering mine inward fire,
Do feed my love and foster my desire.
 And as a sudden and a stormy rain
Makes Flora's children hang their painted heads,
 And beateth down the pride of Ceres' plain,
Drowning the pastures and the flowery meads,
 Ev'n so my tears, that overflow my fire,
 Drown my delight, but not my love's desire.

TO HIS BELOVED

The orient colors fine
 Will fall and fade away,
But let that sweetest love of thine
 Still live and ne'er decay.

The margarital gem
 For praise deserves thy name,
So like you are to them
 As Nature shows the same.

The sun shall cease to shine,
 The moon shall lose her light
Before these constant eyes of mine
 Choose any new delight.

A CONTENTED MIND

I weigh not Fortune's frown or smile;
    I joy not much in earthly joys;
I seek not state, I reck not style,
    I am not fond of fancy's toys;
    I rest so pleased with what I have,
I wish no more, no more I crave.

I quake not at the thunder's crack;
    I tremble not at noise of war,
I swoon not at the news of wreck,
    I shrink not at a blazing star.
I fear not loss, I hope not gain,
I envy none, I none disdain.

I see ambition never pleased,
    I see some Tantals starved in store,
I see gold's dropsy seldom eased,
    I see even Midas gape for more;
I neither want, nor yet abound;
Enough's a feast.   Content is crowned.

I feign not friendship where I hate,
    I fawn not on the great in show,
I prize—I praise a mean estate
    Neither too lofty nor too low;
This, this is all my choice, my cheer,
A mind content, a conscience clear.

CONSTANCY

A solid rock, far-seated in the sea,
Where many vessels have been cast away,
Though blackest storms of blustering winds do threat,
Though boisterous rage of roaring billows beat,
Though it be raked with lightning and with thunder,
Though all at once assault, and each asunder,
With massy bulk of itself's marble tower,
Still, still repels th' inevitable stour,
And seems still firmer and more permanent,
The more the tempest hath been violent.

Right so the faithful, in whose humble breast
Religious fear of God is deep impressed.
Whatever stroke of fortune threat his state,
Whatever danger him discommodate,
Whatever mischief that betide him shall,
Whatever loss, whatever cross befall;
Inflexible, invincible, pursues
The sacred footing he did ever use;
And ay more constant and confirmed is he,
The more extreme his sad afflictions be.

THE SOUL'S ERRAND

Go, Soul, the body's guest,
    Upon a thankless errand;
Fear not to touch the best;
    The truth shall be thy warrant.
Go thou, since I must die,
And give the world the lie.

Go, tell the court it glows
    And shines like rotten wood;
Say to the church it shows
    What's good, but doth no good.

Tell potentates they live,
    Acting by others' action;
Not loved unless they give,
    Not strong, but by a faction.

Tell men of high condition
    That in affairs of state
Their purpose is ambition,
    Their practice only hate.

Go, tell the young nobility
    They do degenerate,
Wasting their large ability
    In things effeminate.

Tell those that brave it most,
    They beg for more by spending;
And in their greatest cost
    Seek but a self-commending.

Tell Zeal it wants devotion,
    Tell Love it is but lust;
Tell priests they hunt promotion;
    Tell flesh it is but dust.

Tell townsmen that because that
    They prank their brides so proud,
Too many times it draws that
    Which makes them beetle-browed.

Go, tell the palace dames
    They paint their parboiled faces,

Seeking by greater shames
    To cover less disgraces.

Say to the city wives,
    Through their excessive bravery,
Their husband hardly thrives
    But rather lives in slavery.

Tell London youths that dice,
    Fair queans, fine clothes, full bowls,
Consume the cursed price
    Of their dead fathers' souls.

Say maidens are too coy
    To them that chastely seek them,
And yet are apt to toy
    With baser Jacks that like them.

Tell poets of our days
    They do profane the muses
In soothing sin with praise
    That all the world abuses.

Tell tradesmen weight and measure
    They craftily abuse,
Thereby to heap up treasure,
    Though heaven thereby they lose.

Go, tell the vicious rich,
    By usury to gain,
Their fingers always itch
    To souls' and bodies' pain.

Yea, tell the wretched poor
    That they the wealthy hate,

And grudge to see at door
 Another in their state.

Tell all the world throughout
 That all's but vanity;
Her pleasures do but flout
 With sly security.

Tell kings and beggars base,
 Yea, tell both young and old,
They all are in one case,
 And must all to the mould.

ENVOY.

Now, kindly host, adieu!
 Rest thou in earthly tomb,
Till Christ shall all renew
 And then I'll thee resume.

Note.—The foregoing poem appears among Sylvester's miscellanies for the first time in the folio of 1633. The version attributed to Sir Walter Raleigh differs slightly from this in the first seven stanzas (omitting the fifth), though each stanza concludes with a couplet commanding the soul in case of a reply, to "give them all the lie." It may be found in full in Spofford's "Library of Choice Literature," in Bryant's "Poetry and Song" and probably in other collections of recent date.

THE WORTH OF VIRTUE

The wise man's free among a thousand chains;
    He only's rich, content with his estate;
Only secure in dangers, eased in pains,
    Only true king of fortune and of fate.

He is not daunted with a tyrant's threat,
    But by his trouble grows more strong and hard;
Knows his own merit; looks not to the great
    For recompense.   Virtue's her own reward.

True virtue's conduct cannot purchas'd be
    By study, treasure, or the grace of kings;
Not by one action, or by two or three;
    But long, long practice its perfection brings.

Virtue, contented without store of treasure,
    Nor feeling poverty's abject desire,
Borrows of none, but constant to the measure
    Of just provision, will no more require.

❧

GUIDANCE FROM ABOVE

Another hand, another eye directs
Both death and nature in these high effects:—
The eye of Providence, the hand of Power,
Disposing all in order and in hour;
So working in, so waking over all
That but by those doth nothing here befall.
Then not as curs, the stone or staff to bite,
Unheeding why or who doth hurl or smite,
Unto that eye let us erect our own
And humble us under that hand alone.

SACRUM MEMORIAE

Ornatissimi Pientissimi Ipsius Amici, Magistri Josuae Sylvester; Qui in Oppido Middleburgensi vicesimo octavo die Septembris, Anno Dom., 1618, annoque aetatis suae 55.

FATIS CONFESSIT.

In verse to personate what art hath painted,
 Craves not Apelles', but Apollo's skill,
 The vein and strain of Maro's learned quill,
Or some with sweet Urania best acquainted.

Yet sith even all whose brows are deckt with bays
 Seem to neglect thee, Pan hath ta'en the pains,
 With oaten pipe, with homely, rustic strains,
To sound, not art's but heart's plain, warbled lays.

Is't not a wonder worthy admiration,
 In this so sinful—sin foul—age to see
 All real virtues in one man to be—
All, met in one, to have cohabitation?

Thou wast no lordly, great cosmopolite;
 Yet much renowned by thy virtuous fame;
 A saint on earth,—no need of greater name,—
A true Nathaniel, Christian Israelite.

Thy wisdom in thy sparing speech was shown.
　　'Tis strange his words should drip whose works did
　　　　stream,
　　Yet words and works shone all with Grace's beam—
Thy piety, sobriety, well known.

Religious, valiant, like good Josua,
　　Religious in thyself and family,
　　Courageous to withstand adversity
And worldly cares, which most men most dismay;

No temporizer; yet the court frequenting;
　　Scorning to soothe or smooth this age's crimes;
　　At war with vice in all thy holy rimes;
Thine Israel's sins, with Jeremy, lamenting.

No Croesus-rich, nor yet an Irus-poor;
　　The golden mean was thy chief love's delight.
　　Thy portion pleased thee well, and well it might.
Than piety, what riches better?　More?

Adorned with the gifts of God's good spirit—
　　I mean the gift of tongues, French, Spanish, Dutch,
　　Italian, Latin—as thyself few such,
But for thy native English of most merit;

Wherein, like former fluent Cicero,
　　With figures, tropes, words, phrases sweetly rare,
　　Of eloquence thou mad'st so little spare,
That Nile in thee might seem to overflow.

Witness Du Bartas, that rare masterpiece
　　Of poetry, to past and future times;
　　By whose mellifluous, sugared, sacred rimes
Thou get'st more fame than Jason by his fleece,

Of which thy work, I justly may aver,
  The radiant sunshine is so fair, so trim,
  As other poets' moonlight much doth dim,
Admired, silver-tongued Sylvester.

Yea, all thy full-eared harvest swathes are such
  As, almost, all thy brethren's high-topped sheaves
  Bend low to thine, like autumn-scattered leaves,
So white thy wheat is, and the weight so much.

Nor wrong I them by this harsh appellation;
  Their pleasing vein was oft too vain, but thine
  Still pleasant-grave; here moral, there divine;
Right poet-laureate wert thou of our nation.

This, then, say I, maugre the spleen infernal
  Of elvish envy, shall promote thy praise,
  And trim thy temples with ne'er fading bays;
Such heavenly offsprings needs must live eternal.

What should I say?   Much more than I can say:—
  A man thou wert, and yet than man much more;
  Thy soul resembled right an house of store,
Wherein all virtues in thee treasured lay.

A blessed death an holy life ensues;
  Thy pious end this truth hath well expressed;
  Such as thy life, such was thy death, all blest,
Thy heaven-born soul her native home did choose.

And hadst thou died at home it had been better;
  It would at least have given thee much content,
  But herein England's worthy to be shent,
Which to thy worth did prove so bad a debtor.

Nor mind I this, but then I blush for shame
   To think that though a cradle thee we gave,
   Yet, O unkind! denied thy corse a grave,
Much more a statue reared to thy name.

But thou wert wise who to thyself built'st one
   Such, such an one as is of endless date;
   A real, royal one, which, spite of hate,
To Time's last time shall make thy glory known.

Now, though thy step-dame country cast thee off—
   Ah, too ungrateful, most unkind to thee,—
   Yet here accept a mite of love from me,
Thy meanest brother, this mean epitaph:—

EPITAPH

Here lies—Death's too rich prize—the corse interr'd
   Of Josuah Sylvester, Du Bartas' peer;
   A man of Art's best parts, to God, man, dear,
In foremost rank of poets, best preferred.
                         —John Vicars.

INDEX

Lightning Source UK Ltd.
Milton Keynes UK
UKOW07f1943231217
314931UK00012B/323/P